Darling R,

   Despite every thing 9/11

will always be a special

day.

         Carole.

          X X .

11ᵗ September 2002.

Greenhill Books

GURKHAS
AT WAR

Dedication

This book is dedicated not only to those whose stories appear herein but also to the many whose deeds have been recorded elsewhere, and to the many, many more whose deeds were never recorded, and to all of those whose voices are now mute.

Also by J.P. Cross

English for Gurkha Soldiers

Gurkha - The Legendary Soldier [text only]

Gurkhas [text only]

In Gurkha Company, The British Army Gurkhas, 1948 to the Present [31.12.82]

Jungle Warfare, Experiences and Encounters

First In, Last Out, An Unconventional British Officer in Indo-China

The Call of Nepal, A Personal Nepalese Odyssey in a Different Dimension

'A Face Like a Chicken's Backside': An Unconventional Soldier in South-east Asia

The Throne of Stone

GURKHAS AT WAR

In Their Own Words:
The Gurkha Experience
1939 to the Present

Edited by

J.P. Cross
and
Buddhiman Gurung

Greenhill Books, London
Stackpole Books, Pennsylvania

Gurkhas at War
first published 2002 by
Greenhill Books, Lionel Leventhal Limited,
Park House, 1 Russell Gardens, London NW11 9NN
and
Stackpole Books,
5067 Ritter Road, Mechanicsburg, PA 17055, USA

British Library Cataloguing in Publication Data
Gurkhas at war: the Gurkha experience in their own words,
World War II to the present
1. Great Britain. Army. Brigade of Gurkhas – History
2. Gurkha soldiers
I. Cross, J. P. (John P), 1925– II. Gurung, Buddhiman
355.3'1'0941

ISBN 1-85367-494-X

Library of Congress Cataloging-in-Publication Data
A catalog record is available from the library.

Edited and designed by Donald Sommerville.

Printed and bound in Great Britain by MPG Books Ltd.,
Bodmin, Cornwall.

Contents

List of Maps

In general, only place names germane to the narratives have been indicated on the maps. Those places named in the Gurkhas' interviews whose whereabouts could not be substantiated by the editors do not appear, though provisional identifications of such places' true identities are indicated in the text by square brackets [ ] whenever possible.

List of Illustrations

Thanks are due to Alison Locke, and to The Gurkha Museum (Winchester), for their kind provision of a number of the photographs. Credits appear with the appropriate illustrations on pages 145–60.

Glossary

A full explanation of Gurkha ranks is given on pages 33–34.

bahaduri bravery award

daku guerilla

Dashera Hinduism's most important festival

Diwali Hindu festival

dukha trouble or difficulty

fakir member of any Islamic religious order

Galla Wala Recruiter

Habsi Black African

havildar sergeant (Indian Army)

jemadar junior grade of Indian Army Viceroy's Commissioned Officer

jogi Hindu mendicant

josh zeal, enthusiasm, guts, spunk

jori 'mate', mucker

kote armoury

kukri Gurkha fighting knife

naik corporal (Indian Army)

nullah gulley or ravine

pani patya ritual purification ceremony after a sea journey or caste contamination; now discontinued

raksi country spirit

sadhu Hindu wandering holy man

Sarkar government, specifically the government of India

shabash well done!

subedar, subedar major senior grades of Indian Army Viceroy's Commissioned Officer

tupi top-knot, by which Hindus can be lifted to heaven on death

Abbreviations

Well-known military terms, such as CO, POW, 2IC, RV have been omitted from this list. Note that CO, Commanding Officer, refers to a Lieutenant Colonel commanding a battalion; OC, Officer Commanding, refers to a Company Commander, normally a major.

AR	Armalite rifle	GE	The Gurkha Engineers
ARO	Area Retired Officer[1]	GIPC	Gurkha Independent Parachute Company
AWO	Area Welfare Office	GMP	Gurkha Military Police
BEM	British Empire Medal	GO	Gurkha Officer
BMH	British Military Hospital	GOC	General Officer Commanding
BOR	British Other Rank		
CGC	Conspicuous Gallantry Cross[2]	GOR	Gurkha Other Rank
CT	Communist terrorist	GPMG	General Purpose Machine Gun
DCM	Distinguished Conduct Medal[2]	GR	Gurkha Rifles
DMS	pattern of boots with moulded soles	GRRC	Gurkha Rifles Regimental Centre
DOBOPS	Director of Borneo Operations	GRTW	Gurkha Rifles Training Wing
DRO	Deputy Recruiting Officer	GTR	Gurkha Transport Regiment
DSO	Distinguished Service Order	IAMC	Indian Army Medical Corps
EY	type of grenade-firing rifle	ICR	Indian currency rupee
FOO	Forward Observation Officer	IDSM	Indian Distinguished Service Medal (=MM)
FUP	Forming Up Point	II	illegal immigrant
GASC	Gurkha Army Service Corps	INA	Indian National Army[4]
GCO	Gurkha Commissioned Officer[3]	IO	Intelligence Officer

---

[1] These officers have responsibility, among other duties, for processing potential recruits.

[2] The DCM and the MM have now been superseded by CGC and MC, respectively.

[3] This rank has been superseded with Gurkha officers now holding normal short service commissions.

[4] Name given to those who sided with the Japanese, through force, conscience or as a method of escaping from being a POW. Also known as JIF, Japanese Indian Force, or Jiff, Japanese Inspired Fifth Columnist.

IOM	Indian Order of Merit (=DCM)	QGE	The Queen's Gurkha Engineers
IS	internal security	QGM	Queen's Gallantry Medal
IWS	individual weapon sight	QGO	Queen's Gurkha Officer
JCLO	Junior Chinese Liaison Officer	QGOO	Queen's Gurkha Orderly Officer
JWS	Jungle Warfare School	QOGLR	Queen's Own Gurkha Logistic Regiment
KGO	King's Gurkha Officer		
LMG	light machine gun[5]	QOGTR	Queen's Own Gurkha Transport Regiment
LP	landing point for helicopters	RAP	Regimental Aid Post
MC	Military Cross[6]	RCT	Royal Corps of Transport
MFC	Mortar Fire Controller	RGR	Royal Gurkha Rifles
MGBG	Major General, Brigade of Gurkhas	RMO	Regimental Medical Officer
m-i-d	Mention-In-Despatches	RPKAD	para/commando unit of Indonesian Army
MI Room	Medical Inspection Room		
MM	Military Medal[6]	S$	Straits dollar, originally used in Malaya, Singapore, Brunei and Borneo
MMG	medium machine gun		
MS	milestone		
MVO	Member of the Royal Victorian Order	SEP	surrendered enemy personnel
NBC	nuclear, biological, chemical	SLR	self-loading rifle
NCR	Nepal currency rupee	SMG	sub-machine gun
O Group	commander's group for verbal orders	TDBG	Training Depot, Brigade of Gurkhas
OP	observation post, sentry	TNKU	Rebel 'army' in Brunei
PIAT	Projector, Infantry, Anti-Tank		

---

[5] LMG 1 and LMG 2 in narratives denote numbers 1 and 2 of the two-man team.
[6] See note 2 on page 9.

Introduction

By the time this book came to be written I had walked over 10,000 miles in Nepal, 5,000 of them with my surrogate son, Buddhiman Gurung. My first visit was in 1947 when only two Englishmen – such were all from the United Kingdom known in those days – a year were allowed into Kathmandu, the capital of Nepal, as visitors, in addition to the four British families officially there. At a guess I and my friend were the 126th and 127th such to visit the country since 1793.

16 April 2001 saw 186 years of close association of Gurkhas, the hill men of Nepal, with the British. I have an interest to declare: I have been personally involved in over a quarter of that time, from 1944 in 1 GR, bold and fearless, full of blood and thunder, then in 7 GR until 1982 and a resident in Nepal ever since, now old and hairless, full of thud and blunder.

Since then my wanderings have taken me from the flat plains abutting India to above the snowline, covering more than 85 per cent of the country. Between 1947 and 1976 I visited Nepal to get to know it and its people better. Mostly I walked with a serving Gurkha soldier, either returning home from his unit or when already on leave in the country. My last posting in the army, 1976–82, was as the Deputy Recruiting Officer for the west of Nepal. I covered just over 1,000 miles a year, even though I lost almost all my sight for 15 months during that period and had to learn to walk again with tunnel vision spectacles.

It was then that Buddhiman Gurung, fatherless from 13 years of age, and I met. Before I had a sight problem he was a porter. As my sight worsened he became my constant companion when I left camp, even after my sight was partially restored, when walking without hitting things or overbalancing was still a challenge. Since then he has been my surrogate son and I live with him, his wife and five children in Pokhara, 125 miles to the west of Kathmandu.

I left the army in 1982 and have lived in Nepal ever since. It was during a visit to England in 1998 that I suggested to Lionel Leventhal of Greenhill Books that we might be able to fill a gap in the historical record of the Gurkhas. All previously published histories of the Gurkhas had been written by foreigners with a foreigner's own unwitting judgmental bias masking or exaggerating the Gurkhas' innate characteristics. Why not, I suggested, get the Gurkhas to tell their own stories themselves?

The result is this book.

The Gurkhas have it that army work is like 'working in the dark or singing by a river', a mountain river that is, which makes its presence noisily known from afar. This is how they describe the many weary, dreary hours of army service when, as a minute cog in a vast engine, their efforts seem to go unseen and unheard.

Both Buddhiman and I can understand the feeling only too well. As a young lad he too knew the weary, dreary hours spent gathering enough greenery to fill a small back basket so that his mother and three other children might have something to eat, so poor was the family. He knew the boredom of following grazing cattle and goats, for the most part those of other, richer, villagers, near the top of a 5,750-foot mountain, especially when misty and cold in winter, miserable in too thin clothes, especially in the rainy season with leeches a constant and wet clothes their own burden.

My understanding of what the Gurkhas say is also profound. Sure, an officer's work is more obvious than a rifleman's and his voice louder but darkness and a loud noise cover both equally. My knowledge comes from service with these men, in war and near-war, near-peace and peace. In the middle two categories comes jungle work, a total of ten years 'under the canopy' in my first 30 years' service, living in its close-horizoned, all-pervading, never-ending green of trees, vines, creepers and undergrowth which prevent the eyes from seeing as far as the ears can hear.

So it was a nice meeting of minds when Buddhiman and I, during our walks for me to visit my recruiting staff and other pensioners, were given unstinting hospitality and, after a meal, were regaled with stories of war as had happened to them. The seed of this book must have been planted then: germinated by Lionel Leventhal's enthusiasm, it has now borne fruit.

Transcripts of all narratives, many more than are written in this book, as well as copies of the recordings themselves will be found in the Gurkha Museum. Any royalties Buddhiman and I might accrue from the sale of this book will go to the Gurkha Welfare Scheme.

Part One

WHO ARE THE GURKHAS?

IMPRESSIONS OF THE GURKHAS

'The English are as brave as lions, they are splendid sepoys ... and very nearly as good as we.' Subedar Prembahadur Thapa, 1GR, to his company commander Captain John Burgess in 1825.[1]

Earl Kitchener of Khartoum was talking about Gurkhas and asked: 'What sort of shots are they?' 'None better,' came the reply. 'Have they good eyesight?' 'They can see through a brick wall.' 'How do they stand hardship?' 'They'll stand anything except abuse.' 'H'm,' said Kitchener, 'pretty useful sort of soldiers.'[2]

'Exceptional in courage and devotion, resplendent in cheerfulness'.[3]

---

[1] Quoted in Khanduri, Chandra B., *A Re-Discovered History of Gorkhas*, Gyan Sagar Publications, Delhi, 1997.
[2] Quoted in Royal Military Academy Sandhurst, RMAS/212/Ch dated 24 May 1983.
[3] Part of the British Army's 'Prayer for the Gurkha Soldier'.

CHAPTER 1

The Gurkha Soldier

No one can understand the approach to and ethos of soldiering in a foreign army of those we now know as Gurkhas without a knowledge of their origins, social background and the chemistry of such a relationship. Æons ago, some Mongoloid people who lived in the north-west of China migrated to the southern slopes of the Himalayas as fractured ethnic minorities. This they still are. They came from a hostile environment, having to battle with extremes of cold and difficult terrain where short-term solutions were the norm rather than any longer-term balanced approach found still farther south in the hot and flat lands of the 'Cow-Belt' territory of northern India. Improvisation rather than finesse was forced on them; being stubbornly parochial new ideas came slowly. They were probably distrustful of strangers and bad at any organization above household level: a strong family and communal ties were their bedrock, refuge and strength. For survival they learnt to be tractable and, if they had not displayed fortitude to the point of fatalism nor had had an unwavering self-belief, would never have evolved into modern military legend.

There is no record of how long these migrations took but Gurkhas have had 'itchy feet' for many centuries, certainly for two millennia. The British connection only started in a positive manner from 16 April 1815, during the Anglo-Nepal War. Until 1947 the only honourable profession hill men could aspire to was military service under British officers first in the East India Company and later the Indian Army, rather than in an army officered by Aryan Nepalis. And therein lies one reason for those whom the British see as paragons of military virtue still being regarded by that same Aryan majority in their own country as spoilt, troublesome and unworthy minorities who deserted their own officers in time of need in 1815.

Nepal has never been a colony and therefore cannot, in all sincerity, be claimed to have been exploited by the British as is sometimes suggested by the politically immature. However, there is no doubt that hill men were exploited by their own ruling classes and were never looked on but as inferiors, so when the British saw their matchless qualities as soldiers, and the Gurkhas found that, probably for the first time ever, they were treated fairly and given a chance to show their full potential, the result was, and still is, a 'chemistry of camaraderie' that has stood the test of time.

Nepal was a closed, caste-bound, autocratically feudal country until the early 1950s. The remaining permafrost from centuries of such rule will still take several generations to thaw completely. Gurkhas, simple, pastoral, hardy hill men at the rip tide of Aryan and Mongoloid influence, only maintained their extended and nuclear family strengths by a combination of strong ethnic ties and an innate understanding of how to survive hardships of hunger and harassment, marred by a high mortality rate and the unchecked scourges of illness and disease. And what is a regiment if not a strong extended family?

Gurkha hill men have 'for ever' been used to a life of poverty, privation, drudgery and weariness closely connected with the soil, with rites of passage powerful constants, a progression of youth and old age, birth and death, regulated by the rhythm of the seasons. In addition, basic tenets of Buddhism and Hinduism inculcate a belief in insecurity, especially so in an age when death and disaster lurked everywhere, hence the mind-set of resignation about progress and change that deeply permeates their culture by being caught in a constricting, repeating, seldom altered circle of time. Against this was no freedom of choice until the opening of service under the British came the way of some and then only for the fittest. With such a background, small wonder Gurkhas so spectacularly outshone their military peers from so many other armies – and still do.

The second main reason why Gurkhas are different from 'other troops' is that the latter seldom make a habit of exerting themselves more than they have to while the former are naturally prone to do so. The constellation of beliefs, attitudes, values, expectations, actions and responses both as hill men and soldiers can be collectively identified as its own culture. The personal pride in belonging to an elite group, enhanced by a courtesy of behaviour ingrained by centuries of a society based on seniority, is accepted by people blessed with both but creates suspicion among people endowed with neither. So it is that the military 'extended family structure', similarly hierarchical and unquestioning, lets Gurkhas accept a regimental life easily, with discipline largely self-imposed. Subordination under both systems was normal and the men were 'biddable'. Successful military discipline is an amalgam of tamed and inflamed instincts.

One great, but seldom noted, difference between a Gurkha and a British platoon has been its commander: the former has usually been considerably older, with much experience and nearing the end of his service; the latter traditionally was at the beginning of his soldiering, with little service, and hardly any experience.

When the soldiers of World War II enlisted, Nepal had yet to be troubled by tourists, contaminated by alien cultures or perplexed by party politics. To me the supreme irony of wartime Gurkhas was that they never realized that they were fighting for democracy which did not exist in their own country.

They rated army life in war comparatively lightly as their wants were simple, having been accustomed to boredom, frugality and a laborious life. This capacity to accept conditions, which many others would find offensive or even excessive, enabled Gurkhas to play a part, especially in the Burma campaign of World War II, at a higher standard for longer, sustained periods than almost any other troops. This was only possible by every Gurkha having his own unique quality that, under the pressure of unusual circumstances, let him prevail. This potential ability particularizes an individual to the extent that even in the mass his individual character is obvious.

The military values of honour, courage and loyalty – core criteria of self-respect – find fertile soil with Gurkhas. Many fought magnificently, others less well, depending on age-old principles of leadership and morale which have nothing to do with colour, caste or creed. Of course there were lapses but these were so seldom as to be remarkable when they occurred.

Gurkhas are not extravert but are tightly self-controlled until a critical point of anger, excitement or drink has been reached. They seem strangers to the feelings many other races have when they react to normal daily intercourse. Behind a pleasant, bland exterior, is a combination of unshakable conviction and iron nerve, along with an ability to survive in a hostile hill environment with dominating overlords, and a protean ability to meld into surroundings well enough to bend successfully where not to adapt would be to break.

So a Gurkha is – what? Only one answer springs to my mind: 'a good soldier' in the context of 'the highest quality that adds something which few others can attain', namely an indeterminate mixture of self-confidence, perseverance, a malleable but defiant character, self-discipline and a good appearance. In fact the Gurkha is many things at the same time in terms of language, ethnicity and social identity, each with its own special characteristics. In sum, he is a unique blend of identity differences that breed their own chemistry but which, in turn, must have a special alchemy for fulfilment, which was, paradoxically, in war against an enemy not theirs, in a foreign country and under foreign officers. But first they had to be recruited, to be transformed from hill men into Gurkha soldiers.

Recruiting

From the earliest days, recruits came from the underprivileged sector of society, with no hope of any other enhancement and not much intellectual curiosity, but with considerable superstitious prudence, an infinite capacity to learn and a marvellous ability for improvisation. The army beckoned the young men beguilingly. Accrued conventional wisdom was that their lives would be changed, probably for better, possibly for worse.

Gurkha hill men possess a positive regard for the symbols of power and a comparatively small regard for personal comfort or absolute safety. Apart from being in honourable employment, in our interviews such details as education and medical facilities were seldom mentioned; food was, chiefly to say that they were nearly always hungry when they were recruits! Peer pressure and penury played a big part as did the knowledge that a successful man could earn money and so cut an impressive dash when on leave, especially that very first time with the certainty of a good marriage when velvet cloth and gold could be brought back to soften the hearts of the most nubile maidens. Occasionally a reason to join was trivial as when, in 1941, one man tried to borrow the recruiter's pen by taking it unasked out of his pocket. He was roundly abused: the only way to buy a pen was to join the army. This he did, buying one after his first pay parade. Some only wanted to run away from an unhappy home. All enjoyed seeing new places, relished the chance to win a bravery award – a *bahaduri* – and, in due course, a chance of promotion, possibly even to officer rank, and finally to have a pension and be of status in retirement. Those who had not received promotion or medals felt that their efforts had been inadequately judged and ill appreciated.

Even up to 1942 many men had no idea that a war was in progress and

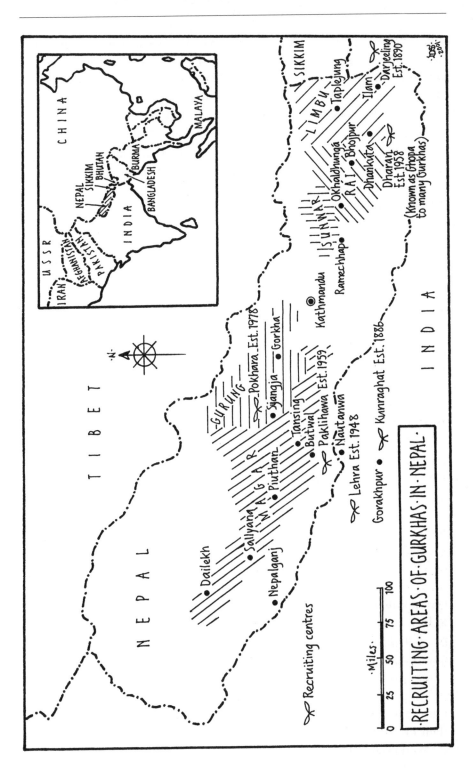

RECRUITING·AREAS·OF·GURKHAS·IN·NEPAL·

a few, even when sent on active service, had no idea what country they found themselves in, even who was their enemy or who their friends – this was certainly so in meeting both Japanese and Chinese early on in Burma. But whether men knew there was a war on or not, it normally made no difference to their desire to be recruited.

Originally regiments enlisted their own men. Although the expression 'traditional martial classes' is anathema to some people, this phrase is used as shorthand for those ethnic minorities in Nepal who, as the British Army has seen them, make the best soldiers. All less 7 GR, 9 GR and 10 GR enlisted Mongoloids: Gurung and Magar from the west of Nepal. 7 GR and 10 GR enlisted Rai and Limbu men from the east of the country. Each group has its own language, some more than one. 9 GR was the only regiment to enlist Aryan Nepalis, Chhetri and Thakuri, from both west and east. They speak Nepali.

Other group names found in the text are: Ghale, close to Gurung; Thapa, Rana and Pun within the Magar fold; and two virtually separate entities, Tamang and Sunwar, from the east. Other Aryan Nepalis mentioned are to be generically subsumed into Chhetri and those very few mentioned herein are Khatri, Sing, Bhujel and Thakuri.

In 1886 a recruiting centre was established in Kunraghat, Gorakhpur,[1] in the United Provinces and in 1890 a recruiting office was opened in Darjeeling. By the time of World War II, ex-Gurkha recruiters, known as *Galla Walas*, were sent out regularly to bring in 'likely lads'. It was almost unheard of for a lad to be enlisted by coming in by himself. The journey down from the mountains to the depots was fraught with dangers – wild animals, thieves and even the men's own families chasing a son to get him back home. Some sons of serving soldiers or pensioners in the regimental lines would be enlisted, mainly for clerical or specialist work. They were known as 'line boys' and were looked on by British officers and their hill men peers as not as reliable material, albeit cleverer and better educated. It is a sobering thought that those from the sub-continent who lasted out the rigours of war best were from areas least visited – and in the case of Nepal, never visited – by the British.

The method of selection was basic. After a clean up, men were measured and weighed, then paraded in bare buff in two ranks, the more

---

[1] In 1948 it moved to Lehra and, in 1959, to Paklihawa, 200 yards inside the Nepal border. The Darjeeling depot moved to Dharan in 1958. Dharan closed in 1990 and recruiting was done in Pokhara whither the recruiting set-up had been moved in 1978.

obvious choices in front, the less obvious behind. The final inspection by the senior British officer saw some men's positions changed: the front rank would be enlisted, the rear rank not. A medical examination was mandatory and, once that was successfully completed, the recruit would go off to a regimental centre for basic training.

There were ways to make up for physical short-comings. To give one example: a father and son both went to be enlisted, the father over 30 years of age, way above the maximum allowed, and the son too short. Both were successful: the lad stood on his toes when being measured as the examiner was looking at head level and the father 'shaved in hot water' to make his face smooth. They were posted to the 3-inch Mortar Platoon of 1/2 GR. The father went home after the war and the son served on to become a sergeant. The son told me about this!

I was the Deputy Recruiting Officer (DRO) for West Nepal from 1976 to 1982 and, as change in the mountains is so slow, I am sure that the attitudes of the young men then cannot have been much different from when I joined the Gurkhas in 1944, although methods had become more sophisticated and there was enough to eat! Recruitment, open to 'all martial classes', meant to me that I had to continue with more of the same, the type of men who had been my comrades in arms for most of my working life. Competition was intense: at a guess for every man enlisted six people benefited. I employed forty *Galla Walas* who each had some 2,000 aspirants to cope with every time recruits were wanted. Only one in every 400 was selected. I enlisted 2,148 men: the putative figure of those benefiting was 12,888 and, for the unsuccessful, some 5,142,312 people must have 'gone without'. Talk about 'playing God!'

A potential recruit did not believe that any foreigner could know enough or more about him than he himself did. I knew what to look for, albeit formulating an exact or even adequate description is very difficult. What is certain is that a man who has not been brought up under hard conditions is more likely to crack when, on active service, he finds himself cold, tired, wet, hungry, afraid, out-numbered by the enemy and far from base. I had experienced all these and seen men crack under the strain. My definition of high morale is 'the ability and willingness to give of the best when the audience is of the smallest' and, based on that, I had a diagnostic fluency in choosing the best material. Recruiting officers in World War II had had many years of regimental service and would be more interested in serving with soldiers than having a higher rank away from them. They would, therefore, have the best knowledge of the men; they would also know exactly what to look for even though the great numbers they were needing would mean a lower standard of men would be recruited than in peace time.

The strength of all military Gurkhas since 1815 lies in the warp and weft of its fashioning, the steady and unspectacular application of the uninspiring and dull but important tasks done properly, without which the foundations for successful action in an emergency would not be strong enough to bear the burden or the consequences. That the Gurkha has stood the test of time is self-evident; that he will continue thus is a tenet of British Army faith.

CHAPTER 2

Interviewing the Gurkhas

The theme of this book is for Gurkhas themselves to tell their story of active service in the pre-1948 Indian Army and the post-1947 British Army. As one who falls, just, into the same bracket as the World War II veterans, with none of us having all that much mileage left, it seemed apposite that I undertook the task of collating these recollections. This I did with my surrogate son, Buddhiman Gurung.

Oral History: Fact or Fantasy?[1]

This book is neither a military nor a regimental history but, rather, a very brief outline of various campaigns interlarded by personal stories. Memories, or their ghosts, of these old men cloud or clear our ideas with dappled spotlights as, with a faraway look in their eyes and fixed expression, they relate and relive that which they remember, or think they remember,[2] of events that happened half a century or more ago: grandsons' activities seen through grandfathers' eyes, unmoved by contradictions, complexities or ambiguities, and sometimes larded by the human frailty of exaggeration so giving yarns a whiff of taurine dung. A certain degree of caution must be exercised by credulous readers if only

---

[1] The historian Professor Arthur Marwick puts oral history eleventh out of twelve types of primary source. Quoted in Addison, Paul, and Calder, Angus, eds., *Time to Kill*, London, 1997.
[2] In a study, reported in *The Economist* of 24 June 2000, 67 14-year-old boys had been interviewed about their childhood memories in 1962. When asked the same questions 34 years later, so many changed their answers that, statistically, mere guessing would have had equal results – so much for what they thought they remembered!

because few riflemen knew much about events outside their own section or platoon, especially in the heat of battle. Men's minds retain events as a series of vignettes which bubble up regardless of the strict chronological order so beloved by serious historians. So it is that many stories differ from official historical accounts, especially so when remembering certain regimental sensibilities – how many Glorious Dead were glorious when alive? In Joseph Conrad's words: 'In plucking the fruit of memory one runs the risk of spoiling its blooms.' And how!

I have tried to produce seamless narratives by judicious prompting of relevant answers. Few stories 'came alive' as the old men were not used to showing emotion, even though some of them wept as a youthful but bloody past overpoweringly mingled with the impotent present. A Gurkha can say so much by leaving so much unsaid.

Names of British officers and places, especially in Italy and Burma, were infernally hard to reconcile as they were almost always mispronounced and, when written, apt to be spelt phonetically. (When the army's phonetic alphabet was changed on 1 January 1956, my company signaller spelled 'phonetic' as 'fanatic'.) I have taken the liberty of amending names of places, as well as errors in ranks and sub-units, where known.

Those who wish to set the stories more fully in context are directed to the list of Further Reading which appears on page 314.

Collecting the Stories

In 1999 and 2000 Buddhiman and I visited 24 places in Nepal and three in India to collect stories. Recording was easier by far than transcribing: survivors of World War II were, in 2000, 75–94 years of age, and many of them only remembered years and months of the era according to the calendar used in Nepal,[3] the attenuations of dotage afflicting some more than others. Only those who were young men in World War II were alive to tell their tales, and this from a narrow perspective usually clouded by the 'fog of war'. None of those who served in the Malayan Emergency (1948–59) were under 60 and none who served in the Brunei Rebellion (1962–3) or in Sukarno's Borneo Confrontation (1963–6) under 50.

---

[3] The Nepalese Bikram era is 56 years, 3 months and between 12 to 15 days ahead of the Gregorian calendar.

These campaigns were remembered by all ranks with senior men having a more structured narrative to tell. Events in Hong Kong, Cyprus, the South Atlantic, the Gulf, Bosnia, Kosovo and East Timor came across 'loud and clear'. The different tempos of the differing campaigns reflected in their stories vary from fascinating, through frightful to frivolous, yet these last almost always contained nuggets and reminded me yet again that, in every case, we all depended on the efforts of a great body of men whose existence, in Field Marshal Slim's words, 'is only remembered when something for which they are responsible goes wrong,' with echoes of Wellington's dictum that 'every man in uniform is not a hero'.

Many war-time men, apart from suffering from 'selective amnesia', were deaf, toothless, sometimes almost voiceless or even suffering from a stroke so were difficult to understand. For some, story telling is essentially a 'liquid' affair best enjoyed with friends – '*raksi* is our diary' as one of them put it – not a 'dry' performance into a microphone. Even the recorded talk of the non-afflicted was sometimes too hard for Buddhiman to understand, so mauled, muted and muttered were the words. The oldest men were also illiterate and innumerate, certainly functionally, when they joined up, as education was forbidden in Nepal before 1951. This, in fact, was a bonus, as the power of recall of the illiterate is often, of necessity, better than that of those who can refer to the printed page to refresh their memory. People brought up on the rote system of learning can, in later years, use the positive properties of mental retention which the system engenders to good effect.

Gurkha Characteristics

Questions had to be correctly framed otherwise 'Who are you?' would be answered 'I am I'; 'Who did he then marry?' 'Somebody else'; and 'What was that [Nepali word] you ate?' 'Something to eat.' It is this addiction to the literal that gave Gurkhas a reputation for being dumb. A Gurkha's facial expression is 'closed when on parade' and therefore gives an often erroneous impression of slow comprehension. This was unfair as many only spoke the common language spoken in the hills, Khaskura, or Nepali as it is now known, as a second language after their particular tribal dialect, and many British officers had pronunciations that at best were inadequate and at worst inaccurate, so correct meanings had to be guessed at. That took a moment or two and it was not unknown for officers to become impatient if what they said was not immediately acted upon. This situation was further exacerbated because the official language of the Indian Army was Roman Urdu and that had to be used for all non-regimental activities, such as talking to hospital attendants, going on courses and reading pamphlets, to say nothing of the fact that British officers were not taught the language of their men, Gurkhas or Indians, until they had passed the Elementary Roman Urdu examination.

Nepali is very good for onomatopoeic ululations, of about 7.2 on the vocal Richter scale, but not so satisfactory for 'grades' of description. Magnificent gestures from our interviewees showing how the enemy were encircled or some such other hair-raising exploit – even once being demonstrated by crawling under a table – were, likewise, wasted for the printed page. While many had a wonderful memory for the mundane, evocative descriptions are rare. Many details of battle have been conflated and become confused. Yet another reason for not giving details was neatly summed up by one man: 'If I told you everything that happened it would be like keeping the children amused.'

Men's descriptive abilities were often strained. Trying to explain continual movement or constant pressure came out as 'doing, doing, doing, going, going, going, here, there, hither, thither, up, down, what what how, what what how, utter distraction'. In cold print is 'one hard slog, on, on, on' really adequate as a translation?

Yet another facet of Gurkhas' reminiscences is that they did not complain of any British inefficiency. They recalled thoughtlessness, yes, as when one young British officer joked to parents, who had lost five sons in the war and were receiving ICR 90 for each son, how much this pension was, saying 'Give some to me.' The mother was so angry she threw all the money back in his face. No complaint was made of lack of rations, ammunition and stores as such and almost never at bad tactics. Defeat in Malaya? Privations in Singapore? Retreat through Burma? Capture at Tobruk? All were seen as the result of there not being enough Gurkhas to deal with the situation and a recognition that, possibly, a bigger need for military stores and equipment in Europe meant less being available elsewhere.

Apart from having taken of the *Sarkar*'s salt and their oath so 'never complaining, never explaining', Gurkhas showed, and still show, a pathological dislike of making adverse comments. Asia presumes an obligation of citizens to obey governments, Western democracy regards governments as representing the citizens. This difference colours, clouds and distorts conceptions of the one about the other. As young men they were (and as old men still are) so used to endemic incompetence and inefficiency that any deviations from normal army arrangements were either seldom as bad as had happened at home or were accepted with the fortitude of a fundamental fatalism – it's all a ploy of the gods. At least, that is my explanation of this phenomenon.

One common plaint was the *dukha*, blandly translated as 'trouble', of and in service. Any discipline has a quality beyond an individual's convenience and low-level *dukha* stretches from having to be permanently on the alert and seldom relaxing, to deprivation of female company, discomfort and boredom, as well as the fretful, nagging constant of inescapable duties of line sentry, inlying piquets, fatigues, and broken sleep for one reason or another alike in the line and out of it. War is drab, dull and dangerous; life in hill villages is drab, dull and sometimes dangerous. These facets are seldom reflected in narratives but both are inescapable; apathy is the opposite of aggressiveness, especially when the latter has lost its momentum. This is the explanation for the wonderful discipline, tenacious to a fault, and uncomplaining stolidity shown under difficult conditions. This has to be the reason why Gurkhas were able so well to accept the traumas of war. This was just as well when there was no particular emotional or emotive issue, other than solidarity, not letting oneself or one's *jori* down, the good name of the regiment and the desire for a *bahaduri*, that drove the Gurkhas to give of their best, as opposed to the Japanese soldiers' loyalty to their emperor and the Germans' to Hitler.

Natural candidates for a high-level of *dukha* are danger, having a hard time involving pain, grief, trouble, distress and suffering, especially on active service conditions, let alone in battle, or when wounded, hungry or under great stress as a POW. Whatever the reason it seemed pervasive then and, with senescence sucking strength from once-lively limbs and the depression caused by 'life not being what it was', is pervasive now.

That the name and fame of the Gurkhas is worldwide is beyond dispute. The Gurkhas themselves are mostly reticent about their achievements and they told their stories dispassionately and, for the most part, modestly. Gurkhas are not fearless but fear of showing fear is strong. Fear before an action was understandable but I believe that 'stage fright' would be an apter description. After shot and shell started to fly and the enemy charged, fear was forgotten. One man put it this way: 'If you think you'll get back home, you'll be no use in war. You're only any use if you think you won't get back.' That leads on to a remark often made: 'We had nothing to lose by risking our lives as we had lost them already,' with the unsaid rider that they gave their all to master the situation as the Law of Vital Interests took over and those 'last few yards' were as 'home ground'. As ever, then as now, a high standard brings its own penalties of expectation.

Strangely most men did not talk about the more horrendous events until, at the end, one of us usually asked them if there was anything else they'd like to add. Then came personal details, from the more prosaic 'I had my hat shot off my head twice,' to 'I was wounded in the neck and my boots were full of blood. I was in hospital for nine months,' to unbelievable stories of degradation and cannibalism. The man who was left for dead with his nose smashed flat by Japanese rifle butts and who is still almost incomprehensible, wounded so he still has pain walking, deafened by gun fire so he has never heard properly since, had to be asked about his terrible condition as he had volunteered nothing.

Also I wonder what will be the reactions of any Indian officer who reads this book to the stories of those who served in 2/1 GR, 2/2 GR and 2/9 GR, were captured by the Japanese and bullied by the INA when prisoners of war and now give vent to their true and long pent-up feelings? Difficult to say as, in the last fifty years, the leading light behind the INA, pilloried by the British as an arrant turncoat and who was an embarrassment to the more sensible senior Congress functionaries, has had his reputation as a successful freedom fighter so inflated that he is still a cult hero on Indian campuses and, unexpectedly in view of what indecencies were perpetrated on the Old and Bold of another country, Nepalese campuses also. If nothing else, the person in question has joined that small band of people of more use dead than alive.

But even if memories of actions are inaccurate, lesser matters are even more so. 'I know that Field Marshal Auchinleck's wife was Queen Alexandra,' from a 3 GR man; 'I tell you, sahib, the Irrawaddy does not flow into the sea in Burma as you said but it comes out at Tokyo'; 'How can you say that aeroplanes damaged in Italy did not have to go to Calcutta for repair?' Such obvious fantasies have been eliminated.

Interviews acted in a therapeutic and cathartic way. A 9 GR rifleman's one ambition since 1945 when he jumped into enemy-occupied Malaya with Force 136 had been to 'chew the military cud' with a British officer. Over 80 when he told his story, he had thought it would never happen and his eyes glinted with gladness and his smile was genuine and broad when he left, telling the Area Welfare Officer (AWO) who had called him in to be interviewed that he could now die happy as he had no more major wishes to fulfil; some spoke almost as at confession and later appeared similarly shriven: 'Sahib, I ignored the advice given to me by my company commander in 1944 and I am sorry. I was wrong. I can't tell him but I am telling you as I have wanted to tell someone all this time.' Fact, not fiction.

In the same vein, three men (one with a broken leg) walked three days to come and tell their stories, many walked two days, while an eight-hour walk was a commonplace. One even wore a wartime shirt he kept for special occasions on which were pinned his medals, including the MM. *Bahaduris* play a very big part in a Gurkha's psyche. The British method of giving *bahaduris* at platoon commander level upwards for 'collective action' or 'sustained effort over a period' is seen as eclipsing individual acts of bravery. What really does upset Gurkhas is not getting an award for something achieved when others were rewarded for, often in the mind of him unrewarded, seemingly doing far less or even nothing at all. That comparatively so few people get *bahaduris* is because military organizations 'work by numbers' as laid down in regulations, whether it be studs in ammunition boots of yesteryear, pieces of Army Form Blank per day, minimum cubic area between bed spaces, probably holes in a mosquito net and certainly bravery awards in a set period of time. This results in lean periods when acts of less distinction get rewarded and in fat periods when acts of great distinction do not. Bravery awards are contentious and delicate. The Gurkha soldiers' holy grails are based on effort being rewarded, whether by promotion or a *bahaduri*. For such not to happen is seen as a negation of trust. Not for nothing did Napoleon say something to the effect of, 'give me enough ribbon and I will conquer the world.' The number of times disappointment in bravery was not recognized is a recurring theme in the stories, resulting in non-return from leave post-1947 and not staying in a unit designated for the British Army pre-1948.

Apart from everything else, gathering data was a wonderful time to meet old friends. The glamour and vainglory of regimental soldiering over four decades had long faded but the magic of camaraderie then formed, dormant for so long, instantly and without hesitation rose to the surface everywhere I went. Many names and numbers of those with whom I had served sprang to mind and almost everybody had his own anecdote about the times we had spent together – some true and flattering, some untrue and flattering, others neither! Looking at the men's animated faces and shining eyes was like looking into a mirror in reverse: smooth-faced, clean-limbed, upright lads of yore were sometimes scarcely recognisable now that they had become shrivelled, wrinkled, toothless and grey-haired or bald. I, too, after so much time, was one of that large army of 'those who fade away'. Even so men of regiments other than mine to whom I had only ever once dropped a passing chance remark remembered what it was, and when and where we had met.

When the magic of the chemistry still works its charm, for me it is proof positive that the British–Gurkha connection is, indeed, based on very strong grounds.

CHAPTER 3

The Gurkha
Order of Battle

The Gurkha Brigade
to 31 December 1947

At the outset of World War II the Gurkha Brigade, as collectively the Gurkha component of the Indian Army was known, comprised ten Gurkha regiments, of two battalions each. These were:

1st King George V's Own Gurkha Rifles (The Malaun Regiment)	1 GR
2nd King Edward VII's Own Goorkhas (The Sirmoor Rifles)	2 GR
3rd Queen Alexandra's Own Gurkha Rifles	3 GR
4th Prince of Wales' Own Gurkha Rifles	4 GR
5th Royal Gurkha Rifles (Frontier Force)	5 RGR (FF) or, in short, 5 GR
6th Gurkha Rifles	6 GR
7th Gurkha Rifles	7 GR
8th Gurkha Rifles	8 GR
9th Gurkha Rifles	9 GR
10th Gurkha Rifles	10 GR

Battalions are identified in the form 1/7 GR, which means the First Battalion of the Seventh Gurkha Rifles or, colloquially, 1st/7th Gurkhas.

In World War II 114,971 Gurkhas were recruited from 168,294 volunteers. There were 23,655 Gurkha casualties in the course of the war, slightly more than there had been in World War I. Third and fourth battalions were raised for all ten regiments with 1 GR, 2 GR and 9 GR also having fifth battalions. This expansion required ten Gurkha Rifles

Regimental Centres to be established for basic training and regimental records. Five training battalions were raised: 14 GR, 29 GR, 38 GR, 56 GR and 710 GR. Other new units were: 25 GR and 26 GR, employed in Burma as garrison battalions for the defence of General Slim's HQ and a corps HQ; and 153 and 154 (originally 3/7 GR) Gurkha Parachute Battalions. Large numbers of Gurkha men were recruited for non-Gurkha Brigade units, including the Kashmir State Forces, Assam Rifles, Burma Rifles, Indian Pioneer Corps, Indian General Service Corps, Indian Army Medical Corps and some others. A total of 250,280 Gurkhas joined the army and there were 2,734 bravery awards, a ratio of 1 in 91.

The Brigade of Gurkhas
from 1948

When British rule in India ended in 1947 it was decided that some Gurkha regiments would transfer from the former Indian Army to the British Army while others would continue to serve with the now-independent Indian Army.

Four infantry regiments were chosen for the British Army, initially of two battalions each. The army of the new India was originally destined to have the remaining 12 battalions from the pre-war cadre of 20. Many more battalions have since been raised, as well as 11 GR being re-established. Gorkhas (the Indian Army spelling) also serve in non-Gorkha units, e.g. Indian Artillery, Indian Guards and Army Service Corps.

The British Army regiments were as follows:

2nd King Edward VII's Own Gurkha Rifles (The Sirmoor Rifles)	2 GR
6th Gurkha Rifles	6 GR
7th Gurkha Rifles	7 GR
10th Gurkha Rifles	10 GR

The following additional Gurkha units were also raised at the dates shown:

The Gurkha Engineers (1948)	GE
Gurkha Signals (1948)	GURKHA SIGNALS
Gurkha Military Police (1948)	GMP

Gurkha Army Service Corps (1958)   GASC
Gurkha Independent Parachute Company   GIPC
    (1965-71)

A Major Staff Band was raised in 1956 and, in 1970, became a Minor Staff Band: The Brigade of Gurkhas (2nd King Edward VII's Own Gurkha Rifles) Regimental Band.

Changes of name

In 1950 10 GR became 10th Princess Mary's Own Gurkha Rifles. In 1959 6 GR became 6th Queen Elizabeth's Own Gurkha Rifles. In 1959 7 GR became 7th Duke of Edinburgh's Own Gurkha Rifles. In 1994 all four infantry regiments were subsumed into The Royal Gurkha Rifles (RGR). This new regiment originally had three and later two battalions.

From 1962-69, GMP was 5 (Gurkha) Dog Company.

In 1963 GASC became The Gurkha Transport Regiment (GTR), which in turn became The Queen's Own Gurkha Transport Regiment (QOGTR) in 1992. In 2001 QOGTR became The Queen's Own Gurkha Logistic Regiment (QOGLR).

In 1977 GE became The Queen's Gurkha Engineers (QGE).

In 1977 Gurkha Signals became Queen's Gurkha Signals (QG SIGNALS).

Exceptionally, as all corps units are part of the Brigade of Gurkhas, these last three named can be looked on as 'infantry' in so far as such things as drill and dress are concerned.

Ranks

Ranks in the Gurkha Brigade followed the pattern used in the Indian Army as a whole. A private soldier was a Rifleman, (Rfn). NCO ranks were Lance Naik (Lnk), Naik (Nk), Havildar (Hav), Company Quartermaster Havildar (CQMH). Naik and havildar can be translated as corporal and sergeant respectively. Warrant officer ranks were Company Havildar Major (CHM) and Battalion Havildar Major (BHM). Between them and the British officers were three grades of Viceroy's Commissioned Officers (VCO) which had no direct British Army equivalents; Jemadar (Jem),

Subedar (Sub) and Subedar Major (Sub-Maj or SM). In the Gurkha Brigade these were known as Gurkha Officers (GO).

The Gurkha Officers were all promoted through the ranks after long service. Jemadars and subedars normally served as platoon commanders or company 2ICs, but were junior to all British officers. The subedar major was the Commanding Officer's 'Gurkha advisor' on all purely Gurkha matters, analogous to a matron in a hospital – all pervasive and not to be done without. The only promotion beyond that grade given to Gurkhas was the very rare honorary lieutenancy or captaincy bestowed on retirement.

Ranks in the post-1948 Brigade of Gurkhas are designated and abbreviated in the same way as are their British counterparts, e.g. Rfn (later Rfm), Lcpl, Csgt, 2lt, Lt Col. The exceptions are the three ranks between WO1 and 2lt: Lieutenant (Queen's, formerly King's, Gurkha Officer) and referred to as Gurkha Lieutenant, Captain (Queen's/King's Gurkha Officer) and referred to as Gurkha Captain, and Major (Queen's/King's Gurkha Officer) and referred to as Gurkha Major or GM. Of these, the two junior are normally employed at platoon/troop level and company/squadron 2IC level. The Gurkha Major has the same role as the subedar major.

The change in nomenclature of ranks, from Viceroy's Commissioned Officer to King's or Queen's Gurkha Officer, was only introduced in 1949 when the Royal Warrant that renamed The Gurkha Regiment – a temporary appellation from 1 January 1948 – as The Brigade of Gurkhas was promulgated.

As we enter the 21st century Gurkhas commissioned from the Royal Military Academy, Sandhurst, and Short Service Officers regularly fill appointments in ranks up to major, as did the now obsolete Gurkha Commissioned Officer. At the time of writing two Gurkhas have been promoted to lieutenant colonel. Theoretically there is no bar to reaching the top.

There was a great disparity of pay and pensions troubling alike to British and Gurkha personnel from 1948 until 1997. Now the 'take home' pay of a Gurkha equals that of his British counterpart. From 2000 pensions have been increased by a two-fold minimum and all ranks, regardless of date of discharge, receive equal amounts.

Part Two

GURKHAS OF THE INDIAN ARMY

The Gurkhas in World War II

Gurkhas fought from Jitra in north Malaya to Singapore; from the Thai border back through Burma to Imphal in India and then forward again to Rangoon and Thailand; from Syria through the Western Desert of North Africa to Italy. One of the eight battalions from the Nepalese Contingent sent to relieve manpower shortages also fought in Burma, the rest were deployed in the Imphal area or on the North-West Frontier of India where Indian Army Gurkha battalions were also guarding that vital area against any enemy invasion from the west and tribal unrest.[1]

In the aftermath of World War II, trouble in Greece, Palestine, and South-east Asia and the tormented division of India needed the Gurkha Brigade to help restore order.

---

[1] 38 per cent of peacetime establishment was deployed there.

CHAPTER 4

Malaya

In 1939 Britain's regular army in Asia, equipped only for colonial warfare, was far less ready for a continental war than in 1914, and a complete inability to envisage, let alone counter, any aggression from the east, after years of apathy, inertia and inadequacy at the highest levels, resulted in no British forces, Indian or colonial, being ready or able to withstand the Japanese assault.

The tragic, hopeless and bewildering events that resulted from the Japanese invasion showed the British colonial apparatus in as bad a light as possible and worse than any previously imagined. The retreat down Malaya to Singapore was a pitiless rout and a nightmarish military disaster. The three Gurkha battalions in action, 2/1GR, 2/2 GR and 2/9 GR, had been 'milked' – some would say 'bled' – of their above-average officers and NCOs to form new war-time units and were filled instead with raw recruits whose inadequate training was slanted to warfare in the desert, not in tropical rain forest. The inexorable and traumatic mauling the battalions suffered, followed, when prisoners, by inhumane treatment meted out by the Japanese, and by Indians who thought they could gain independence by soldiering for the Japanese, have had to be lived with by those few survivors who were still alive in 2000.

In order to escape from captivity many 'volunteered' to fight with the Indian National Army (INA), the force raised by Indian 'nationalists' who put survival and a misplaced hope of national glory ahead of their oath of loyalty. Hill Gurkhas excoriated the INA and only a very few Indian-domiciled Gurkhas joined it wholeheartedly, those others who did saw it as the only method of escape. Unfortunately these men's evidence against the main Indian bullies was not allowed in the post-war trials, relevant though it was in many cases.

Jangabahadur Sing, 2/9 GR, *moved north, with a recently-arrived batch of young soldiers he had helped to train in India, to join the battalion as fighting began.*

One morning a small aeroplane flew low over us and without an order an LMG 1 shot it down. We crowded around and found a dog, a man and a woman, all alive. But who were they? We captured them and sent them back.

We reached a rubber estate in Thailand. The adjutant was on the point of giving us orders in an abandoned British camp, with the mosquito nets still over the beds, when we were attacked by Japanese aircraft. We made ourselves as scarce as possible wherever we could. The Japanese fired on us all that night. We did not know friend from foe so we shot at anyone we saw.

I was a signaller so had to go around delivering messages. Next morning at 0400 hours we should have started our withdrawal but we could not break contact from the Japanese. We did get away and tried to leave by convoy but we met seven Japanese tanks and their artillery. We had a battle, then retired quickly with our personal weapons but there was no way of looking after the wounded or burying the dead. It was every man for himself.

By evening we had started to join up but the CO, adjutant and the majors who had given us so much encouragement when we were fighting were nowhere to be seen. None of us knew if they had got away, were dead or had been captured. We later met Yam [*sic*] sahib who told us we had to cross a river but the bridge had been blown by our own people so we had to move off to find another. We would cross by a ford if we found one. We walked on a compass bearing all night. Next day we found another crossing, not a bridge but a single wire over the river. Eighty of us got across, one at a time.

Before the others moved off three of us were detailed to stay at the crossing place to see if there were any stragglers. We stayed there all night but none came so we moved off by ourselves, down a railway line. Eventually we saw a light in the distance and it was a British unit. We were challenged. "Halt!" "Second Nine!" "Come on!" We were given a meal and moved on immediately with the British soldiers.

Maniratan Pun, 2/2 GR, *started fighting at Jitra.*

… and the Japanese attacked from Kota Bahru, swarms of them in lines. 2/1 GR was on our right, 2/9 GR on our left. They withdrew without letting us know and left us. That made it worse for us. The CO, Woollcombe sahib, gave the orders for us to withdraw in haste. An Indian battalion, 1/14 Punjab Regiment, stayed behind and helped the Japanese. They only went through the motions of fighting.[2]

Japanese aircraft bombed us and tanks came from another direction and cut us off. We had nowhere to go. There was a lot of firing.[3] When I got to the Slim River many men had already drowned and I saw the Gurkha hats[4] floating downstream. The transport was bunched up and we were ordered to abandon it. We left it behind.

The bridge over the Slim River had been blown but we managed to catch hold of the girders at water level and, with our arms slung, got across. I can't tell you how many men were drowned.

We eventually got to Johore Bahru and went over to Singapore. The Indian battalions did nothing. The Australians were better than the Indians and their artillery supported us well, they covered our movements and gave us clothing. Sometimes when we were on fatigue together they shared their water with us. They only wore shorts at work. I don't want to say that the Australian infantry was good or bad, only to say that it was through its lines that the Japanese advanced into Singapore having attacked them with incendiary bombs.

We lost because we did not have enough men, not enough heavy weapons, not enough of everything.

Chandrabahadur Chhetri, 2/9 GR. The day after the surrender order came we were ordered to "ground arms" at 0800 hours. I wept as if I had lost my parents. No one was to blame.

---

[2] 'Capt Mohan Singh, 1/14 Punjab Regiment, was in the pay of the Japanese before the war started. He showed 2/1 GR into their positions before the first battle – defected to the Japanese and showed them our positions.' Letter from Capt, (later Lt Col) C.G. Wylie, 2/1 GR, dated 31 January 2001.

[3] The battalion left Jitra on 10 December 1941 and reached Slim River on 7 January 1942. The regimental history commends Maniratan for rescuing wounded under fire at River Batu south of Jitra. He only has a confused recollection of the whole 550-mile 52-day retreat to Singapore.

[4] Wide-brimmed hats, doubly sewn together.

We moved to River Valley camp where Captain Mohan Singh and a woman came with a crowd of Indians two or three days later. We were told we had to join up with Congress. I was very angry and didn't understand. I was threatened three times and sent to a concentration camp for a few days. Some 350 of us were fallen in and a machine gun was set at each corner. We were asked if we would join the Indians but we all refused. Three of us were pulled out and shot in front of the others and we were asked again if we would join them. We still refused. We had to be true to the salt we had taken. We had all given up any hope of staying alive.

We were three years and eight months in River Valley camp.

Balbahadur Rana, 2/2 GR.   The Indians ran away. If the Gurkhas had been at the same strength, the Japanese would not have won. Indian troops, British troops and Australian troops were not good enough. The whole plan was weak; everything was weak.

The Japanese are not all that talented in war they are merely very forceful. The INA was very bad. I was stripped and had a bucket of night soil and urine poured over my head in front of the others as I refused to join them. I fainted and was not allowed to wash for a long time after I regained consciousness.[5] Since coming home in 1946 I have never spoken to an Indian, nor will I ever.

---

[5] This last disgusting episode still so hurt the man, in 1999, that he had the greatest difficulty in mentioning it at all.

CHAPTER 5

Burma

The Burma campaign was one of the longest in World War II, lasting more than three and a half years. Its causes were differently seen: the Japanese wanted to protect their troops in Malaya, to close the overland supply route to southern China and capture a stepping stone to India. The Maharaja of Nepal, fearing Japanese retribution after a subsequent Japanese invasion of Nepal, forbade his own army, the Nepalese Contingent,[1] from leaving Indian soil and tried to have all Indian Army Gurkha units recalled.

The British wanted to hold India against Japanese invasion, regain lost territories and avenge defeat, yet Slim only had 'smashing that evil thing, the Japanese Army', as his ultimate aim. Churchill envisaged by-passing the rigours of a land battle by capturing Rangoon from the sea prior to a sea-borne capture of Singapore. Re-conquering Burma by land was, to him, like 'munching a porcupine quill by quill.'

The American aim was to clear the road north to China as they only wanted northern Burma, the air route and pipeline, and the Ledo Road into China. The rest of Burma did not interest them. Field Marshal Viscount Alanbrooke stated that the campaign was conducted with inadequate forces, largely out of deference to America's delusion about China: 'If ever there was a campaign mishandled it is the Burma one, and mainly due to the influence exercised by Chiang Kai-shek [Jiang Jieshi], through the President, on the American Chiefs of Staff.' The fact that transport aircraft belonged to the USA and that the conquest of lower Burma did not concern the Americans were critical factors that militated against British interests. None of those points would be known by soldiers in the jungle but their influence would be felt throughout the campaign.

Burma had an impossibly low priority for its defence arrangements and was woefully ill-prepared for any military attack as the jungle was

---

[1] One battalion managed to escape the ban.

thought to be impenetrable. The Japanese had made successful efforts to undermine Burmese cooperation with the British and advanced with a momentum and ferocity that took everyone by surprise, so giving the impression of being 'supermen' compared with pre-war colonial inertia.

Japanese soldiers were given basic training in the intangibles of battle – spirit, loyalty, sacrifice and obedience – to a greater extent than in minor tactics and weapon handling. The words 'retreat' and 'defence' were not in the Field Service Regulations (1928) for the Imperial Army. This, and an unquestioning faith in the inevitable victory of Japan, led to cruelties and self-sacrifice unseen in, and unsurpassed by, other armies. The Indian Army's doctrine and training never envisaged such fighting so its men started with a grave moral as well as serious material disadvantages. Such tactics as battle drills, designed to implement instinctive and instant reactions, were only later introduced. But drills and regimental pride were poor counters to Japanese fanaticism.

The war was fought with a tenacity, savagery and drama seldom witnessed, over a country that has mountains, jungles, open plains, fast-flowing and deep rivers, few roads, and a monsoon that restricted ground and air operations. On the one side were the Japanese with some Burmese and Indian support, and on the other were British, Gurkha, Indian, Burmese, Chinese and African troops. Fighting took place on a large and small scale, presenting a bewildering array of withdrawal, thrust and counter-thrust, attack, defence, patrols and ambushes. The course of the campaign was difficult enough to follow for planners and participants at a high level, utterly impossible for others of lowly status in a rifle section. Making sense of it half a century later, even with maps and in outline, is not easy.

Narratives have been divided into four phases, with the caveat that many of the men interviewed, being muddled as to dates, places and sequence of events so long afterwards, have made even these four phases overlap:

The Loss of Burma, 1941–42
First Chindit Operation, 1943
The Arakan, Kohima and Imphal, 1943–44
The Reconquest of Burma, 1944–45.

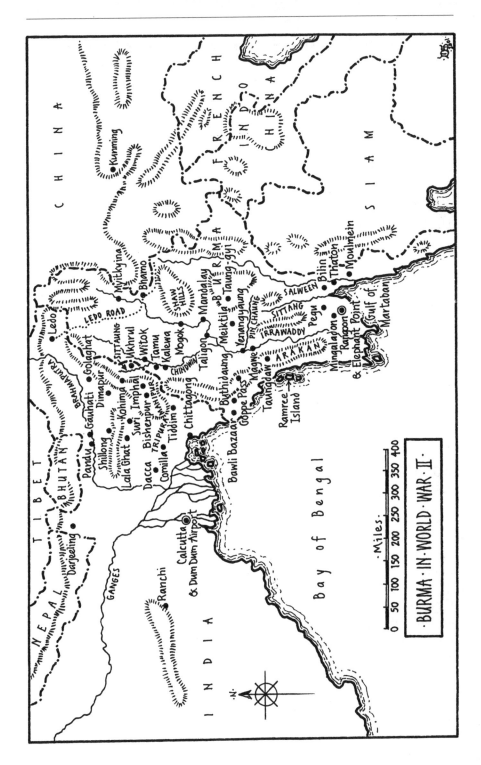

· BURMA · IN · WORLD · WAR · II ·

The Loss of Burma, 1941–42

The event that indelibly seared itself into many of our interviewee's minds was the blowing of the bridge over the Sittang River on 23 February 1942 which left many men hopelessly stranded on the far bank and vulnerable both to the hungry river and the ferocious Japanese. Such a catastrophe, unimagined and unimaginable, caused so much trauma among Gurkhas that none could believe that a responsible commander could possibly have given such an order – it could only have been given by a spy.

It was later alleged that Subhas Chandra Bose, leader of the INA, gave the order but it was only in May 1943 that he transferred from a German submarine to a Japanese one off the coast of Sumatra. The spy theory had many permutations, some of which are quoted, even though they are very likely unmitigated fantasy.

Rangoon fell soon after the Sittang disaster and the retreating forces failed to regroup and hold on to central Burma. The Japanese deployed on a two-divisional front, one to the north against the Chinese who were unable to stop them and the other towards India. The retreat continued.

Balbahadur Gurung, MC and Bar, 1/3 GR, *finished the war as a subedar.*

I enlisted on 1 March 1927. After war broke out we went to Secunderabad where the old NCOs were sent back to the depot and I was promoted to CQMH. There we did jungle training. We were sent to Calcutta and on, by sea, to Rangoon. We had no idea about the war but what a shambles it all was. We had to take positions in holes when Japanese aircraft flew over. We were in Rangoon for about a week.

We were sent over the Sittang River, crossing by the road and rail bridge, to contact the Japanese somewhere near the Thai–Burma border but they were advancing so we soon met them. We were given an order to return to the Sittang but we were late in returning. 1/4 GR were in time and crossed over but 1/3 GR, 2/5 GR, 1/7 GR and 3/7 GR were stuck on the wrong side.

The Japanese were in a commanding position, flying a large flag. 1/3 GR was ordered to attack their HQ which was near a large temple. The

CO, newly posted in from 2/3 GR, was killed.[2] Others were also killed or taken prisoner. 1/3 GR approached the bridge at 1800 hours and tried to cross the river individually but the Japanese killed many of them and the others disappeared. We stayed where we were, surrounded by the enemy all night. Then, at 0600 hours the next morning, with a fearful noise, the bridge was blown. We did not know where to go nor what to do.

At 1500 hours we got an order to try our luck as best we could. We had eaten nothing all day but did not feel hungry as we felt we were soon to be taken prisoner. On that order everybody took to their heels and ran to the river, making a deep thrumming noise as they ran. A rope had been drawn across the water but we could not use it because the Japanese killed all who tried to cross over using it. The acting CO, Major Bradford, and Subedar Major Gagansing Thapa took out their pistols to try to prevent the rest of us from going across. Many more died, including Bradford sahib and the subedar major, who shot each other dead rather than become prisoners of war, which seemed inevitable.[3] I was there at the time and saw it happen.

We went to prepare what we could, individually, for flotation. I had been forward on a recce so had had no time to prepare anything. At the river's edge there was a tremendous crowd and many, many more men died there. I decided to wait a bit. I saw a lot of black-haired heads bobbing in the water as they floated downstream, dead. None of that lot got across.

By then we had been ordered to throw away our weapons and equipment into the river. All I had were the clothes I stood up in. With me were Naik Chintaram Thapa, who could swim a bit, Subedar Harku Thapa and his orderly, Bhaktabahadur Thapa, who could not swim a stroke. Harku Thapa, an Almorah "line boy" and senior GO of C Company, was taken prisoner and Bhaktabahadur sank. I told Chintaram to cross as best he could and I fixed Bhaktabahadur up with

---

[2] Lt Col G.A. Ballinger. On 22 February 1942, he came across some Japanese who held up their hands in surrender. Telling his escort not to open fire he went to take them prisoner. As he did so they fell on their faces and he was killed by LMG fire from behind.

[3] According to the regimental history, a Japanese officer came forward to accept Maj F.K. Bradford's surrender but Sub Maj Gagansing Thapa, refusing to surrender, fired his pistol at the Japanese and then shot himself through the heart. The Japanese officer who had accepted Bradford's pistol used it to kill him. A naik then shot the Japanese officer through the head.

a few pieces of wood on which he floated. I told him how to move his legs and I pushed him across. He finished up as an honorary captain and still calls me father, praising me to his wife. I never saw Chintaram again.

Halfway across was a small island on which we rested. The Japanese were firing machine guns on fixed lines. Bhaktabahadur was helpless, but got away with it. I kept my head below water much of the time. When we started again the sun was setting and I used a particular tree on the far bank as a marker. Fish killed by the blowing of the bridge lined the river's edge. I saw a British officer who looked as if he was sitting down but he had sunk into the mud. He asked me my unit and I told him. I tried to pull him out but could not and he ordered us to go to an RV and have a meal with 1/4 GR. I suppose he drowned in the mud, or maybe the Japanese got him first, I don't know.

The 1/4 GR CQMH, who gave me a meal in a leaf, was Lalbahadur Gurung, my brother-in-law whose house is next to mine in my village. Before I could finish my meal a train whistled. I had to rush to it, throwing away my meal. We were told to get off at Pegu. Had we gone on to Rangoon in it that would have been the last of us.

We waited a week in Pegu for reinforcements and rations and Cameron sahib, a well-known man, made 1/3 GR and 2/5 GR into one battalion. On leaving Pegu we were badly ambushed by the Japanese who fired continuously at us. We were dressed in PT kit and armed only with rifles and one bandolier of ammunition. All our wounded died and we burnt their corpses. When we tried to escape, the Japanese hit us with artillery and ambushed us once more. Our own 3-inch mortars returned fire and I made my escape.

Eventually we got to Manipur, having made our own way there, living off the land. All parachute drops of food sent to us fell into Japanese hands. We were there three months, during which time we were given 20 days' leave. I managed to get home for ten days, having walked very fast. Many thought I must be dead. I got no more leave till the end of the war.

Chandrabahadur Pun, 1/3 GR.   We were posted to Secunderabad in Hyderabad and trained for war. No one told us where the war was or who were our enemies. We were then stood to and went to the railway station in a hurry and finished up in Madras. But from there, where to? We saw the officers weeping because they were leaving their families so we knew we were going away to fight. But where to? No one told us. I also saw our Gurkha officers take some soil and dab their foreheads with it as a prayer for a safe return.

In Madras harbour I counted 36 big ships in lines. We moved out to sea and heard firing. Our NCOs told us it was artillery from the land being fired to encourage us. But no, it was covering fire with a range of 75 miles but still the officers did not tell us where we were heading for. We sailed past an island to our right and sailed on into the "black water". One old NCO told us that we were on our way to Burma. None of us had heard of Burma. We reached a place called Rangoon. There were lines of ships there also and 2/5 GR lost 18 men in a Japanese air attack. I was ordered to fix an LMG on top of the ship and fire back at the aircraft. I don't know if we hit any but the bullets snapped the boat's wireless wiring which all fell on me.

We disembarked in a hurry. Some of the other troops started to panic and the subedar major drew his pistol to ensure that we had an orderly disembarkation and said he'd shoot anyone who didn't heed his warning. My group had to stay up top till the very end. We were driven 32 miles out of the town to a rubber estate and camped there. That night we saw Japanese aircraft bomb Rangoon and we were afraid we would also be a target. A British officer told us we were going to Singapore but, even then, we heard that the Japanese had taken it. We entrained for Penang instead but went up a branch line that night. We heard cocks crow and thought we were in a big village but the birds were jungle fowl so we knew we were in deep jungle.

Next day the officer told us that the enemy would attack us and we had to make a stand so we dug a defensive position. I was a naik by then and my section was sent on a patrol. I was given a compass and map and told that there was a very big tree and a track and we had to reach there. We got there, walking through long grass and met eight Japanese at the place. I saw the long grass moving and told my men to lie down. That was the first time I'd seen the enemy. Before that I did not know what the Japanese looked like. The eight men stayed at the tree. We heard a noise, "kerek, kerek, kerek". I told the section I would go forward by myself and see what was happening and they were to cover me. I moved stealthily and saw that the Japanese were cutting the tree down with a long hand-saw to make a road block. I had a good look at them and moved back to my section, slowly. Once there I told the gunner to give me his LMG. I fired three magazines rapid at them and killed them all and brought back eight rifles. We doubled back to the company lines to escape any follow up.

I was given a big *shabash* when I reported what had happened and handed over the rifles. We continued to dig defensive positions. Another platoon took a patrol to a field of sugar cane near the tree. It was attacked by 15 Japanese and we heard the firing so we stood to. We went to search the sugar cane field and found 15 Japanese corpses. Everybody was shown the dead men to see what the Japanese looked like – like us but with longer hair and different uniform. It had not been a big fight.

One British officer, Foster sahib, told me and one other to go with him on a patrol and we went ahead with him following on behind. We saw a big man embracing a tree and went to see what was the trouble. He was a Garhwali CHM. The Japanese had nailed his hands and feet to the tree. He was dead. Foster sahib was horrified. He said: "One bullet could have been enough; why kill him so cruelly?" We went forward with our rifles at the hip position and found two men from 2/5 GR, wearing their Gurkha hats, tied together by their red lanyards and who had been stabbed to death by bamboo slivers. Foster sahib said that the Japanese were very wicked and stopped talking to us, he was so shocked. We had a short break. He took out his map and sent us over a river to where he thought the Japanese might come, to take up an ambush position. Once we got there we saw ten dead men hanging with their ankles wired to the bridge. Foster sahib could not contain his disgust.

We took up a position and our own artillery came up that way with the pieces on mules. We went to help them unload but, before we could get to them, 15 Japanese appeared and tried to capture them. But we captured the Japanese, all 15 of them. The Punjabi gunner officer said he could not cope with the prisoners so Foster sahib, in anger, ordered us to go back to our tents, cut the ropes off them, bring them back and tie up the prisoners. We were ordered to tie them in twos and threes. Foster sahib said his mind was so unhappy that we had to lay them on the ground while he went to fetch a carrier. Once back he drove the carrier over them, backwards and forwards, killing them as they lay on the ground. He then said he was feeling better.

He said he would go back to our base on the carrier and made us walk back. By that time we had been in that area for about a month altogether.

That was our life, fighting and resting in turn. 1/4 GR joined us so we were three Gurkha battalions with 2/5 GR and my own 1/3 GR. We were half way between Penang and the Sittang. The Japanese had come into that area before as they had close relations with the Burmese. I spoke to an Indian who told me that the Burmese had been offered a hundred rupee reward for the capture of a British officer and fifty for a Gurkha, so we had to be careful where we went.

One day a British officer told me to take my platoon and all the weapons 17 miles away to an all-weather road and dig trenches on both sides. Jemadar Manus was sent with me to help. We used many wild banana plants to camouflage our positions. We set up the three LMGs and Jemadar Manus said they were correctly fixed. A Burmese *sadhu* came along the road and we beckoned him to us. He told us that that evening 7,000 Japanese would be attacking there and we were to be alert. He was a Japanese spy. That evening, as it became dark, we saw lights flickering and flashing and I told the men to stay vigilant in their fighting positions. Lights then appeared on a second side, then on a third.

I told Manus that the men were scared and to give them encouragement. He told them not to open fire before he did and if they did he'd shoot them. Seven Japanese, wearing camouflage, came along the road and Manus did not open fire so we did not either. A little later long lines of Japanese came along the road. Manus still didn't order us to open fire so I gave orders to fire with every weapon, including all three LMGs on fixed lines. Manus was struck dumb by it all and fell down in a faint. We killed as many as we could. Manus came to his senses and shouted "barrel change" but we continued firing. He found his walking stick that had fallen on the ground and came over to us and hit the gunners on the head, shouting "barrel change". The barrels were red hot by this time so we did change them. We then ran out of ammunition.

I was called over by Manus who told me to take some men and collect hats, rifles and identification marks from the dead men. Nobody wanted to go with me so I went forward alone. Dead Japanese were all over the place, for all the world like a lot of sheep that had been killed by fighting. Manus joined me and put some white paper on their bottoms to count them. We did this but Manus and I fell into a swamp of quicksand and started sinking. Manus called the men to cut a tree and rescue us with a branch by pulling us out. This they did and we were so covered in mud that we changed into spare clothing there and then.

Manus said we'd have a rest and, if we wanted to smoke, we'd have to roll over with our mouths near the ground. We had started to smoke when the Japanese opened artillery fire on the road block for two hours, not where we were on the edge of the swamp. No damage was caused. We watched the shells hit the road. Only on the third day did we rejoin the battalion.

I was given a big *shabash*. I am an unlucky man as in a former existence I gained no merit, which has meant that in this life I received no *bahaduri* for anything I did.

Then the Japanese surrounded us and the fighting started in earnest. Bullets were flying everywhere and the company commander said that 36 British tanks were coming to give us support and my section would have to help them. The tanks came and I went to report to the commander, a major. He wanted a briefing from me and I got on the tank with my section and away we went.

We were told we'd go and attack after our artillery had fired on the Japanese. The Japanese are fools: they'd kill themselves with grenades as they were trying to kill the tank. Our job was to shoot them before they tried to do this by mounting LMGs and rifles on the outside of the tanks. On we went. The Japanese were quiet in our sector but were pressing elsewhere. The Punjabis had sent their 3 Platoon into that sector to help our men but they were driven back. 1/4 GR then went in but they were unable to make any difference. It was night time and the turn of 1/3 GR. I was ordered to attack the Japanese at 0330 hours. 2692 Havildar Chandrabahadur,[4] son of a jemadar, was with the CO when I was called by name and was told that the Japanese had a strong defensive position. "The other battalions have not been successful. Anyone can go but I'd like you to. I'll give you an IOM if successful. Take a box of grenades with you." I said I'd go and the CO said I'd have to reach the Japanese position by 0300 hours, 0330 at the latest.

So we went, carefully, crawling in places, showing no silhouette. I

---

[4] Because there are comparatively few Gurkha names in use it was common for there to be several men in a unit with the same name. When this happened, as in this case, part of each man's army serial number would be given with his name to identify him correctly.

met what I thought was a bank of earth and realized I had got to the very heart of the Japanese defensive position. I moved back a little, fixed my LMG and prepared the grenades. In all I threw three grenades. By the light of the first I saw a straw hut, the Japanese guard room. That grenade also set up a Japanese alarm. I threw a second and a third, which hit the hut and the ammunition inside exploded. The place lit up and we were engaged in hand-to-hand fighting. I was bayonetted three times, in the left shoulder, head and leg. I did not lose consciousness. My right hand automatically reached for the pistol I was carrying and I shot six rounds and saw six Japanese fall. That cheered me up. A large stone was dropped on me from somewhere on the bank, hit me in the chest, breaking a bone. I became unconscious.

When I regained consciousness I was covered in blood. It was nearly dawn. The Japanese fired three Very lights and artillery fire opened on all sides and set the jungle alight. When it was a little lighter 2/5 GR came to give us support. I was lying on the ground half conscious. I had no idea how many of my section were dead or wounded. I heard a Gurkha officer who saw me say "Here's a dead one." I was put on a stretcher and taken away. In that Japanese bombardment the CO and Havildar Chandrabahadur were killed, along with many others, so my IOM was lost.

I was sent back to hospital, crossing the Sittang before the bridge was blown. I was flown out to Dum Dum, Calcutta, and sent to a hospital in Lucknow. When I had recovered I was sent on 84 days' leave. By then it was sometime in 1943.

Chakrabahadur Tamang, 1/7 GR, *joined the army on 5 August 1940.*

When we were at Rawalpindi we were told to make ready to go to Malaya. We carried one change of clothes and a blanket. We went by train to Calcutta and embarked at night. We were told that the Japanese had attacked Malaya and we were to go to Burma. However, two days out bugles were blown and gongs were rung so we all gathered in one place and the CO told us that one ship was unable to move so we had to return to Calcutta. I had a thousand rounds always ready for my Bren gun. After waiting 48 hours in Calcutta we set off for Rangoon. Communication between ships was by semaphore.

I was on duty at the top of the ship's masts as we approached

Rangoon. I had my Bren gun and binoculars. I had been told that Japanese aircraft were red and ours were white and to shoot down the red ones if they came to attack us, but they did not come. I had a telephone with me and I was told to come down. Rangoon was a big and busy place. We went off to Mingladon airfield. After a day or so we went by rail to Martaban, crossed the river and went by vehicle to Moulmein. B Company had to move forward to the Thai border which took us three days to reach. Once there we dug trenches. We had no weapons heavier than a 3-inch mortar.

The border was a small river and the OC used binoculars to observe into Thailand. He saw some soldiers he took for Thai Army men and told us they would come to the border to contact us as both we and they had to guard the border. That night the Japanese cut our telephone line and fired artillery at us. We exchanged fire. At dawn we retired as with no telephone we had no information. It was a hard march back, sometimes through jungle, sometimes through scrub, with the Japanese always chasing us. The Japanese were already at Martaban and had two aircraft on the ground there. After a lot of bother we managed to cross the river higher up in small boats by night and met up with the battalion. When it was daylight the Japanese bombed us and caused casualties, dead and wounded.

We managed to get to Thaton and had hoped for tank support but they had been knocked out. We had no air or artillery support. It was chaotic. We retreated to Bilin where the platoon commander was evacuated wounded. My Bren 2 took three bullets in his chest and we had to leave his body in the jungle. The section to our right fired back at the Japanese as they saw their heads approaching above the undergrowth. Contact was broken off. After a quiet night we were bombarded again the next day by when we were near the Sittang. We were told 16 Brigade would help us from over the river but the bridge was blown before that happened. It could only have been the work of a Japanese spy in our army to have blown the bridge and left us on the wrong side. We felt we would die there as we had been defeated. All was ruined. And how many dead there were!

We made floats from what we could but Japanese aircraft were flying up and down shooting those trying to cross. The group I was with received orders to try and make our own way back to Meiktila, Mandalay or Rangoon, whichever was the easiest to reach and to throw away our weapons. But I kept hold of mine. We looked up and down the river and saw the enemy firing all round. We kept quiet, moving from place to place as best we could. We went back to the river but couldn't cross it, so we went back to hide in the jungle. The Japanese were everywhere.

By then there were five of us. We hid, evaded and retreated. Next morning we were very hungry as we had no rations. As we had a bit of money we went to a Burmese house and said we'd buy some food from them. But they would not sell us any, saying they had none.[5] As we were so hungry we decided we had to break into a house and see what we could get. This we did. Two men went and came back with a pot of cooked rice. As we were scooping out handfuls and eating, a Japanese officer and three soldiers, with bayonets fixed to their rifles, came upon us and shouted to us to put our hands up. The Burmese we had asked for rations must have told the Japanese of our presence.

So, with hands up, I approached the officer who shook me by the hand. He took us to the bungalow he was using and we were told to sit on the grass outside while he went inside and had his meal. When he came out the soldiers saluted him and we were told to stand up. We were on the move all day, no food and no water, walking through rubber estates. We were taken to a wired-off piece of land where many of the battalion were, British officers as well. "So you've come to join us?" one asked. "We thought you had escaped." "We tried to but could not. Now hunger will kill us," I replied. "The Japanese give us a handful of rice, about as much as we feed the chickens with," he said. "Sit down. We've been here four days."

At 1700 hours the Japanese brought four of the vehicles we had put out of action, shouting "*Wei wei*" and a lot else at us in a loud voice. We were pushed inside, packed tighter than a load of goats. We were shut in and sentries were placed. As we drove off into the night we passed groups of Japanese soldiers and the sentries shouted out that enemy soldiers had been captured.

By next morning we were back at Martaban and taken over the river in small boats tied to a river steamer. Many of our battalion were there, including the British officers. In mid-stream two of our fighters came and strafed the place. Our officers took off their hats and waved at

---

5   Chakrabahadur related the entire conversation in Burmese which he had learnt and had not forgotten 58 years later. Likewise his conversations with Japanese, Chinese and British people were first given in the appropriate language and only later in Nepali for our benefit. Remarkable.

them. Two Japanese aircraft appeared but ours shot them both down.

We were put into the civilian jail, packed tightly together, for the rest of 1942. We had no new clothing, no hair cuts, no washing, never enough water to drink and mosquitoes the whole time. There were 42 of us on the upper storey. British officers were separate. Some time in 1943 we were taken out. We were in bad physical shape. We were taken to Taunggyi in the Shan hills where we had to make roads, build bridges, clear the undergrowth and do coolie work generally.

I overheard the Japanese talking on the telephone and understood them. They said that the Chinese and Americans were advancing towards them and there was to be no falling back from that position. "We mustn't retire as we are getting reinforcements." As we listened to their talk I saw the situation was going against the Japanese and that we ought to escape but a subedar of 5 GR said we were not to try. I felt we ought to run away and try to join the Chinese. I had made friends with a 5 GR man who knew Chinese and I had written what he taught me in a note book. This man said he was a boatman and he could take us over any river we had to cross.

There were 11 of us. I took some cutting tools and one night cut the wire and we escaped. We were soon in thick jungle. One morning we saw some troops on a far hilltop, but we could not tell if they were Japanese or Chinese. Through some binoculars we saw artillery fire. I said I'd go forward and see who those troops were. There was a track but it was dangerous so I decided to go through the jungle. It was a most difficult route, involving much scrambling up and slipping down. I got to within shouting distance of a sentry and called out in Japanese but got an answer in Chinese. I went straight back to the others and took them forward. "I'll go in front, you follow me," and went along the track. The Chinese had ambushes in three places on the track. The Chinese shouted "Hands up. Come here," so we came and saw a corporal, lance corporal and a private soldier sitting down drinking tea.

We were interrogated, all in Chinese, and I told them we were "Indian sahibs" who had escaped from the Japanese camp. We were told to sit down and have some tea. We were asked if we had eaten and we said we hadn't eaten for a few days so the Chinese, expressing their sorrow, cooked us a meal. A little later two Chinese officers came and, in English, asked us who we were. "Are you Surkha?" [*sic*] "Yes." "Good." He took a map out and I showed him where we had come from, and what route we had used. I also showed him the Japanese positions, their fuel dump, ration stores, where they had already been hit and where they had not been hit, where the Japanese senior officers' accommodation was and a lot more.

The Chinese officer said we had been at a place called Bosee and he contacted Kunming for an air raid on the Japanese position on the morrow. We were told we would have an escort for a four-day journey to a road-head at Lungling and from there transport would take us on. So, with rations and an escort, we walked for four days and, on reaching Lungling, were given a vehicle and two drivers and were driven 188km to Posang. We started at 0900 hours and on the way went over the Salween. We got to Posang between 1600 and 1700 hours where there were a lot of American and Chinese servicemen on the road and the hills who shouted their welcome at us. Only American aircraft were there, no Chinese.

Next day we motored the 160km to Kunming and met a major and a captain of 9 GR. We were asked if we had been in Chinese hands on 11 October. "Yes." We were allowed to clean up and were given rations by the Chinese quartermaster so we could cook on our own. We were completely kitted out, including bedding. We were asked if we could drive and we said that there was a driver in our group.

The major told us we had had a very rough time so we were to relax for a couple of months when he'd get us an aircraft to fly us out, in the meantime to write a letter telling about our journey and where we now were. During our stay more 1/7 GR men came in from the camp, including the 5 GR subedar who had told us not to break out of camp. Two 1/7 GR men had died in the camp since we left.

So we were put into an aeroplane and were flown to Dum Dum in Calcutta.[6] We said we'd started out from Shillong but were told that Shillong was no more and we had to go to Palampur. Once there we did our *pani patya* and were extensively debriefed and sent on three months' leave. All was as usual at home; my parents had no idea what I'd been through. I returned as an instructor. We celebrated the end of the German and the Japanese war. We were all sent home after that and I finished my service on 5 August 1946.

---

[6] A most wonderful sigh of relief escaped from Chakrabahadur here, he had been reliving it all!

Padamlal Pun, 1/4 GR.   I am very pleased to be able to have this heaven-sent opportunity to talk today. Although I am old it makes me feel young again to be able to talk about my war experiences. We old men feel uplifted by being asked to tell our war stories.

Britain, USA and China joined together to fight the Japanese and Germans. The whole world trembled. That was how dangerous it was when I volunteered, on 20 November 1940, to join the army and help the British.

I was enlisted in 4 GR and trained in Bakloh. We were busy for nine months after which I was made lance naik and sent to the MT Platoon in 1/4 GR. 1/4 GR moved to Secunderabad. We went to Rangoon by boat and I was posted to 48 Brigade HQ as a driver. We had to retreat in the face of the Japanese. The Japanese told the Burmese to kill the British and all the Indian civilians had to be sent back to India. We reached the River Sittang and at 0600 hours the order to blow the bridge was given and it was blown at 0800 hours. It fell into the river.

At Sittang was a senior officer, a German. He was our commander. His secret wireless was on his wrist, like a watch. He talked into it to the Japanese saying that he had done his bit and now it was up to them. After that Clark sahib said, "Oh, our commander is a spy" and arrested him. He stripped him of his badges of rank. He was taken to Manipur where he had to wear a garland of boots, was put in chains and tins were beaten behind him as one would scare away a dog. After that I don't know what happened to him.[7]

At the Sittang half our forces were on the far bank when the bridge was blown. These people became distraught and some jumped into the river. The mules were left to look after themselves. I saw about 25 men take off their equipment and clothes and try to swim across. Only ten were successful and the others were drowned or eaten by crocodiles.

We eventually got to Mandalay where we were engaged in a ten-day battle. There were not many survivors when we ended up at Manipur.

48 Brigade Commander told us to take tank ammunition to Pegu. I loaded it up and took it there where 17 Division HQ was. I had driven all night and at 0600 hours reached a bridge over a river and crossed it. There was a convoy in front of me in which was the division

---

[7]   However outlandish this tale might sound, variations on this theme crop up in other stories. How much is pure gossip, how much is the result of crude Japanese propaganda or how small a kernel of truth there is in this tale will probably never be known.

commander. There was a space with tall plants in it, like a garden, on the right of the bridge and an open plain to the left. All the officers went into the garden but found many Japanese who were hiding there. A battle started. The general was shot and a British sergeant carried him to the road towards my vehicle. He died as he was being carried. I left my vehicle as that was no place to hide. I saw a cement bridge I thought I could hide under so went there but found an enemy LMG post so didn't stay there. I went up a small re-entrant but the Japanese there threw a grenade at me. Before it exploded I jumped to the left and escaped.

I was very hungry by evening because the battle had continued all day. I went back onto the road when the firing ceased. I was just starting up my vehicle when a section of British troops arrived. They put their LMG in the body, jumped in and I drove off at high speed. Corpses were everywhere for the next two miles. There was a railway line after that and I saw ten division HQ men. I spoke with them. A soldier from 2/5 GR was with me and we spent a night in that location. There was a camp of reinforcements on the main Rangoon–Manipur road and next morning we met them and had a meal there. As we started eating we were attacked by many Japanese aircraft. The reinforcements fired back, single shots and rapid fire, and shot some down. Then more Japanese aircraft came over. *What* a din! I went to hide in a ravine and the 2/5 GR man followed me. For an hour we were bombed and there was dust everywhere. I was not hit.

The Japanese aeroplanes flew away and the dust settled. They had dropped up to 400 bombs on the reinforcements, the cookhouse, which was destroyed, and on the artillery. The guns were smashed. Our vehicles had been lined up at the side of the road on the right. Those drivers who had lain on the ground on their chests had been killed by the vibration while those who had knelt and leant forward were alive, shaken and deaf. Some vehicles had also been destroyed. The 2/5 GR man had had his right arm ripped off by a bomb splinter. I left him to be looked after by the reinforcements, got into my vehicle and chased after eight division HQ vehicles which were moving to the north up the main Rangoon–Manipur road. Two other vehicles of brigade HQ were with me.

That night I witnessed an area of scorched earth. In that area every living thing was dead. It was quiet with no shooting. I drove through it safely and caught up the convoy. Ahead of it were British tanks and we were now 11 vehicles. We had no food, no sleep and were constantly stopping and starting, stopping and starting. I wondered what it was all about. There was fighting ahead of us. Between 0400 and 0500 hours we reached the Pin Chaung river where the Japanese had set fire to the petrol stored there. Flames spread to the sky. As we had heard no noise of artillery or aeroplanes we were very surprised. At Magwe on the right was jungle and the left was open country and in the middle a slope where fighting was taking place.

A British captain came up to us and said "Gurkhas, Gurkhas. Form up!" All 11 GORs of my group went to form up. He pointed out where we were to patrol. On the left was some open ground, so nothing was there, but the jungle was full of Japanese. Transport animals – elephants, camels and mules – were corralled there but there were no handlers. We told the captain that there were many Japanese so we couldn't do anything but he said "Fucking Japs" and went to the wireless and asked for artillery support. Fire orders were given. The machine guns fired and killed many Japanese whom we found next morning. I left my vehicle there and moved off on foot to the left, up a ravine which was stacked full of dead men. If I stay here I'll die, I said to myself, and if I go to the right or straight on I'll die, so I'll go to the left, I decided.

I moved off and came to a field of ground nuts where I was fired on. In fact firing was all round but I wasn't hit. I reached a hillock. It was quiet. I was tired and thirsty. I saw a spring of water and drank from it with cupped hands. I sat down to think. In the rear, Japanese. In front of me, Japanese. More Japanese to my right. On my left was a big river and I felt I could get across but I was afraid of wild animals in the jungle over on the far side. So where could I go? There was nowhere at all! I had seen a gold-leafed pagoda so I decided to go there. I made my way along a small track towards it. I got there and saw *jogis*, *fakirs* and Japanese working on captured 17 Division equipment and one man exploded a round of tank ammunition. I called to the *jogi* but he knew no English, no Hindi, no Khaskura.

He looked at me in a scared way and I saw it was no use to talk with him and it would be dangerous for me to stay as I would be killed. I left and saw a place where 2,000 people were enclosed. They were Indians trying to escape to India but who couldn't go forward because of the fighting. I saw a couple of elderly people and tried to make contact with them but they started shouting "The Japanese have come, the Japanese have come." "No, no," I said and told them who I was.

"The Japanese often come to check us and you won't live when they see you. If you stay with us, take off your uniform," I was told. I took my clothes off and put on the ones they gave me, a green shirt, a red hat and a loin cloth. I also painted my face black, with soot from their cooking pots, so as to look like the Indians.

And Japanese soldiers did come. Speaking in Burmese they asked the children in the crowd if anyone new, any enemy, had got into their midst. The children said that no one new had come. The soldiers put their rifles in the corner and started playing with the children. I saw they enjoyed that. They left and more came. I drank some tea and spent the day there. The Indians also gave me some food.

Next morning I rose at 0400 hours and the Indians cooked some food for me. The man in charge of the crowd shouted out for us to move off and the Indians gave me some of their bundles to carry. I moved off in the middle of the crowd. At one place I passed between Japanese and Chinese who were having a battle so I was encircled. Some of the Indians were killed and some ran away. I, being a soldier, lay flat as the bullets came overhead and only stood up when the firing stopped. I escaped by following the Chinese. I would not be accepted as a civilian so I stripped the clothes off a Chinese corpse and, picking up the dead man's rifle, continued my journey behind the Chinese soldiers.

I reached the Chinese camp where the huts were made of leaves and straw. I didn't go in straight away because I saw men and women bathing together in the nude without shame. They *had* to be communists. I couldn't stay with such people but I was called forward and spoken to. They did not speak Hindi or English and merely stared at me. I was hungry and ate some food they had thrown away and carried on by myself. Two miles farther on I met up with a company of Indian Army Sappers and Miners. There was an English captain who asked me what I was doing. "I've come back from the firing line," I told him. "Tell me all you know," he said. The men who had fallen in were surprised to see me. I was allowed to stay there the night.

During the night a message came from the Chinese that they had taken the firing line and if we had left anything there to go and collect it. Next morning I was told by the captain that we had to go and fetch the vehicles and a tank that the Chinese I had met the day before were guarding. I was to go with the fatigue party of 15 to collect them. So I went back to the firing line but the Japanese had destroyed them. They had set fire to them and the metal parts were still gleaming red with heat.

There was a civilian truck with the ignition key in the steering column. I found it could be started and had fuel in it. In the truck I found brigade HQ's money and kit. A section of British troops who had escaped from the Japanese encirclement arrived. I took them in the truck up to the Sappers and Miners' camp. I told the captain what I had done and he praised me. I was told to separate what was needed of the stores from that which was not needed. I gave the three boxes of money to the captain, and gave the rations to the company. We moved off in the truck with the Sappers and Miners and reached a river with no road bridge but there was a bamboo bridge made by the villagers. We left the truck there and crossed over with what we could.

On the other side we met up with some ox carts in each of which we put three men. All day we continued on our way in the ox carts. We spent the night in a cultivated place by the side of the road and after our meal went to sleep. We were fired on heavily. The Indians had no weapons, nor had I so where to go? I and two Indians walked off on our own for eight days, sleeping and eating when we had the chance. Villagers had been told by the Japanese to kill us, so as soon as we heard dogs barking we veered off to a flank.

We saw two boats on the Chindwin with a British officer in each. They looked at us through binoculars and beckoned us forward. We went to the edge of the river. It was like meeting our parents again! We got into one of the boats and were taken to Kalewa. There I was told to go and spy on some villagers who were said to be pro-Japanese. The Indians were kept on board and hidden. I put on village clothes and went to spy on the villagers.

I met a subedar from the Tripura State Forces who could speak English and the local language well and he managed to get me some food. We got back to Manipur together and the Indians also managed to get back there. There had been heavy fighting. I stayed at 0 Mile Stone and another bombardment was expected. But my battalion was at Kohima so I went there. I found the two Nepalese Contingent units, the *Kalibahadur* and the *Sher Dal*, were there already. Why were they in Kohima? Because the Manipur raja had married a Nepali princess Nepali troops had to go and guard her.

I was interrogated and the staff of officers and men there were very surprised at my tale. "You have had so much trouble and experience.

We are going back that way. Stay with us," the soldiers said to me. We went back a little to another camp where wounded and lost men were collected. Rations were issued from there. I stayed there. The rations were in short supply so one day I was sent out to collect jungle produce. Then I was told that all the fit men had to go to Manipur and rejoin their units. I was so happy to be able to meet up with what was my lost family. The CO, Walton sahib, and Lokendrabahadur were there with nine others. Only 11 of us. They all congratulated me on surviving, patting me on the back. I did likewise to them.

Five days later many of our men trooped in, all with matted hair. Then, with my friends around me, the CO told us to get our heads shaved.[8] There was no knife to shave our heads with so a canteen knife was brought and sharpened. As each man's hair was taken off, it was found to be full of bits of metal from bomb and grenade splinters. We were re-kitted. There were no parades, no timetable. We were free to wander around as we pleased. We couldn't understand what was happening. We played British and American board games. Those who wanted to have a woman were allowed into the villages. For us who had been in such a war it was like heaven.

Purnahang Limbu, 1/7 GR and 154 Gurkha Parachute Battalion, *joined the army on 7 December 1940, having been taken down to the recruiting depot by a Gurkha officer.*

I had no idea what I was being enlisted for but, after I had had my head shaved, I hoped I would not be sent home as I would feel disgraced.[9] I went to Shillong and was told to stay on after I had finished recruit training. I was first posted to 4/7 GR but later to 1/7 GR. As I had taken of the *Sarkar's* salt I had to stay. Eight months after joining the army I was sent to Ranchi for another six months and on to Poona for a watermanship course when I nearly drowned. We were motored to Calcutta and embarked.

That ship was taking us over the sea. Next morning I could only tell east by the rising sun but had no idea of direction until the sun went down that evening. If the ship sank we had nothing to catch hold of. We got to Rangoon which was in flames. On the ground we walked

---

[8] All military Gurkhas had shaven pates and *tupis* until 1946.
[9] For not being good enough for enlistment.

over logs still hot and bent tin, treading on ash. We heard a noise and I asked what it was. Aircraft, the NCO said, but could give no answer to my questions when I asked him what it was all about. We were all in the dark.

We reached Martaban but I still did not know what it was all about and why we were going there. We were shown a track and told the Japanese would come along it. We made fire positions and then stood to. We were told to fire if the Japanese came. Many Japanese did come and I fired and killed one. I did not see where the others went. Later we were surrounded by swarms of Japanese. We pulled back. I found that some food and rum were being given out so I had some. A British officer was wounded and was asking for water. He later died.

We were ordered to make our own escape. But how? Moving off I was startled when I slipped down a slope and into some water but did not hurt myself. I got up into a field of grass. I told myself that I had taken my oath and had to be ready for what came. There were 11 of us and we had no rations. A jemadar said we could catch and kill anything there was to eat but, because there were so many Japanese around, we could not fire our rifles nor light a fire. Anything we got hold of would have to be eaten raw. We did fire at a pig but missed it.

In Pegu, I think it was, I and another GOR, 10010 his number was, were moving along and a Japanese tried to fire at us with his machine gun. It jammed. I fired at him with my Tommy gun and it jammed. 10010 took his kukri and killed the Japanese who fell on me. We exchanged blows even as he was dying, so strong was his ardour. We also saw Japanese snipers in trees.

We came to thinner jungle and on a small rise was a village. In one shop the man said "Inggli", three times. I suppose he meant English. I showed him I was not a Japanese. He used his hands to say that there were Japanese everywhere. He took a knife and a roll of cloth which he cut into lengths some of which we wound round our bodies and some round our heads in Burmese style. He also gave us some ash to put a caste mark on our foreheads. We moved off and at a larger house we were stopped. The owner asked the other man who we were, Japanese or English troops? By that time we were nearly dead with hunger. When he found out we were not Japanese he cut some bamboo into small lengths and cooked rice for us in these.

There were three girls in that house and one of them said we were Gurkhas. After their meal the others left but one of the girls told me to stay and marry her and the man of the house said he would keep me as his son-in-law. "You marry her," he told me. I thought why not and had a night in the house. But the next morning there was firing all round. I could tell from the noise that our rifles were firing as well as Japanese machine guns. I thought I had better try and rejoin my battalion as I had joined the army under oath. If I die, I die; if not, not. The girl said she couldn't cajole me to stay so she cut a sliver of bamboo which she tied round a puppy's neck and gave me as a souvenir to take away as I wouldn't stay with her. She gave me 11 annas and waved at me as I moved off, without boots, puttees, trousers or shirt, dressed as a Japanese. She said the puppy would be lucky for me and that the Japanese wouldn't harm me. I was not so speak if spoken to except to say "*Tu wa me*," – "going far".

On my way I wandered into a crowd of Japanese who were eating a wild bison. I walked on, pulling the puppy after me. The enemy thought I was a local and let me walk through them and on. I reached a dry *nullah* and saw a vehicle with a USA flag on it. I went up to it and the men said "Johnny", three times. They said something else about getting to their unit the next day. They sat me in the vehicle and offered me some food but I did not eat it as I thought it was beef. I asked for some tea instead. They drove off with me in the vehicle. I had no idea where to but it was a two-day journey.

We reached Yenangaung where there were some large structures on legs[10] in amongst some cotton trees so I knew I was near a village. The vehicle stopped. I saw an irrigation ditch like we have at home and I thought of my hill village and tears came to my eyes. Now I won't die, I said to myself. I was taken into an office where a Kachin woman was writing at a table. I was given bedding, cigarettes and matches. I was also given three balls of something tasty and a cold drink made of bananas. I was given a meal of rice and duck. I stayed there nine days.

A signal was sent about me. I heard transport and found 1/4 GR had arrived. I told them who I was and they took me with them. I was completely re-kitted and issued with a Tommy gun. Three Chinese lorries driven by women came into the place which had been surrounded by the Japanese. The women bared their teeth at them and the Japanese ran away, to east and west, so giving us a chance to escape. What *was* the power those three women had?

I got back to 1/7 GR. We reached a river and were told that a brigade

---

[10] There were oil fields in the area and Purnahang had seen the oil derricks.

had to blow a bridge across it before retreating and we had to cross before it had been blown. A Burmese officer said he would stay behind and fight the Japanese so we also had to stay on the near bank. We stayed on some flat ground near the river. There was a travelers' rest house there. It was dark by then and some of our men did cross the river. The Japanese came to the high ground above us and fired. The night was alight with tracer bullets and Very pistol rounds. I have no idea how many of us and the enemy died that night nor how many of our men got away. Only 311 men of the battalion remained.

Then a very clever young British officer, to whom I had taught map reading when he was a second lieutenant, managed to get us across the river in motor boats and on to Manipur. By the time I got there I had been 11 months in Burma and had been surrounded by the Japanese 22 times.

Back in Palampur we were put separately in tents and were treated as outcastes because of we had eaten food cooked by lower caste people and because of what we had done. We were kept roped into the tented area and were not allowed to go to the cookhouse until we had done *pani patya*. I felt deflated.

Purnahang's fighting days were over.

We were sent to Amritsar to join 154 Gurkha Parachute Battalion. Our new CO came and said to us that we had all done much fighting, much to our credit, and now we would be called "Royal". He also gave us a lanyard.

We did ground training and had to jump from an aircraft. Some of us had to be pushed out of the door and some of us wet ourselves we were so scared. We all volunteered to go home on discharge or leave because we did not like peeing in our pants. But we had to stay. There was a lot of talk about flying to Japan to drop but that did not happen as the Japanese surrendered.

I had managed to do all I could to the best I could. Looking back now, at 83 years of age, I see I was strong, resolute and resourceful.

Lilbahadur Rana, 4 Burma Rifles, *joined the army in October 1939, at Gorakhpur and was sent to "Peiwai" [Pyawbwe?], in Burma for three months' training.*

Our battalion had one company of Muslims, one of Nagas, one of Punjabis and one of Gurkhas. We guarded oil wells for 15–20 days and went to another place for an equal time. The Japanese encircled us and, as the CO had given us orders not to fire, we escaped without firing. After two or three days' march about 35 of us "fell out". The Japanese surrounded us three times and we still had no orders to open fire.

We decided what to do if we were attacked again because we were not allowed to open fire at the enemy. We covered ourselves with sand and when the Japanese came along we jumped up, threw sand in their eyes and made good our escape.

It was only after I came back from some home leave in 1943 that we were allowed to open fire on the enemy.

Lilbahadur did not show any irritation at being put in such a position.

First Chindit Operation, 1943

The history of the first Chindit operation, a thrust behind the Japanese lines in north Burma to cause havoc by blowing up rail and road links, and the order to retreat in small groups, abandoning wounded and dead, men and mules alike, remains controversial. Poignant stories are still graphically told and nightmares still disturb the sleep of the dwindling band of survivors.

Harkaraj Gurung, 2/2 GR and 3/2 GR, *joined the army on 16 October 1929.*

In about 1936 we were on the North-West Frontier, in Waziristan. We were posted to Bannu, Razmak, Malakand and other places. One was Damdil where a battalion from Abbottabad suffered heavy casualties, a company being destroyed by Pathans.[11] The Pathans captured some of the men at night when they slept. 2/2 GR was also posted there. I was in the Machine Gun Platoon. We went on column, using flags to signal, and mules, not vehicles. One day when we were playing football the Pathans sniped and killed the goal-keeper, even though we had pickets on the high ground to left and right. I was involved in four or five sniping incidents.

The Pathans were really wicked, almost the most wicked I ever met, but the Japanese were even worse. Why, even one Japanese soldier could hold up a brigade. A sniper would hide up a tree but we could never find him. In 1939 we heard that we were fighting a war. I was posted to 3/2 GR when it was raised. I can't remember any names of our officers. None in 2/2 GR could speak good Khaskura but they were worse in 3/2 GR, except one who had been a tea planter in Darjeeling.

We were put into a Chindit column with 1,500 mules. I was a muleteer and my mule carried two machine-guns. We crossed the Brahmaputra being pulled over by rope. The war with the Japanese was very far away. We moved by night and slept by day. We went through

---

[11] 2/5 GR lost 1 British officer and 5 GORs killed, and 14 GORs wounded; 1/6 GR lost 1 British officer, 2 GOs and 24 GORs killed, 1 British officer, 1 GO and 27 GORs wounded. 92 Pathans were killed, 64 seriously wounded and they suffered ±300 casualties in all.

Kohima, Manipur and Tamu. We crossed the Irrawaddy and the Chindwin. Nothing but jungle. One of our elder majors lost the way and we had to wait until he sorted things out but an English-speaking major with a beard came and took over, sending the old major back to brigade HQ. We reached a village and made a recce for the enemy. We stayed near there for the night and were fired on from the village. The bearded major ordered me to fire my guns and I fired in the direction of the enemy fire, seeing nothing, but the enemy fire stopped. I was given no orders to advance and yet, when I stopped firing, I was on my own. All the rest had moved off.

I also moved off and found all the mules stuck in a swamp. I found my two and, as they tried to leap clear, I pulled them and helped them get out. There were no other mule handlers so I did not know whether to stay until they came back or go on by myself. I tracked forward and, that evening, caught up with the rest. I found that the wireless had had its aerial shot off and was useless. We saw some Japanese and stayed there seven days. When I fired my guns my mules immediately took cover behind a tree without being told to, much cleverer than a person.

We had insufficient food and no liaison. By then there was an ox in the column. We were ordered to kill and eat a mule but we didn't. However, we may have eaten the ox as it was no longer there.[12] Then a recce party went to a village and the villagers signalled not to advance because there were Japanese there. Later, after the Japanese had left, the villagers signalled to go forward. With what little money the patrol had some rice was bought and we had a handful to cook that evening. Those who were unlucky in not getting any rice picked edible leaves and stuffed their equipment and pouches with them. We were all very hungry. We found some jaluko[13] and caladium. We cooked it out of sight of the Japanese and suffered no ill effects.

There was nothing but walking. We chased the Japanese away. The locals seemed to like us Gurkhas and did not let us down by informing on us. I suppose our operation served its purpose as an in-depth reconnaissance as we did find Japanese. We had no training for the operation and there were no tactics, just walking and walking. It was very hard work. We were like a condemned army and nobody cared what happened to us. In No 4 Column we had no sickness and only one young British officer wounded in the arm but he came back with

---

[12] Being sacred to Hindus, it could never be acknowledged that it had been eaten.
[13] A plant found in marshes seldom used except as pickle or curry.

us. In the other columns I heard it was not like that and people were left behind if they could not walk. At the end it seemed that we would either go on till we got some *bahaduris* for dying or go back without any results. I can't remember how long we were on this operation. It could have been a month.[14]

We went back to Tamu. We had not taken our clothes off and we were covered in lice. We were given new everything, including weapons. I managed to take my own two machine-gun mules back to Manipur, the only two to survive.[15] I gave them back into the mule pool where there were thousands more. In Manipur we stayed near the hospital which was bombed by Japanese aeroplanes. Our people tried to shoot them down but were unsuccessful. We stayed there two months and our men came back during that time in twos and threes. Then Colonel Scone sahib of 2 GR came from Eastern Command to command us so we had an officer who looked after us properly.

Ramkrishna Limbu IDSM, 3/2 GR, 2/10 GR and 4/10 GR, *was another muleteer.*

I joined the army when I was 21 years old and I am now 83. I trained in 10 GRRC and after eight months was sent to Lalitpur to learn how to be a mule driver. I then joined 3/2 GR. We marched into Burma. It was Wingate's fighting patrol. We took explosives and mines but our column did not destroy any bridges. Other columns did. Each platoon had a Burma Rifles man to be the interpreter. I picked up a few Burmese words but had no real knowledge of the language. It was essential to get news of the Japanese. Weatherall sahib spoke very good Khaskura.

Some of the Burmese were pro-Japanese and gave us *dukha*. When the Japanese were seen to be weak the Burmese became pro-British. Many of our men and mules were killed. I was in No 6 column and my mule was number 373. I have no idea how far we moved in any day nor where we went. We had airdrops on the way in. We moved by night. The bridge over the River Sittaung was blown. We had to make our own way out after that and had no re-supply. I and my mule went hungry, as often there was nothing edible for either of us. I killed a few Japanese on the way out and many of our men were killed. I can't

---

[14] It was, in fact, four months.
[15] But see next narrative.

remember the names of any of the places we went through. The leader of our small group paid for boats to take us back over the Chindwin.

Out of all the mules that went into Burma I was the only man to bring mine out and return it when we reached Manipur. All of us went to hospital for three or four days. We were skin and bones. Horses die easily, mules don't.

I was awarded an IDSM *bahaduri* in 1943. Lord Wavell came to give it to me and photos were taken but I never got a copy. After two months in Manipur we were sent on home leave. I went from Dehra Dun and returned there. 3/2 GR was disbanded[16] and I went back to my own regiment and was posted to 4/10 GR.

4/10 GR went down the Tamu road then retired. The Japanese wounded six of us when we attacked the RAP that they had captured. It was a grenade that damaged me. I was evacuated to India by air and after I was better worked in 10 GRRC hospital in charge of the medical orderlies for two years. I was promoted to naik for that.

Tilbahadur Thapa, 3/2 GR, *is a survivor.*

We crossed the Brahmaputra River in boats and continued by rail to Gauhati. We met a waggon load of *Habsis* who laughed at us because we were so small.

We moved by day and night to Manipur and stayed at brigade HQ. The Nagas were all engaged on building roads. We were there three weeks.

The subedar major took all those too weak for war – the blind, lame and ill, all malingerers in my view – back to Dehra Dun. We went on to Tamu, another three miles away, and held a ceremonial parade for a general. The whole brigade paraded and the general spoke in English and Khaskura. After that companies were sent to different places.

OC C Company 3/2 GR's name sounded like Calpat[17] but he was known by his nickname, Brigade Major.[18] He told me we'd be together.

---

[16] No. Platoons from other regiments that had augmented 3/2 GR for that operation returned to their parent regiment.

[17] C Company 3/2 GR was in fact commanded by Capt G.W.N. Silcock who died at Chittagong on 14 January 1945 from a broken neck caused by falling from a first floor of a house at Akyab while sleep walking.

[18] This would be Maj, later Brig, J.M. Calvert, who commanded No 3 Column.

I was now in the 3-inch Mortar Platoon. Each rifle company had two 3-inch mortars with it. We were in Tamu for two days. There was a large dry river there. On the other side the terrain was flat and covered in scrub and jungle.

On the third day we advanced to a village near the River Ringnasi [?] and asked if any Japanese were there. We were told they sometimes came and we went on day and night, with mules and horses.

We reached a hill early one morning where we stopped to brew up tea and I started cooking myself a snack as well but a firefight immediately started. I put my half-cooked food in my pocket and on we went, day and night and day and night through the jungle. Monkey calls sounded everywhere.

One night at 2100 hours we reached the banks of the Irrawaddy and stayed near a bamboo clump. We were told that we'd cross at 0800 hours next morning and to keep quiet, no coughing, no smoking except under cover, because the Japanese were on the far side.

Next morning we loaded our heavy weapons on mules and horses and half C Company moved upstream. As we moved out bombs started falling, "grum-kigrum-grum-kigrum", and small arms fire, "parara-parara-parara", came from the far bank. Nonstop it came, "parara-parara-parara", and hit the bamboo and undergrowth, "chim-chim-chim-chim-chuiaa-chuiaa-chuiaa".

2IC C Company, Subedar Siribhakta, his orderly and myself fell to the ground and many of the company were killed. Havildar Hirasing, the platoon havildar, was hiding somewhere else. Some men scattered and went where I knew not. Many animals were killed; many, including the one elephant, ran away, "haa-haa-huu-huu". The Japanese pinned us down and we could not fire back.

The OC sahib shouted "Hirasing havildar, where are the 3-inch mortarmen? Are they there?" "Yes, yes," he shouted back. The OC told him to fire the mortars but I shouted back that the Nos 1 and 4 were dead. "I'm by myself. No 2 is somewhere with the animals."

We told ourselves we had to fire back and we tried to but we could not lift our heads. Bullets zinged all around us. Siribhakta's orderly stood up and was immediately shot. His body fell on top of us, covering us in blood, he babbling as he died. The bullets fell around us like hailstones. Siribhakta cursed us for not firing but kept his own head down.

Our ammunition was with us but the mortars were on mules which were dead or scattered. Which one of us remaining three was to fetch them? We were all squatting down and as I'd have to die one day why not die now? I got up to bring the tubes with bullets zinging around my head. I was not hit.

I pulled a mortar, bipod, base-plate and ammunition from a dead mule and went into action. The OC sahib shouted "Fire, on a line of 11 o'clock, with a range of 500 yards." I fired one round then thought of our men being in that area so fired another at 700 yards. Even heavier fire came from the Japanese.

On and on the bullets came and the OC sahib shouted "A little right, 12 o'clock." I fired by myself, as the others were still hiding. The second bomb hit the Japanese position and they stopped firing. And then our fire opened, "bhutu-tu-tu-bhutu-tu-tu, bhutu-tu-tu". The OC sahib shouted "Stop" so I stopped. Then other mortar sections also stopped firing. Our wounded men were groaning. We collected as many weapons as possible from the dead men and dead animals and buried them in a pit. We also buried the dead.

It took us three days to cross the river and we gave a lot of covering fire. I crossed over last of all. We took up positions on both flanks on the far bank.

We met our platoon commander and I sternly rebuked him, reminding him he was under his oath of loyalty and how was it that he had hidden and not fought back? We were only three and even then I was the only one to fire the mortar.

We had no rations and were so hungry we were utterly exhausted. Some Burmese villagers brought up rations for the Japanese, sacks of rice, beans and other vegetables, which we captured. The Burmese ran away. We were so hungry we ate the rice uncooked. We only left that which we did not recognise. After feeding we went to the top of a high hill and sent a message for an airdrop and reinforcements. When they came they were from Abbottabad, 6 GR I think. We took up all-round positions and put up smoke from three places having been told we'd get an airdrop at 2200 hours. A fighter aircraft came first and the supply aeroplanes followed it. We only managed to distribute the rations the next day.

We were ordered on to a village near the River Syaulilebar [?]. On our way we walked through a sal[19] forest and red mud. It was very hot and there was no water so we were very thirsty. We had not been allowed

---

[19] *Shorea robusta.*

to drink from our water bottles all day. We were only allowed to drink after patrols had secured the river area. We got to the river at around 1800 hours. When we saw the village we mounted our mortars and the remainder advanced. At night we camped there and started to cook our meal. We were told to move at 0600 hours next morning.

As we were cooking the Japanese attacked us on all sides with small arms fire as we had stopped in the middle of a Japanese position. At midnight they attacked us and a free-for-all developed – man to man, kukris, bayonets, swords, hand-to-hand, Gurkhas killing Gurkhas and Japanese killing Japanese by mistake in the confusion. Both sides fired bombs blindly, even killing each other. It was like a nightmare, so noisy was it that we could not hear each other clearly. The jungle was set alight. Pandemonium all round. We were all shouting, "gun-nu-nu-gun-nu-nu-gun-nu-nu". The jungle reverberated with our shouts.

Around 0200 hours, we saw a man armed only with a raised kukri running towards us. We thought he was mad but he came to give a message that his platoon was completely surrounded and could not move forwards or backwards. "How far in front are you?" we asked. "About 500 yards in front," he answered.

We were also fighting but I reckoned that if I fired at 800 yards I'd hit the Japanese. Siribhakta mounted his weapon and fired rounds one at a time right and I one at a time left. We fired and fired, working by the light of the forest fire. The platoon in front managed to withdraw. No one had any idea of casualties, dead or wounded.

The next day we took stock of the situation and by evening we were organised enough to move off into the night. We walked till dawn when we stopped in some low-lying ground. We set up our wireless and were told to return to India. We went back the same way and, on reaching the Irrawaddy, started making boats and rafts from cane and bamboo.

By late evening we were ready to cross but were fired on from the opposite bank. We scattered and a British sergeant was shot. He fell over. He took some gold out of his shirt pocket and offered it to me as he was about to die but I declined it because I was in a hurry to join my platoon as we moved to some cover.

Eventually we reached some high ground and asked for rations to be dropped the next day. We were told to conserve our matches and salt but no airdrop came. We were also told to eat any and everything we came across, horses, elephants, buffaloes and cows – once we got back to Kunraghat we would do *pani patya* for eating forbidden meat.

We returned to our section formations. The OC sahib said he'd stay with the British troops and a Burmese officer and his Burmese soldiers would stay with us Gurkhas and we would have to obey him. Our first task was to cross the Irrawaddy. We were to bury all heavy weapons and only take light automatics, Stens and Tommy guns, and rifles. We were to let all our animals go free.

The British battalion moved off and so did we, but we soon became two groups, the Burmese by themselves and we Gurkhas by ourselves, making our best way forward. Subedar Siribhakta told us not to move in a group but to make our way individually so as to avoid leaving tracks the Japanese could follow.

I found myself in a group of six, all muleteers who knew nothing. I made all the decisions. One of them was my wife's elder brother. I had a compass. We found wood-apples and ate them. There was nothing else. Later we killed and ate deer. We lived off the land. We tried nettles but they made us piss many times during the night, always hot. We moved like that for three months. We were afraid of elephants, bears and apes. Sometimes we slept in trees and sometimes on the ground, where possible in caves.

By now it was the rainy season and we eked out our matches and salt. We took counsel. We had some rupee money so we decided to go to a village, buy some rations and if possible rejoin our troops. I put 180 degrees on my compass and aimed for a village called Waibang, remembered from before. I said "If we meet up with our forces, we'll get home; if we meet the enemy, let us die." We had no hope of survival.

We went on for one and a half miles and saw the village. We lay up, hiding, as we watched it. That night we slept separately so that we would not all be killed at once. Next morning we joined up and discussed if we should go into the village or not. We decided that three of us would go and the other three would stay behind.

We took off our socks and boots and all clothing that would identify us as Indian Army and, carrying our rifles, I took two others into the village. I had told the other three I would bring back rations if at all possible. Staying on one side of a dry ravine at the village edge I called out to the villagers, in Burmese, if there was any food. I spoke Burmese

A Burman sent us to a Japanese storehouse. The men there asked us, in Hindi, where we had come from. "How much do you want?" they asked. "I'll take one sack of everything," I replied.

They told us the price by sign language. One sack of rice for eight rupees. By then the other three had joined us so we were six again. We were all given a large glass of tea. "Drink up, we are friends," we were told. "Drink up quickly, take your rations and go."

We had only drunk half our tea when a meal of rice, meat and vegetables was brought for us, in six dishes. "How hungry you must be! How much *dukha* you must have had in the jungle," they said. As I drank my tea I said to the others there might be poison in the food. "No worry," they said, "if we die, we die." We still had our rifles slung and we started eating. "Eat up, lads, we are fated to die today," I said and one answered, "if we die we die, if we don't we don't."

We started to eat. We were told not to hurry. "Even prisoners can eat without weapons. Put your weapons behind you and eat comfortably. The Japanese don't come often, only occasionally," we were told. We put our weapons behind us and someone came and took them away. I turned round and asked why they had been taken away and was told that, were the Japanese to come suddenly and see them, it would be dangerous. It were better to hide them.

We thought that, though we had escaped from enemy bullets, now, with no weapons, we were in the enemy's hands. We were bound to die now. But we had two grenades each in our pockets.

Japanese surrounded us. We were caught. We thought we'd use the grenades on them. But no matter how many of them would die we would be captured, our chests cut open and raw chillies be rubbed in. So we didn't throw the grenades. We kept them hidden.

Three of the others, including my wife's elder brother, said, "No, let's kill them and die ourselves," but I stopped them by saying, "Let's surrender and see what happens. If they kill us, they kill us and if they don't, the gods will save us." My wife's elder brother and one other said they weren't going to stay and tried to move outside but were prevented by a crowd of Burmese, ranging from eight-year-olds to 84-year-olds, armed with all sorts of knives.

A Burman killed my wife's elder brother with a heavy-bladed knife and cut his body into pieces, throwing his hat and shirt away. His remains were thrown into a ditch. I asked the Hindi speakers why they had arranged that and they said, no, it wasn't they but the Japanese who had done so. The Burmese bound the second man and knocked him over. They fetched a cart, put us four in one corner and threw the bound man in after us. They saw him as a bad man.

We were taken into the jungle and, still in the cart, were stripped. We wore only underpants but were allowed to keep our money. That night we reached a town and were fed. Then off again, for a day and a night. Next night we reached Mogok. On the way we hid from aircraft. At Mogok we were fed with the remains of some burnt rice, scraped from the bottom of the cooking pot. Then we were taken to a prison where there were about twenty other Gurkhas.

We asked about each other. Next day we were left alone and the following morning some Chinese were brought along and we five were called out by the Japanese who gave us picks and shovels. We dug a deep pit. One Chinese was brought to the pit and we were ordered out of it. The Chinese was bayonetted in the stomach and fell into the pit. We were ordered to bury him alive. O-ho, I thought, that'll be our fate.

We dumped our tools and were led off back to the jail and given something like biscuits and water. O-ho. Our friends asked us what had happened and I told them. We decided to ask to be shot instead. Someone said that how they killed us was up to them.

That evening the Japanese told us was that they would bring some officers – we called them subedars and jemadars because they had three or two rank stars on their uniforms – to us on the morrow. Next morning the Japanese took us outside. They were dressed in smart uniform. The jail commander turned to us and said "Look how smart our men are. You are useless mouths." He asked us how many Japanese we had killed.

We told him we had no idea. He told us to put our hands up and took our money away from where we had hidden it and gave it to the Burmese. We were locked in the jail for another three days and three nights, then marched off, walking day and night, to Rangoon jail. We were put into the ground floor and the officers were on the upper floor. There were 700 people of all kinds bound arm to arm, lying on their backs, unable to stretch their legs. A trench under them took their urine and faeces. We were also trussed up like that.

The smell was dreadful; mosquitoes went "gu-nu-nu-nu-nu-nu" all night and flies buzzed all day. And so hot! We were let loose after one month and taken out. We were fallen in in two ranks and lectured by a Japanese and a Burmese officer who asked us if we were willing to work for them or wanted to go back to jail. "Those who want to work put up your hands." Every hand went up as we opted to work.

We were taken into wooded country full of tethered elephants and horses and our task was to look after them by preparing their feed and clearing up their dung, three times a day. We worked till 2200 hours.

We lived in long huts and were woken up every morning at 0200 hours with the command "*Shaw-shaw-shaw*" and made to prepare the fodder until 0600 hours, when the Japanese commanded us to feed them, "*Mis-mis-mis*". After that it was our turn to feed with some rice and gruel. We were not allowed to use our hands but had to use small sticks. If we ate with our hands they hit us in the face.

At last the weather became colder, much colder. Among the 700 were some Burmese and one morning, before 0200 hours, one older Burman had collected kindling and had lit a fire. When the Japanese came in the Burman and I were warming ourselves. He asked where the others were. I told him I didn't know but they were probably asleep somewhere. The Japanese sentry started hitting me in the face. The old Burman ran away. I was so angry I picked up a brick and, whether I died or not, made to throw it at the Japanese, who ran away. The Japanese told the other Gurkhas what I had done and that they were to watch me being shot when it was light. We went out as normal to feed the animals and at our meal time I was called over by that Japanese to have a meal with him but I was so angry I did not go.

A 3/2 GR subedar and jemadar had also been captured and the Japanese said that these two would be told our faults next day and they would look after us. We all thought we'd be killed.

"Why be afraid?" I asked the others. "Only I am to be killed as I am the only one who has done wrong. You have done nothing wrong," I told them.

Next day at noon the subedar and jemadar came. The Japanese fell in on one side and the Gurkhas on the other side. The case was discussed and the Japanese officer ordered the sentry and the person who had done wrong to step forward. I stepped in front and pointed out the sentry who had hit me and called him forward. I explained what had happened in Hindi as the Japanese officer spoke Hindi. "He always hits everybody every morning and many cheeks are swollen from continual hitting. My cheeks are very swollen. As I have done no wrong and have worked well, when he hit me I picked up the brick." I explained what I had said at the time.

The sentry said I had driven the other prisoners outside. My answer was I was a coolie so were the others, so how could I send them away? The Japanese officer told the sentry that we Gurkhas were there to help, not to be hit. "Why have you hit them so much? Everybody's cheeks are swollen."

The Japanese officer then struck the sentry very hard and the other Japanese took him away. A new sentry came in his place. The Japanese officer told the other Japanese that, "The Gurkhas' mothers and fathers are not here and there are no mail facilities and so no one knows they are here. They are prisoners and have to be here. Our fathers and mothers are not here either but we are here to fight. Will we die or stay alive? These men will have to work as long as they're here. If they are sick they must be treated."

Some time after that we were moved and eventually reached Mandalay where we saw the Irrawaddy, vast as the sea. The bridge had been smashed and we spent the night crossing in boats, some way downstream. Next morning we moved onto high ground in very thick jungle. We rested up at a small stream. That day we sent Damarbahadur Chhetri to forage for some *raksi* from a village. I could not move because an aeroplane flew very low, "gun-nu-nu-nu-nu". I said out loud how lovely it would be if we could fly away like that. The Japanese commander heard me and that evening came over and told me never to move when any aeroplane flew over. "What would we do if you had a wound in your feet?" he asked.

Damarbahadur came back with *raksi* and a chicken which we killed, cooked and ate. Next day at noon three aeroplanes came over and dropped bombs, "gun-ki-gun-ki-gun-ki", and fired on us, "gut-tu-tu-tu-tu", one way and over again, "pa-ra-ra-ra-ra". We did not know if they were British or Japanese aeroplanes. Some Gurkhas and many Japanese were killed and wounded. I was distraught; how to escape? I found a ditch and lay in it.

I was joined by a "jemadar" Japanese officer who kept on saying in Hindi, how bad the English were. After the aircraft flew away Damarbahadur and I decided to escape. Blood was everywhere. We took one blanket each from dead Japanese. It was late afternoon and there were still one or two Japanese around the place so we stayed where we were. Another aeroplane came over and this time we heard the Japanese cry out that it was a British one. It was then we slipped away.

We moved all night through thick undergrowth. We heard some Japanese shout "*Hangku!*" – "Halt!" We evaded them, moving along a stream, sometimes in deep water, sometimes in shallow.

At dawn we reached high ground. We found some water so we decided to rest and have a wash. No food, no weapons, no matches, only one bottle of *raksi*. We agreed to drink only half and leave the other half for later. We saw that our blankets were covered in blood so we threw them away. We had on one thin shirt, one pair of pants and a pair of boots, all Japanese – nothing else. And it rained all day.

Eventually, seven days later with only water to drink during that time, we met two Gurkhas, Subedar Narbahadur Gurung and a rifleman. We were now four. The other two had seen a jungle clearing and some villagers so we decided to go there and ask for fire so we could cook bamboo shoots. Narbahadur and I were to go but, if either of us were wounded, the other would stay with him.

On our way there we met some British soldiers who, on seeing us, took aim. We halted. They halted. They talked. We didn't understand what they said and they did not understand us. A bearded Punjabi soldier was fetched as interpreter. "How many of you are there?" he asked. "Four of us." "Where are they?" "Up the hill." "Call them down."

We called them down and we were told to sit. We sat down. We were asked all details, home village, date of enlistment, place of enlistment, number, rank and name, where we went after recruiting. "Dehra Dun," I said. "And after that?" "Fort Sandeman." "Then where?" "Loralei."

And all the details of where we had been, the names of all our officers, British and Gurkha, what weapons we carried and much more. Eventually we told them we were running away from the Japanese.

"Who was your OC?" "Major Calpat." "Oh? Now he's a general. What is your brigade number?" "I do not know. I can tell you everything except that. I have heard it is 77." "If you don't know your brigade number, you can't be a genuine Gurkha soldier." "I don't know for sure. No one told us but I heard one soldier say it was 77."

After that we were told to spend the night there. "Our HQ is eight miles away and another four miles on is the Gurkha HQ. If the Japanese don't open fire between 1800 hours and 0600 hours tomorrow, I'll take you there. If there is any Japanese attack we will kill you." "Fine. If we are killed by a British bullet rather than a Japanese bullet, we'll go to heaven." We were happy. A British soldier gave us biscuits and tea.

That evening three of us were bound together by our hands. One had his hands so tightly bound he started weeping. I told him to keep quiet as our captors would not understand as we had no common language. We other two managed to loosen our bonds sufficiently to relieve the pressure on the third. However, before our captors came to us in the morning we had tightened the knots again.

The Punjabi came in the morning and told us to follow him. We met the brigade HQ officers who were sitting down as though waiting for us and asked where we had come from. We were asked many questions which we answered. One officer told his orderly we were very hungry so quickly make some tea and bring biscuits. As we ate and drank we gave them full details of our experiences.

Two men were detailed to take us to Calpat sahib and some other Gurkhas. When we got there we were asked the same questions. "Good. You've escaped. I don't want to see your Japanese clothes," he said. We were given new clothes and told to burn the old Japanese uniforms. The subedar major ordered the cookhouse staff to feed us three times a day because we were so weak.

Next day we were fully debriefed and we told all we knew, in detail, just as we had told the Punjabi, from the beginning. At the end the officer said that he'd tell the general about us and we would meet him next day. "You will get an MC [sic] even if you don't get a pension." They again asked me my name, number and rank. The paperwork went everywhere, including Gorakhpur. Later I learnt that my *bahaduri* had been given to someone else. I believe that the paperwork had the name altered before it was given to the general. The GO who wrote down the details changed the name to that of his cousin.

In the evening the general came, "ghap-lyak-ghap-lyak-ghap-lyak". We had met before and he called me by my name. "Do you want to continue fighting or go home?" he asked, in Khaskura. "We want to fight. Please give us weapons."

The GOs said no, because the Japanese had treated us so badly and we were too weak for military operations. The British officer said that we still had to capture Myitkyina so these men could stay looking after casualties in brigade HQ.

We heard the attack on Myitkyina, bombs bursting, "gu-du-du-gu-du-du", and machine guns firing, "da-ra-ra-da-ra-ra". There was heavy fighting. There were British troops, Hindu troops, Muslim troops, Gurkha troops, Chinese troops, *Habsi* troops but the Japanese were in prepared positions. The battle lasted a month. It seemed as though both sides suffered dreadful casualties but eventually we took the town.

We were taken to the airfield and were flown to Pandu Ghat railway station. There we met Siribhakta who had been captured and escaped. We went to Gauhati where again we were asked many questions. I was asked what I had been doing and I told them I had worked with mules. I was detailed to go to Calcutta next day. When Siribhakta was asked what he had been doing he said "This and that". He was rebuked and the officer ordered him to be locked up. I learnt that Siribhakta had, in fact, helped the Japanese. A previous group had reported against him.

Dalbahadur Pun, 3/2 GR. From Manipur we invaded Burma in Wingate's column. I remember a big battle when our ammunition finished and we had no re-supply. We were told to make our own way back to India. It was an unpleasant situation. Weatherall sahib, who spoke very good Khaskura, had been killed and we were surrounded by Japanese, had been for three months. We searched for jungle produce, especially yams, to eat. We tried to buy food in Burmese villages with "king's money" that had been dropped in to us with the earlier rations. There were mosquitoes everywhere. Our clothes were in rags, footwear was worn out and our feet were in a bad state. Our hair hung down our shoulders. Those who were too sick to move were left with some money near Burmese villages or left to die where they were.

I, a machine gunner, was with two GOs. We dumped our weapons. The GOs wanted to surrender but I said "No, let's escape or die. If we stay alive we'll meet in India, if we die, we'll die here." We separated. I reached the Irrawaddy and the problem was how to cross over. Just short of the near bank in the jungle I met Major Conron who had a biscuit in one hand and a life jacket in the other. He asked me where I had come from, where the subedar and the other GOs were, and where was my machine gun. I told him I didn't know where the GOs were. He said "What's gone has gone. You and I have to cross the river. Let's go together. If we live we live, if we die we die." He was so weak he could not swim so I went to look for a boatman.

It was evening. I went to a house and all inside were very scared. I pulled one man out and took him back. He trembled a lot. The major put his pistol to the Burman's head and told him either to take us across in his boat "Or I'll kill you here." That made the Burman even more scared. He put us in his boat and started rowing us across. There was enough moonlight to see a bit. We finished up on the other side exactly opposite a Japanese post. They opened fire and killed the major. I was unhurt. It was around 0100 hours and I started walking. At the top of a bamboo-covered hill I stopped. I was worried; the major was dead and I was by myself. We had come 700 miles from India. How was I to go back the same distance? I had a compass. At Mandalay we had been told that if we had to escape we were to march on a bearing of 300 degrees to reach Manipur. I started on 300 degrees and moved between 300 degrees and 310 degrees. Three months after that I reached Manipur.

That night it was moonlit and I sat down to rest under a tree and got covered in red ants. Did they bite! A large herd of fifty to sixty elephants came my way and smelt me. They started looking for me but I avoided them. I had to avoid the Burmans also as they would have speared me to death. They had already killed many of us that way as I had seen for myself. They were as dangerous as Red Indians.

I was afraid of being captured by the Japanese but only once was afraid of one animal, a ferocious type of deer that was big, red and horned. I knew it would attack any human it smelled. I was only once attacked by one and I escaped by hiding under a large fallen tree. I saw many tigers, man-eating, singly or in groups. The first one I saw did frighten me and I managed to jump into a river and swim across. I nearly bumped into a group of Burmese, who were all smoking. They didn't see me but they would have killed me had they caught me.

When I came across tigers they took no notice of me. I put that down to the fact that my body smell was different by then. They do not have a sense of smell but have good eyesight. Bears, on the other hand, have dim sight but a good sense of smell. I only saw the red-nosed type, not the black-nosed type we have in Nepal. Once, trying to cross a broken railway bridge, I came across a group of Japanese riding on elephants and I hid from them. One evening I was fascinated by finding myself in the middle of a large herd of deer.

I was always hungry. I started fishing with my hands in one river and caught some prawns which I ate alive as I did two fish I caught in a teeming pool formed by the monsoon at the side of another river. I scooped some out and ate them alive also. There was no salt but they were good. I once came across a nest of 12 eggs of jungle fowl. I ate six straightaway and kept the other six for later. I came across a nest of two young doves. I killed one, plucked it and ate it raw – I had no method of making fire – and kept the other for later.

After one spell of three or four days without any food I came across a Burmese village. The Burmans were afraid of me and ran away. I found some dried maize and carried as much as I could away with me. The Burmans were very scared of the Japanese. The Japanese would come and check on such things as the number of chickens or eggs and if the amount was inexplicably less punishments were meted out, extra work or death. Women suffered badly; they would be gang raped and then stabbed to death.

I was happy to find wood apples which were most sustaining. They kept hunger away for up to three days. The fruit of the ebony tree kept hunger away for 12 hours.

One day I came across three boxes of cigarettes that had been dropped from an aircraft so I knew I was on the correct way out. Three months after I started back I saw a 3/5 GR post on the far bank of the Chindwin, with artillery near by. 1/8 GR was to a flank. They knew about our column. A British captain aimed his weapon at me as I approached the near bank. I waved a leaf at him hoping he'd take that as a recognition sign. He signalled to me to stay there and a boat came over to fetch me. In great haste I got into the boat and when we reached midstream firing broke out from both sides of the river, British and Japanese. I felt I was finished. I almost collapsed when I reached the bank and the captain sahib pulled me into safety in dead ground. He gave me a drink of rum from his water bottle. I drank it. I was told to hide there and food and drink would be brought to me.

I stayed in a trench. The sahib spoke good Khaskura and gave me a towel. My morale soared. I had not had a rice meal for three months so when some was brought I ate four mess tins and slept for the rest of the day. That evening the captain came to see how I was and woke me up. He told me he had contacted battalion HQ and I had to report in there. It might be difficult as reports from an agent had been received indicating an enemy attack.

I was to be sent by mule with a squad as I had sore feet but I did not know how to ride a mule so I went by foot. At battalion HQ the RMO looked at my feet. I was not allowed to stay there because of the attack so I was sent on to 3/3 GR. I got there in the evening. I was told how dangerous it was so I would have to move on. I had a havildar cousin in 3/3 GR and I told them his number and asked if I could see him. He died in 1998 aged 87. I did spent the night there. There were three attacks over the next three days but next morning 3/3 GR contacted Imphal by telephone and I was sent there.

I met Bain sahib who had raised 3/2 GR and was now a colonel. He asked me if I knew him and I said I did, telling him his name. He asked me all about what had happened to 3/2 GR and I told him as much as I knew, which was not much. Of the 1,700 men of the original column 665 had returned to Imphal. I made the total 666. I was given a medical inspection, re-equipped and, with the other Gurkhas, sent back to Dehra Dun.

Sancharbahadur Rai, 10 GR, *was posted to 3/2 GR for Chindit work.*

One mule between four men was issued to carry rations. We moved to the Naga hills, taking five days and reached Manipur. We were given money, 4 anna pieces and another coin with a head on it.

We moved off for another four days and had to cross over the Chindwin in inflatable boats with the mules. We crossed the Mu River. A Burmese major taught us not to leave off eating salt and to eat any green foliage that animals also ate. At Mongmit we were surrounded by the enemy and were told to make it back to the Irrawaddy. We were very hungry. We stripped our weapons, mortars, machine guns, everything and abandoned them, throwing away the bolts and springs. We kept a couple of 36, 77 and 69 grenades each. We were ordered to strip the mules and abandon them also. They followed us for five days, whinnying all the time.

One Japanese brigadier showed us kindness. He let us out of the encirclement as we made our way to the River Sittaung and then ordered his spotter aeroplane to fly him back.

There's no doubt about it, teaching us how to use the Pole Star during recruit training was of great use. Each evening we would look at it to get our bearings for the next day.

We made our way back towards the Irrawaddy. Weatherall sahib with us was the best. He spoke to us as one of us. He said that we ought to be able to move 30 miles a day but we had no food so we did not move very fast. "I'll get you to the Chinese in two days and then, by air, we'll fly to Manipur," he told us. If only we'd had a full stomach! But we felt as if we'd die as we were only eating grass.

On reaching the Shweli River we cut bamboos to cross over. Ten Burmese pulled us and 12 pushed us. British machine guns fire slowly, "trk, trk, trk, ra, ra, ra": German and Japanese guns fire very fast, "trrrrrrrr". Twelve of us were halfway across when the Japanese opened us on us, "trrrrrrrrr". The bamboo raft overturned and many died. Only a few survived. What were we to do and where were we to go? A Burmese major went back and the Japanese cut him to pieces, taking his head off. The river ran red with blood.

We had an airdrop of hard tack to last us for five days, biscuits and tea, not much of either. We were in the middle of brewing up that evening when we were attacked by Japanese aircraft. We scattered. By then there were about 300 of us. We reached the Irrawaddy. We had five Burmese with us and, dressed as civilians, they went and searched for boats. They brought back two, one that held fifty men and one that held thirty. In single file, I in front, we got into the larger boat at dawn. We got over. In broad daylight the Japanese opened fire on the boats on the second trip over, "trrrrrrrrr". The current took boats and men downstream. Crocodiles, or big fish, gobbled up the bodies, live and dead, like chickens pecking insects.

With a few others we continued on our way. We licked salt and ate grass. Like monkeys, we shat green. Our heads were very heavy. Indeed, it is true like one British officer had said, "Gurkhas brains are as heavy as horse dung."[20] It was only with the greatest difficulty that we staggered on, our heads hurting. Eventually we survivors crossed the Mu River.

By then I was with three friends, one of whom was a signaller from Abbottabad. When we got to the Chindwin we were fired at from across the river by our own troops who took us for Japanese. My signaller friend took off his shirt. It was filthy, full of lice and ragged. He stuck it on a piece of wood and sent a message. On the other side was 3/5 GR. Firing stopped and a message came back: "Stay there all day and we'll come and fetch you after dark." So we stayed there all day and were fetched over after dark.

We were told not to eat too much, only a mouthful or we'd die. Next morning we were given new clothes, told to eat a little more and our heads were shaved. The third day we had to move on. Four or five hours' walk took us two days, we were so weak. We got to a road and were taken to Manipur, Imphal. Then we were sent to Dehra Dun.

---

[20] *Gorkhaliko gidi, ghorako lidi.*

The Arakan, Kohima and Imphal, 1943–44

These battles relied on a new factor, re-supply by air. Although totally surrounded by Japanese forces, 'boxes' of troops managed to hold out successfully enough to blunt Japanese attacks. Enemy records show that they expected captured supplies to help them reach India but, when these did not materialise, attacks lost their impetus and the 'March on India' was halted.

By this time some units of the INA were operating with the Japanese. Of doubtful quality, they were looked down on by both sides. Militarily their effect was nugatory; politically they managed to make themselves into credible heroes with certain sections of society in the subcontinent, then and, especially, after the war – but not, tellingly, once independence had been achieved.

Harkabir Gurung, 4/1 GR, *well remembers his early army life.*

Our recruit training was strict and the adjutant was the strictest of all. He was called Hedderwick and I can remember when he gave one sentry 14 days punishment for going to have a pee without permission. Our NCOs were strict but never bullied us. Our recruit training was curtailed as a new battalion, 4/1 GR, was being raised. There were a thousand all ranks in the battalion and by September 1943 we were on active service. We went to the Arakan and observed *Dashera* of that year in Bawli Bazar. I had been made into HQ Company pay naik and was also in charge of the arms *kote* in which weapons not being used were chained at night and British officers' binoculars, pistols and compasses were stored. After chaining the weapons last thing I would take the key to the subedar major and get it from him at 0600 hours next morning. It was during this festival that we first came under fire. We stood to and companies deployed. Then it was time for the *Diwali* festival and Subedar Major Dilbahadur Pun, the QM jemadar, the adjutant jemadar and the BHM were gambling. Though this is usually allowed during this festival, Hedderwick sahib, now the battalion 2IC, caught them and that very night the subedar major was forced to leave the battalion. He and his orderly were given two mules to carry their kit, including their weapons. They went to Chittagong and presumably went back to the regimental centre. When I went to get the key from Dilbahadur Pun sahib I found that Subedar Ransing Thapa of A Company was there instead. *Was* I surprised?

In January 1944 we started fighting the Japanese in earnest. We were on one hill and they on another. A three-company attack was launched with one company in reserve. As normal the attackers were issued two ounces of rum before they went in. The mules carrying the 3-inch mortar ammunition made a noise and the Japanese were alerted before the attack was due. The 3-inch mortars were to be sited only 100 yards in the rear. Deadly fire was opened and the men charged but they were stopped by wire and caught up in nets. Sixty GORs were killed and 200 were wounded.[21] I saw it all happen.

Those many casualties meant we needed reinforcements. The wounded were evacuated to hospital. In my part of the camp we were only 26 strong. Hiding in the jungle we were invisible from Japanese aircraft. After reinforcements came we relieved a British battalion. They were happy to hand over to us, saying "very good, Johnny Gurkha." In February 1944 7 Division, that included us, was besieged in the "Admin Box" with the Japanese all round us. We had dug in well. Always from 1800 to 1900 hours we were hit by artillery. It was big, heavy stuff and one piled into the British officers' mess-cum-cookhouse and killed seven people without exploding. Then from 1900 hours the Japanese would charge us, shouting for us to surrender and scattering leaflets into our perimeter positions. Our orders were not to open fire until the perimeter had been breached. We never shouted back at them.

Airdrops were attempted by night but some packs dropped on the Japanese and some on us. We kept wireless contact with higher formation all the time. On 7 or 8 March 1944 we were ordered into our bunkers as 5, 20, 23, 25 and 26 Divisions[22] tried to break the blockade with their artillery from 1800 till 0600 hours. We were deafened. At 0630 hours the fighters strafed the Japanese positions for half an hour then the bombers came over for two hours. We broke out and saw tanks and carriers like a flock of sheep.

The Japanese had run away and we saw very few dead ones. During

---

[21] 14 GORs were killed; 2 British officers, 1 GO and 40 GORs were wounded: total 57 casualties.

[22] Only 26 Division from Chittagong and 36 Division from Calcutta were involved.

the siege we had suffered many casualties by Japanese attacks and when on patrol. The Japanese also suffered heavily. After we were relieved we were allowed to rest near a river for a week. We were covered with lice as none of us had washed for about six weeks. Rations had been short so they were conserved because no one knew how long we could hold out. We had one spoonful of rice in the mornings and one chapatti in the evenings. We had also run out of cigarettes. We were re-kitted.

We left the Arakan and, as the Japanese were attacking Kohima, we moved there, by foot, vehicle and aeroplane to Dimapur then forward to MS 35. We were not on the hills surrounding Kohima. We started attacking in earnest after that. In D Company the OC and the company 2IC were wounded and I do not know what happened to them. The brigade major and the brigade IO were killed as was the recently appointed CO, Hedderwick. Horsford sahib came to command. We advanced against the Japanese under his command and eventually Kohima fell and the Japanese had so many casualties that they fell back.

In June 1944 we were sent on leave for 90 days and after reassembling we started fighting again in January 1945. I had been looking after the pay but now the CO made me part of his special bodyguard. At one river seven miles away were a rail and a road bridge near a village and the CO wanted to know the condition of both, whether they were being used and whether the river could be crossed. A Company was sent to make a recce but did not succeed. Seven patrols failed to get an answer so I was sent. I was shown the position on a map and moved out by night with two others on a compass bearing. I carried a Tommy gun. I saw no one on the way there or back but heard a tiger. We heard noises of men on the road but found no one in the village. We did find some empty trenches. Using the back bearing we returned at 0600 hours next morning and I reported in. That coincided with stand-to and we were fired upon. I shouted out the password and we were allowed back in.

The Defence Platoon was ordered out that morning at 1000 hours and I was ordered to go with it. If I had told a lie I would die! We got back to the village and received a message that we had to stay there as a base and patrol forward. I chose an upstairs room and then moved out another two miles to check the road. The railway bridge was upstream and the road bridge downstream. I took one man, Lokbahadur Thapa, and we covered each other's advance from tree to tree by bounds. There were no bridges over the river there, though it could be forded, and the road had been damaged. I sent back that report that evening. Back in the battalion the OC said he would put my name in for a *bahaduri* but it seems that he forgot as nothing happened. Our own tanks advanced and a section from HQ Company accompanied them.

I was ordered to go and help A Company who had suffered losses. I filled my mess tin with a meal and off I went with nine men. I pointed out which route we would use to get back to the battalion if we became separated and had to withdraw. There was wire round the command post. I was shown where I was needed to lay an ambush and moved off quite some way. I divided my men into a rifle and a gun group. There was not much of a moon. In the area I was told to go to the villagers had dug big, deep trenches that could hold over a dozen people. At 2100 hours the Japanese put in an attack on 2 Platoon, A Company, on the left and on D Company over on the right. The Japanese came very close to us, shouting loudly and we opened fire on them. I don't know if we caused any damage. I don't think they saw us. However, when I looked round I did not see any of my men, only their weapons. They had all jumped into a trench as they were so frightened. A Company started firing our way and at 0300 hours we returned.

I had been wounded and was in hospital for six months. I only rejoined the battalion shortly before the atomic bomb was dropped putting an end to hostilities. We moved off to Thailand to disarm and guard the surrendered Japanese.

Major (QGO) Harkabir Gurung was made MVO in 1972.

Balbahadur Gurung, MC and Bar, 1/3 GR, *back from a spot of home leave after escaping from the Sittang disaster, continued his story.*

Back in Manipur we were issued with worn-out weapons and kit, all the good stuff was in Europe, sent there when the Germans were 30 miles from Britain. After the Russians cut the Germans off in the middle and won the war in Europe we got those weapons back in Burma. There was a great battle in Manipur when we attacked and I won my first MC, which only came through after the war.

It was after we were in Tiddim that an officer called Smith came from being staff captain and sent me to a rifle company. I was promoted to jemadar from CQMH, having been in charge of 70 mules and 11 chargers, and Smith was made CO as the CO had been dismissed. He asked me if I wanted to fight the Japanese and I said I had already fought them a lot. The new CO gave out orders on the wireless that I was being sent to C Company. I took over my platoon and was on my way to do some jungle training but that night we had to fight the Japanese when Smith and I attacked a large concentration of them. We killed a lot of them and there was so much artillery fire that no leaves were left on the trees. We threw grenades and we killed snipers. Heavy casualties were accepted and inflicted when we went into close-quarter fighting after the artillery barrage lifted. My hat was shot off my head. I sent the wounded back to get treatment. The Japanese defence had wire and bunkers. B Company came up behind us but I advised against it as we were so close to the enemy. There was no fire control. I was fired on and fell over, rolling away. As I got up I was fired on by my own side.

Smith then took A Company into the attack and was hit three times, the last time fatally. He kept on going forward till the end. We then retired.

I took my platoon down to a bridge to prevent the enemy coming there and that evening my promotion to jemadar came in writing. We could not dislodge the Japanese from Tiddim to Manipur and Imphal. They were all over the place, despite air and artillery support.

One day C Company was sent to attack a hill, with my 14 Platoon right and 15 Platoon left. The division commander watched my attack. We killed many enemy, who had many sorts of weapons, and every man in my platoon, including my batman by my side, was killed. Only I survived. I killed all the remaining Japanese and managed to get all their weapons taken to the general. We retired and an Indian company relieved us on the hill.

In the battalion all were told how I had given a wonderful display. Extra rum was issued. The CO asked for my red book[23] and the general awarded me an immediate MC.

We were sent to a bridge over a dry *nullah* which the Japanese held and were preventing a division from advancing. It was night time when the CO ordered OC C Company to send a platoon to dislodge them and spend the night there in combat readiness. I was detailed to attack the

---

[23] Pay book.

Japanese at the bridge, clean it up and stay there. We all knew that we were dead men if we attacked so nobody wanted to go forward. After some discussion I was ordered to attack and was asked what help I needed. I said tanks and machine guns. The OC would give me the signal for the advance and we would talk by tank telephone, he being inside. We shouted *"Gorakh Nathko jay"*[24] and attacked. There was much firing and many grenades thrown and we took the position. The OC came up to it, even though he should have stayed in the rear. We made camp for the night. Two Japanese remained in their foxholes and I popped a grenade in. Both ran away, one into our men and was killed. The other escaped.

Next morning I was once again asked for my red book and was told that I had done great work. I was recommended for what would have been my third MC. At battalion HQ they thought I should have had an IOM.

Nardhoj Limbu, 3/2 GR, *had a special note about an incident in Kohima.*

I was posted to 3/2 GR which was in the Arakan. Destruction was everywhere, with the Japanese madder than the Gurkhas. They shouted all night as they attacked us. I was LMG 1. I can't tell you how many firefights I was involved in. The whole scheme of things was no good and the tactics were no good. I killed one Japanese in an ambush when their LMG fired at us. I was given an m-i-d.

It was scary. It lasted for two months, with a lot of air activity and being bombed daily. I was wounded. We were completely surrounded for about a week and a convoy rescued us.

We were taken to the Kohima area after that and when that was over we went to Akyab. In Kohima a Japanese spy, dressed as a British officer, had a private lavatory with a telephone in it. He used that telephone to let the Japanese know where we were. It was uncanny; wherever we Gurkhas took cover Japanese aeroplanes came to bomb us. The pilots knew where we were. After the Japanese spy was caught no aircraft came to bomb us because the pilots were not told where we were. The spy was hanged.

Eventually African troops came to relieve us. We went back to India

---

[24] 'Victory in the name of Lord Gorakh.'

and were sent on some home leave. We came back to Dehra Dun and were taken to Madras but the atom bomb was dropped on Japan and the war was over. 3/2 GR was sent to Penang. After a year in Malaya I went back to India and was sent on release.

Army life was a good life.

Birbahadur Pun, MM, 4/8 GR.   I was put in C Company and the OC's name was Myers.[25] Two days later we withdrew in the face of Japanese attacks. We went to Rangoon then north to Legu or Pegu – I forget so many names after all these years, places and even my old COs' names. Our company was used as a listening post and six days later each of our rifle companies had been surrounded by the Japanese. There were no communications as the telephone line was cut and the wireless was unserviceable. That night Myers sahib ordered two of us, Karnabahadur and me, to take one Sten gun and two magazines each and, in any way we could, make contact with battalion HQ.

We were told only to open fire if we were fired upon, otherwise to be as silent as possible. We were to find out what was the password between 1700 and 0500 hours and return with it so that we could escape later on that night. I could not say "No" to that as I had sworn an oath to obey orders but what was the best way of carrying out those orders? To go along the easiest path would mean we'd be fired on; to go along other, more difficult, tracks would put us in danger of losing our way. If we were shot at then we would have to jump to one side and into the marshy surroundings, get wet through and very cold. So which was the best way of getting to battalion HQ?

We went by a roundabout route and arrived exactly opposite a gun post. We had approached through water making a splashing noise so the sentry was fully alert. He called out "Halt. Stand fast!" and then opened fire on us. Our own man had not recognised us. It was no use arguing at being shot at, so I said "It's C Company's Birbahadur Pun coming to make contact." He opened fire at us again. I shouted out "Its Karnabahadur and Birbahadur coming to make contact." "Is that so? In that case what is the name of your company commander?" "Major Myers." "Did he send you?" "Yes." "So come on," but he did not lower

---

[25] Maj, later Brig, P.O. Myers, OBE, MC, felt that much of Birbahadur's story (see also page 118) was 'a load of nonsense and the result of years of vivid imagination'.

his weapon. He continued aiming at our chests. At last he saw who we were and dropped his aim. We sat down.

He asked us why we'd come and I said that his lot were surrounded here and our lot were surrounded there and we've come to find out the password. "Tonight's password is Calcutta and the answer is *pani*."[26] We went back as quickly as we could and, although I did not have a watch I guessed it was about 0200 hours when we got back. The way back was just as difficult as was the way forward. On arrival at our company, without finding out who we were, the sentry threw a grenade at us and a small fragment stuck in my bottom. We reported to the major sahib who had already received orders on his wireless for us to make our own way back by best individual efforts to reach Pegu. We had a quiet mouth signal, "ch", to get ready and a "ch ch" to move, so with a "ch ch", off we went. We had been surrounded for a week and everybody's feet were rotten.

There was a railway line at Pegu and our battalion rations were to be brought up from Rangoon in a small goods van pulled by a Jeep fitted with railway wheels. I led the way to where there was a ration dump at a bridge over a river and we were ordered to destroy the tinned rations in the dump by piercing them with our bayonets and throwing them into the river.

The area echoed with "gwanch, gwanch, gwanch" as we split the tins. We finished that at 0300 hours and threw the bolts of the spare rifles into the river. We also had to take the blankets from the dump, American ones, camouflaged red, yellow and green, fill up the trenches with them and put soil on top to hide them. The 2-inch and 3-inch mortars had their sights taken off and pins taken out and thrown away.

After all I had done for the company, gone for the password and been fired on, brought it back to the company and had a grenade thrown at me and then gone in front of the company up to Pegu I was not happy when we got there. I had done more than anyone else, but no one had said I'd done well, nor promoted me nor given me a *bahaduri*.[27]

At Pegu we had a week's rest and painted our feet yellow and blue. Two men of C Company had got lost and been left behind. A Punjabi battalion had charged our old place believing the Japanese were still

---

[26] Water.

[27] Birbahadur's voice choked with emotion at this point. He eventually won an MM in Java.

there and found our two. They were only returned to the battalion two months later. Both were given an m-i-d. Can you believe that I, who had done so much from before Sittang and afterwards, got nothing while those two, for doing nothing, were both given an m-i-d?

How unfair. Some of the company had only turned up after four, six or seven days and Chandrabahadur sahib's only comment was "Ram, Ram, Ram," in disgust.[28]

One of my special friends, a Rai, whose tea I used to bring and whose clothes I used to wash, had his leg smashed a week later by a Japanese shell. During that bombardment the men moved to another position and the Rai begged me to stay with him or to take him with me. He won me over and I carried him with me for two miles. I fell into some deep water with him and I only just managed to get out alive. The Rai disappeared in the water for ever. I was also sick and we were in another place for two months when an Indian battalion went ahead instead of us. We were put into aeroplanes and flown to Imphal.

Padamlal Pun, 1/4 GR, *had escaped from the Sittang disaster. After rejoining his battalion his service continued.*

By now it was 1943, monsoon. Operations were quiet for three months. In that time we started building a road to MS 109. We carried various tools. There was no transport. In places we fished and searched for jungle produce, especially the koirala[29] tree whose buds we ate. We reached Tiddim where the Naga king had his base. The Japanese were in front in trenches. We were on the higher ground where we dug in. Turn by turn we went on patrol to the firing line.

Military life is strange. When the enemy were there we couldn't do anything to them; when no enemy were around we had to go and look for them. If there was no enemy at all we quarrelled among ourselves. Military life makes for a fighting spirit.

We celebrated *Dashera* that year as best we could. One day we were told to go and attack No 3 post some four miles away, at night. We were given covering fire by artillery with shells whistling overhead. I was 2IC of the section. At dawn we reached our objective. The artillery fired again and Japanese artillery opened up. One soldier had his nose shot

---

[28] Birbahadur laughed in derision at this point. Ram is the name of a god.
[29] *Bauhinia variegata.*

away and I bandaged him. At the same time the LMG 1 started groaning. He pushed his gun away, rolled over and I called the stretcher bearers. We loaded him on the stretcher but, as he was lifted off the ground, another bullet killed him. I told the man with no nose to make his own way back. Our section should have gone ahead to attack but was now in the rear. I took the LMG and went forward and took up a position by a rock where I was pinned down by Japanese fire. I had about 50 rounds on me which I fired at the enemy who fired back. When I stopped they fired, and when I fired they stopped. When my ammunition was finished I took my clothes off and crawled back, then dived like a frog jumping into a pool. As I slid down the hillside I took off a toe nail and sprained my ankle.

We met a British company on the road with many dead. I ran on back and my section was well in the rear when I caught them up.

Back in the platoon I was asked where LMG 1 was and I told them he was dead and only three men of my section remained, one naik, one rifleman and me. One other rifleman who had said he would not return until he had won a *bahaduri* stood up straight and was shot dead.

We went into our next attack some three hours' walk from Tiddim. We were unable to take our objective. We went to Bishenpur where we got stopped by a road block. So we were told to return. But, on our way back, we were stopped by another road block which took eight days to break through.

In the Manipur area was a strong British force with many Japanese around the hills. We were fired on from all sides and could not prevail. The Gurkhas fought bravely but the Indians just carried their weapons with them and did not fight, so the Japanese came through the Indian positions and cut us off. The Indians let us down by dropping their weapons and running away. We therefore had greater contact with the enemy, in fact more than our fair share.

By early 1944 at Kohima we were surrounded for three months with a great shortage of rations.[30] I was weakened by my war activities and was smitten by malaria. There were no beds in the forward hospitals so I was evacuated to Comilla hospital. For a week or so I was well looked after and my fever left me. In my ward were some Indians. In war men's souls do not stay in the earthly domain. They go to heaven. How can I prove that, when sleeping with the Indians? I dreamed that I went to heaven. I was told by an angel I had not come to the end of my life on

---

[30] 1/4 GR was not at Kohima at that time.

earth. That I accepted. The angel gave me a wooden container with two pints of holy water in it and told me to drink it. This I did. After that I made my way slowly, in descending circles, back to earth. As I came down I repeated, loudly, in my sleep the words the angel had said "Drink holy water, drink holy water, drink holy water."

The noise of my sleep talk woke the Indians who shouted at me to keep quiet. They woke me up. I felt completely free from sickness and fresh, just as I was before I was struck down with malaria.

As my days were not over and having had so much fighting when I wasn't killed, I knew that those who go to the firing line and fight leave their souls behind them. I was sent back to 4 GRRC by a British officer and, when I got there I was told that the war was just about over so what should they do with me? I was sent to the women's hospital to help weigh the infants. I was suddenly told to go on a havildar promotion course of one week in Darjeeling. I felt that, having been through all the war, uncaptured, unwounded, I had no heart for further service and wanted to go home. Of four brothers, three were serving and the youngest was still at home. My second and third brother could carry on serving but I, the eldest, should go home. I left the army on 5 August 1945.

Shamsherbahadur Rai, MM, 1/7 GR.   From Tiddim we went to Kennedy Peak and the Japanese were not far away at MS 52. We attacked that feature but were unsuccessful as the Japanese defence was strong. 2/5 GR tried to dislodge them but could not. Not even aerial bombing could do that.

Ten of us were sent on patrol to discover the layout of their defences. I was on the right but near the objective we lost contact. Above me the ground was high, below me it was sloping down. Those below me were all caught and taken into the Japanese bunkers. I was farther up and three Japanese came to attack me. I had two grenades, one with a 4-second fuse and one with a 7-second fuse. I threw the 4-second one and killed them all. Throwing the other against any who came to attack me, I ran off. Above me was a Japanese listening post and I was fired on from it. I lost my footing in a branch that had been blown off by bombardment and fell flat, hurting my chest and leg. I was not hit but the Japanese thought I had been so they left off firing at me.

I was alone; the others had been taken into the enemy bunkers and had probably been killed. I waited till I had caught my breath and made a dash for some tall trees. The Japanese once again opened fire but I was not hit.

Back at the company base, I found we had been surrounded so we had to make our own way out. The brigadier gave the order to abandon our packs and personal kit and only to take our weapons. So away we went, on and on and on, till we reached division HQ. There we found that the staff had made their escape but the many captured had been decapitated, including the patients in the hospital. The sisters had been killed by having bayonets thrust up their private parts. What greater sin is there than that?

We moved off again, by night, still surrounded. A jemadar was killed and others were badly wounded. So thirsty were they and so short was water that they asked for us to spit into their mouths for comfort as they died but we had no spit in our mouths, so dry were we.

The Japanese set fire to the undergrowth below us and some men were burnt to death. The heat of the flames affected my left eye but, nursing it, I managed to escape.

We were sent to Ranchi for a rest and were sent on twenty days' leave which meant I had about a week at home. My parents were very pleased to see me, not knowing what had happened to me.

On my return we went to Manipur and moved off to contact the Japanese at Bishenpur. Inconclusive, we went back. The division commander's scheme was to surround and ambush the Japanese, who were on a hill. There was a path leading up to the top and we had to ambush that while others surrounded the feature. Later on a Japanese convoy came and the Japanese on the feature moved out from the jungle to meet up with it. The convoy came with a tank that evening, headlights burning. I thought we would be squashed by it.

But it was an unlucky day for the Japanese. With us was a man called Ganju Lama. He was so dumb we used him as a cook. He did not understand much Khaskura. He was armed with a PIAT. He fired at the tanks and destroyed two.[31] We all breathed a sigh of relief. We didn't think he had it in him to do that. A tank is dangerous as it has many weapons on it. He won an MM for that.

The main convoy came on and we managed to kill all the men in it

---

[31] The regimental history reports that all five Japanese tanks in the battle were disabled.

so the vehicles were out of action. Next day we stayed there and ate the Japanese rations, amongst which were some very small biscuits.

A Japanese battalion attacked us from the right. The white Very lights made the night like day. By next evening we had killed most of them and they lay around like clods of earth and bits of stone. We were soldiers and when the fighting had finished we went collecting watches from the corpses as we had been told that all Japanese wore gold watches. One, not dead, jumped up and bayonetted the soldier who was trying to take his watch off him. Another soldier immediately shot him dead with one round.

After that we went back to Bishenpur. Much later I was just behind Ganju Lama when he fired his PIAT at more Japanese tanks in the engagement that won him the VC. The first round he fired hit a tree and rebounded, wounding him. It was put out that he had knocked out nine tanks. The CO and subedar major wondered what award to put him in for. The subedar major said he should be promoted to lance naik but the CO recommended him for the VC.

We moved off, chasing Japanese. The water we waded through was so hot it made the skin of our feet as white as chickens' eggs. It sent many men sick and we only had three men left in the section. We were sent on an ambush. I had an LMG, the naik a Tommy gun and the rifleman a rifle. Off we went in a Jeep up a track in open country. It was monsoon weather and raining much of the time. We picked our ambush site and I smashed down the undergrowth in front of me to make a good field of fire. It was like a field firing range. The naik asked me if I thought the Japanese would come in such open country and I said, yes, they could.

The soldier, in position on my right, said he was hungry. He took off his hat and started to eat some biscuits. It was a bit chilly so he bent forward to light a cigarette and then shared it with me and the naik. The naik said he was sleepy, told me to stay awake and he would give me the chance to sleep afterwards. The soldier, hat off, had already fallen asleep. I also fell asleep and, in a dream, heard an elephant breathing down my ear and sniffing at my weapon, "swaah, swaah". The elephant then turned into a buffalo and that, too, made the same noise. I woke up to see Japanese soldiers, marching in single file on both sides of the track, rifles with bayonets fixed carried over their shoulders. I heard the noise of their boots, "swaah, swaah". They were 25 yards away.

By the time I had got into a proper fire position they were only ten yards from me. The day before my LMG had jammed. What would happen now, today? "If I'm to die you won't fire. You'll have to fire today," I told it. I cocked it and fired. It worked! I fired three magazines and, reloading with the fourth, found I had "double feed" so it jammed. The naik woke up and asked what was going on. I told him that the Japanese had almost killed us. He opened fire with his Tommy gun but didn't hit anyone as by then they had retreated. I won my MM for that action.

The OC, Major O'Donnell, sent a message telling us to stay the night there. He sent up some more ammunition and some cigarettes. Next morning he brought up some more men. We went some way down the road and found Japanese wounded. They begged us to spare them but the OC didn't accept that and they were all killed with kukris.

I saw several cases of Gurkhas crucified on trees. The Japanese never killed outright, they condemned captives to a slow death. I do not like the way modern Nepalis go and work in Japan.

Jaharman Sunwar, 1/7 GR, *was a pre-war soldier.*

Eventually we got to Manipur. We were in 17 Division and we retrained. We moved off to Ningthoukhong, north of Manipur. After dawn stand-down we saw three Japanese light tanks and B Company, 2/5 GR, went to attack the position. They were beaten back and some came running our way without their weapons, saying that the Japanese had finished them off. Our B Company was ordered to go into the attack. I was commander of 1 Section, 5 Platoon. We were ordered to move, inconspicuously, the 800 yards to where there were three Japanese tanks. It was very slippery. It was hard work getting there, moving through bamboo. We got up close to the Japanese tanks at dawn. There was no firing. We opened fire from the standing position as we attacked the tanks which were all stuck in the mud. Rifleman Ganju Lama carried the infantry anti-tank weapon, the PIAT, and he fired at the first tank. The crew dashed to safety and were killed. Ganju fired his PIAT at the second tank and about ten men jumped out. The second tank opened fire with its machine gun but, except for Ganju who was hit in the foot, we suffered no casualties. As the Japanese from the second tank ran away we killed about six of them. The crew from the third tank also ran away. We had captured the position. I had seen it all with my own eyes from start to finish as I was Ganju's section commander. Ganju was evacuated for medical treatment.

We were withdrawn after that and I was sent on a three-month weapon training course at Sagar and three days later we heard about Ganju Lama's VC. We were very happy and celebrated with rum, singing and dancing. General Slim, a one-time officer of 7 GR, lectured us on what was needed to be done in Burma. "Now we're ready to beat the Japanese," he told us.

We reached Meiktila. Our troops came from all sides and the Japanese became flustered. At one cross-roads we had machine guns on fixed lines and the Japanese came in crowds. We slaughtered them and their corpses were like grains of rice spread out to dry. A dozer buried them. After that their attacks became much less. There was almost a competition who could get to Rangoon first. Our parachutists dropped on Elephant Point and three days later peace was declared before 1/7 GR got to Rangoon. We had more celebrations because we had won: dancing, singing, rum drinking and we re-hoisted the British flag.

Jaharman Sunwar was awarded an MC in Malaya in 1951.

Buddhibal Gurung, 3/8 GR, *had an exciting war.*

I joined the army on 12 October 1940 and went to Shillong for 11 months' recruit training. I took the oath of loyalty to the regiment and went to Loralei camp, on the North-West Frontier of India for six months.

We enlisted at 16 rupees a month. I wanted to save 10 rupees a month so I lasted out on 6 rupees for all expenses: cigarettes, ink, pencils, note books, soap and polish.

We then moved to near Bangalore, to Trichinopoli. Hot wasn't in it! So hot our blood overheated and we thought we'd die. We became nervous. The soldiers went to hospital in droves and reported they were pissing blood. I said that it was because they were eating raw *simrik*.[32] This cools the mouth and the blood but causes the urine to turn red. I said, "I don't eat it: I don't suffer. Leave off eating it." The CHM told the men to listen to me and to take me as an example and not to eat the

---

[32] Simrik is a kind of red earth that is used for religious marks on the forehead, poultices for mending broken bones and also acts as a contraceptive.

stuff. They left off eating it, became better and went back to training.

We moved to Ranchi, where we underwent more training and route marches and on to Ceylon where we formed a brigade and took part in much new training, including with motor cycles and other vehicles.

In Ceylon I met a Tamil captain near the camp. I said that I'd heard there were guerillas in Ceylon and I asked him if there were any? "Yes, you want to learn guerilla training?" Two others wanted to learn guerilla training, Gamanbahadur Ale and Birbahadur Gurung, and we learnt in our spare time, daily from 1600 hours to 1700 hours and every Sunday all day, for nine months. We learnt many things, including jumping out of trees and jumping into water. The CO told me that he had three extraordinary men but, "You are too thin. Fatten up! Eat more!" I said, "No, because a fat soldier could not fight."

Then the battalion started such training and we three were the "exercise enemy". On one occasion the umpires said we had beaten the battalion. After 14 months in Ceylon we went to Ranchi. The Tamil captain said that it would be dangerous when the British left Ceylon. If the British were to stay it would be good. Now you're off to Burma. I told him that a battalion had to go where it was sent, even to its death. "Burma is ours and we have to regain it."

In Ranchi we continued training. In the officers' mess truck was such stuff as whisky, beer, bread and a lot more. By night, when the battalion was on duty, we three broke into the truck, ate what we could and put the bottles, unopened, on their sides to show that we'd been there. The British officers were asleep under the truck and heard nothing. They never woke up. We had a torchlight and a dummy bomb made of maize leaves. We lit it with a fuse, threw it and ran away. The umpires said we had beaten the battalion. Later we infiltrated brigade HQ and captured enough men from different parts of the camp to make a section.

Horsford sahib was with us.[33] He liked us and was good. He had joined in Shillong when I did and we trained together for 11 months. Then Milne sahib came. Milne sahib also liked me. On the range, during fire and movement, I beat him at 800 yards. At night Milne sahib would give a goose and have *raksi* but I was a young soldier who did not drink so I only ate the meat.

We moved to Gauhati and nearby Dimapur. I was made section commander of 2 Section, 2 Platoon, A Company, over the heads of a

---

[33] A close relation of CO 4/1 GR.

number of my seniors in service. A Guerilla Platoon, Z Platoon, was formed and I personally picked 30 men from other companies for it. The platoon commander was Jemadar Adjutant Chingbahadur Gurung who was later promoted to subedar. The other two guerillas were also given merit promotion. We were met by a Brahman, originally from Nepal, who told the CO that there were 60 Japanese ahead of us and he had been ordered to feed them with rice gruel daily at 1800 hours. I said we had to surround the position and I would take six men to within 25 yards from where they fed and kill them. Although we waited till midnight none came. They had escaped between A and B Companies. We chased them after eating the food although the Brahman told us not to.[34]

On the way forward was a precipice. Our driver was a Punjabi who had drunk too much. Another vehicle drove towards us from the other direction and, trying to miss us, drove off the road, falling down the cliff. One platoon of soldiers was written off. We drove on to Manipur and were dropped a mile short. The driver told us that the Japanese were there. We put in a night attack. I became angry and threw a 77 smoke grenade. "Who threw that? Who threw that?" someone queried and I said the Japanese had thrown it. "The enemy doesn't have 77 smoke grenades so it wasn't them," came back the answer. "How many Japanese units have been around here and looted our arms?" I answered. We attacked, drove the enemy back and captured Manipur.

We went away towards a small river. We felled a tree for a bridge and only our platoon, commanded by Subedar Singabahadur Gurung, went over. We went on and on. In front was No 55 British battalion [*sic*] who wanted help. So we went there. It was 500 to 600 yards ahead. I was in front, a rifleman behind me, the platoon havildar behind him and the platoon commander behind him. I turned and said, "Keep quiet for the next 600 yards," but the platoon havildar said, "Either much money or many bones."[35]

There was a precipitous hill in front. The air force and artillery had turned the jungle into red mud. The Japanese were to one side. They had killed many British soldiers. We prepared our attack. There was a

---

[34] The action described is probably at the Yu River (17–20 Jan 1944) when the Guerilla Platoon was attached to the Northampton Regiment and Lt Horwood, DCM, was awarded a posthumous VC. Letter from Lt Col E.T. Horsford, MBE, MC, dated 2 Oct 1999.

[35] 'Win some, lose some.'

major sahib who spoke Urdu and English. He asked us why we had come and we said to kill the enemy. "How?" he asked. "We have only 45 men left." So it was up to us. The men said why not make a head-on frontal attack but I said no. Instead I decided to climb the cliff, with the other two guerillas by using the hanging vines on the trees. From the top we saw that the Japanese were in a lying position at the base of the other side of the hill.

We climbed back the same way, "punglung, punglung, punglung, punglung", back down to the river and joined the others. We planned to attack at 1600 hours, 3 Section covering. I took 18 men back up the hill to throw grenades all at once from as near as possible to the Japanese and attack. The OC and the platoon commander were in the rear.

At the moment of the attack one of my men went forward alone. I told him not to but he was instantly killed by a Japanese machine gun. I threw two grenades at that LMG and jumped on the firer. I had a Tommy gun with me – what a useless weapon! It jammed after the second burst. What sort of weapon is that? I broke it in two and threw it away. I took out my kukri. One of our sections was driving the enemy away so, hiding behind a rock, I managed to cut the heads off the Japanese as they ran past me, one by one. During that battle I cut off 80 heads – 80, I tell you![36]

There was so much blood all over me I couldn't move my legs or let go of the kukri as the blood stuck everywhere. It was all over my body, too. It was very difficult to clean up and I had to have help in taking the kukri out of my hand. By scraping the blood off one leg and then the other I managed to move them.

That battle to take the Japanese post lasted half an hour and we stayed there till 1800 hours. The British battalion[37] CO came to congratulate me and said I deserved a VC. That night two of our oldest riflemen, aged at least 50, had such dreadful nightmares that they screamed. So what was to be done about that? We tied their hands and gagged them. At midnight the Japanese returned to attack us. Our mistake had been not to have collected their weapons earlier. They only fired three flares but did nothing else. The platoon commander asked

---

[36] 'I hate to throw cold water on his treasured memories but I think someone would have reported it. Even so one wonders how much gallantry had gone unreported.' Letter from Lt Col Horsford.

[37] Northampton Regiment.

me if I was afraid. "No, they're men and we're men." It was then 0100 hours.

At 0500 hours No 2 Section received an order to attack but I was ordered on a recce first. "I go to die by myself?" I queried. "Instead, I'll take my section and do the job in one." So, at 0600 hours I took my section away, on and on and on and on, uphill. We travelled far and saw a line of elephants bringing up Japanese rations. I saw a drum on one of them, a drum like we carry *raksi* in, so I went up to it and cut the drum off. The elephant was scared and ran away. We all had a drop of what it contained, some kind of hooch. We made for a pass in the hills and saw the Japanese digging a big hole. We watched and saw the elephants bring the corpses of those we had killed the day before.

One small group of Japanese was on a flank as protection. The remaining forty-odd were working in the hole. I split my men into two sections, with me were my guerillas, the rest in the other group. The larger group was to attack the Japanese as they were about to bury the dead and my group was to attack the smaller party. After the attack we were to get out of there as quickly as possible. So we attacked and had no idea of how many we killed. The larger group returned to the company but my group missed the way and only got back five days later. There was such a difference between the map and the ground we didn't know where we were. On day one we moved and got lost. We didn't stop that night but moved on guided by the Pole Star. When the star was no longer visible we veered off to the right. Later that second day we came across a river and related it to the map. We felt we were now safe. We saw a hill and thought B Company should be on it, but it wasn't. On day three we met a party of Punjabis who had been lost for 17 days.

There was a major and a captain in the group, as well as a subedar and a jemadar. To start with we thought they were enemy and I took aim at them. The captain saw me and took off his hat in recognition. We met up. The captain told us to show him our map but I didn't show it as I wasn't sure if they were enemy or not as I had heard that one such group had been guilty of capturing Indian Army soldiers[38] and using such prisoners to fight so I was on my guard against such people. They showed us their map and then I did show them mine. We saw a river on the map and made for it. We reached it and made four waterproof-cape boats. They did not know how to do that! We crossed

---

[38] Buddhibal was correct in being suspicious lest the group was INA.

the river and ferried the 17 across also. I saw a sentry of B Company in a tree and waved my hat at him. He climbed down and we met up.

In camp Milne sahib asked us where we'd been. I explained what had happened. "What did you eat for five days?" he asked. "We survived," I said. Then we went to the artillery cookhouse and had a lot of hot chapattis and they sent me to sleep for an hour! I was told to go and dig trenches for brigade HQ. I went over and sat by anti-tank guns on the road, manned by a British sergeant. He said he was going off to have a cup of tea and no sooner had he left when seven Japanese tanks came up the road. An Indian unit was so frightened all its men ran away. Wretched people! I loaded two shells and the British sergeant, who had not had time to have any tea, ran back and fired, knocking out two tanks. The other five turned tail and left. I was so angry with the Punjabis for running away I shot three of them dead. That made them run away even farther and leave us alone which was good.

Early next morning the Japanese attacked and drove us back all the way to Manipur.[39] It was only when they couldn't climb some high ground that their attack petered out. We climbed Wireless Hill and saw a Japanese flag tied to a small tree. A Company was sent in front of us and I asked the subedar if he had seen the flag. No, he had not. I pointed it out to him and told him to take care. A bit later the Japanese opened fire and killed an A Company Bren gunner. The OC, who loved his men, went forward to the dead man and was himself killed. A and B Companies retreated.

It was now our turn to go ahead. We three guerillas and one named Imansing Gurung were told to see if we could capture the flag. In that area there were lots of ditches where tapioca had been planted. We moved along those ditches and reached the tree where the flag was. The ground was very slippery. One man stood at the base of the tree, another on his shoulders and a third on the shoulders of the second. The fourth had started to climb up but we collapsed as the weight was so heavy. The enemy heard the noise and came to see what was what. We ran away and hid in the tapioca ditches. At 0400 hours we returned to the company.

Horsford sahib said, "I sent you to get the flag because you said you

---

[39] Not true: 3/8 GR were outflanked much farther north so the battalion withdrew to the Bishenpur area almost unscathed. The big battles then took place on the Silchar track, with 3/8 GR around Wireless Hill. Three company commanders were killed attacking it.

could get it but you didn't." "I want a saw," I said, and Horsford sahib ordered one from the Pioneer Platoon. After our evening meal I thought I was a survivor so I decided to go and get the flag with the same four men. Off we went, very slowly, keeping in cover as we went. We came across two deep trenches at the base of Wireless Hill. At midnight all was quiet and we started to saw the base of the tree. The Japanese shouted at us so we slipped back to the tapioca trenches. We talked about what to do next. We decided to go back to the flag as all was quiet and by 0300 hours we had cut the tree. As we were lowering it with our hands above our heads six Japanese, armed with swords, suddenly descended on us. The rear three men ran away and I was left with the flag in my hands. The Japanese put their swords on the ground and tried to pull the flag from me. Six of them and one of me, pulling, pulling, pulling me uphill towards their position. If I were to call my men the other Japanese would hear from the top and come and help the others. I drew my kukri and tried to cut the rope, which the Japanese were holding on to but I cut the flag and ran away with my bit of it. I took it to Horsford sahib who was very surprised and I explained how it all happened. Horsford sahib said, "Aha, if you had brought the whole flag back we would have rejoiced even more."[40]

Not far from our post was a British battalion. I went to talk with a British soldier friend. At that time a dog trotted up, a strange mixture of red and black. What a strange mixture! "That's an enemy spy," I said in a whisper. The soldier laughed. "Shall I kill it?" he asked. "No," I said, "there'll be another behind it," and as I spoke a bigger black dog turned up. The British soldier fired at it and missed. The dog sat down. I took the rifle from the British soldier and shot the first dog which ran away, yelping. I said that the shot dog would mean that the Japanese would run away but the British soldier did not believe me.

Next day an aircraft dropped two lots of rations, both near the Japanese positions. I took two men on spec. We retrieved four sacks, three of pulse and one of rice. There was enough for a small bit for everybody. We sent a sack of pulse to HQ. Horsford sahib asked me if the enemy were at the drop. I said none of us had gone to the other side of the drop area so we did not know. I took 11 men and saw no Japanese near the drop. We went on through undulating country and, at the far side of the fourth rise in the ground, saw the Japanese cooking two mules. After eating them they left and we came back to our base.

---

[40] Lt Col Horsford had no recollection of this incident in 1999.

We were told to return to Manipur. Five hundred of us were to go on 61 days' leave.

I rejoined the battalion only just in time. As soon as my section saw me the men cried out, "He's back, he's back." In less than an hour we were on our way. If I had arrived an hour later I'd have missed the battalion. I didn't even have time to finish my meal of chapattis which I put in my mess tin. I carried three days' rations and 100 rounds of ammunition. We had been issued with only 50 but I insisted on 100.

We moved off on the right bank of a river, I forget its name, and that evening the Japanese attacked us. Next morning the Japanese moved back and we followed them up all day, reaching the Chindwin that evening. The Japanese crossed over. So Horsford sahib and Milne sahib asked me if I could go over the river and I said I could if I went upstream a bit. I decided to go with the other two guerillas. "Can you take your rifles?" "Yes, we can. We can tie them with a rope to our bodies but how can we keep the grenades dry?" We tied the grenades to our shoulders and crossed the river. Once over, we threw our smoke grenades from slightly different places and set the undergrowth on fire. The Japanese made a noise, "ha-ha, hu-hu", and ran away.

When it was all quiet again we went back upstream and a bridge was built to take tanks over. The tanks crossed at night and we went with them the next morning. We crossed over flat and empty spaces and what a battle we had! A splendid show! After we got off the tanks a jemadar and I found ourselves in a shallow dip when the Japanese started shelling. One landed almost on top of us but left us both unscathed. Even so one of my companions died! We advanced and set fire to more ground and we heard the Japanese once more make the "ha-ha, hu-hu" noise. We drove the Japanese like beaters on a shoot, shouting "ha-ha-ha-ha-ha-ha-ha-ha".

The Reconquest of Burma, 1944–45

Immense preparations were made for the reconquest of Burma and the momentum was almost wholly on the side of British, Empire and Gurkha troops. Operations south from China by the Chinese Army as well as a second Chindit expedition, also in north Burma and more successful than the first, played a minor part that reached a crescendo at Meiktila. Thereafter the pursuit of the Japanese southwards, their attempts to escape east and the recapture of Rangoon took centre stage. In this last operation Gurkha paratroops were used near Rangoon at Elephant Point.

Mopping up operations culminated in the final battle at Sittang and the surrender of the Japanese on 15 August 1945 saw the end of the war. Burma was the most complete defeat of the Japanese anywhere, any time, ever. The collection of their arms and stores kept Allied troops busy in the aftermath.

The Second Chindit Operation

Chhabe Thapa, 3/6 GR, *remembered that time well.*

As I had been champion mortarman when a recruit I was posted to the 3-inch Mortar Platoon. We moved to Lala Ghat in India, near the Burma border, and trained with US aircraft. Then we were flown by gliders to White City and after 13 days reached Maluka [Mesa?] railway bridge. By night the Recce Platoon fixed gun cotton to blow it up but the first attempt failed because the fuse could not be lit as none of the matches worked. On the second attempt the Japanese sentry spotted us and gave the alarm so we retired. We went out the next night and blew the bridge up, "barang burung". My task was to give covering fire with the mortars. The OP told us where the enemy were and Jemadar Karnabahadur told me, as No 1, on what degree to fire. I went forward and planted the aiming post, went back and fixed the angle and range on the sights.

As No 1 that was my job. No 2 put the bomb in the tube. No 3 prepared the bomb for firing by inserting the fuse in the tail, unscrewing the head cap and giving the bomb to No 2. No 4 took the bombs out of their case. No 4 was Rifleman Tulbahadur Pun who later won the VC. He was put as No 4, not because he was more stupid than the others, but because he could not get his tongue round the English words. For instance, when he should have said "Cross Bubble" he said "Kanest Bhupal" and when he should have said "Longitude" he said "Landi Kotal".

We were about half a mile from the bridge. A Japanese train came as we were blowing it. As there was no bridge it stopped. We opened LMG fire at it and the sentries jumped out of each goods waggon and ran away. We fired 14 or 15 rounds and took no casualties.

Before another engine could come and take the train away we went over the river and unloaded as much of the stores and rations as we could because we had been living on American K rations for 11 days and they had finished that day. We uncoupled the waggons to make it harder for recovery.

K rations were in three meals for one day and we always felt we could eat a little more. We did not go back to White City but advanced towards Bhamo. By now the Japanese knew we were in the area. They came from Bhamo to attack us so we dug defensive positions in the jungle. There were rice fields at the edge of the jungle. With us were the South Staffordshire Regiment and the Lancashire Fusiliers and they suffered many casualties because they were in the open rice fields and not in the jungle.

At first 3/6 GR were in both Left and Right Columns but after that we were all in Right Column and were sent to look for the enemy. The British troops were in Left Column.

Our wireless mule fell and our set was broken so the CO decided to turn back. But two Japanese supply vehicles came along the road, saw us and hid, then made a loud noise with their engines. The CO shouted "Double march" and the column split with one lot going forward and the other lot going back.

A Gurkha lance havildar mule leader was shot in the left thigh and I bandaged him up with my first field dressing. Ninety-five of our men became involved in a Japanese attack. The wounded man was in great pain. The 95 men rejoined the CO and, on the way, burnt the two Japanese trucks. I was stuck with the lance havildar who said he could not move. I buried his Tommy gun and carried his magazines and him also. I met up with five men and we each thought the others were Japanese but luckily we did not open fire but ran away in opposite directions. They ran away downhill to the rice fields at the edge of the jungle. Some time later the moon rose and I saw the five men at the bottom of a small hillock. I put the wounded man down and rested. I saw the bayonets of the five glinting as they came towards us and I thought they were enemy. They aimed at us from a standing position. I gave the password, "*ago*", and they correctly answered "*khorsani*".[41] They were the rest of the 3-inch mortar detachment less the jemadar. We joined up together but we were separated from all the others.

I had a cloth map and a compass. A Limbu of C Company turned up. The wounded man said "Let's go back to India!" How could we do that over the big rivers like the Irrawaddy and the Chindwin? Impossible. I said we ought to rejoin the battalion. By then the other five had started to move away as they did not want to try and rejoin it. So I started with the wounded man, who could walk slowly, and the Limbu followed us two. A bit later the other five came back to us as they had no map or compass. I ordered two to go in front, two behind and one either side of the wounded man but nobody agreed to go in front. I went in front and at one bridge saw 70 Japanese. Some were cooking and others were bathing. All their arms were stacked. They did not see us. I decided not to fire at them so as not to give away our position. I gave a hand signal to move to a flank. We moved through jungle, uphill and spent the rest of the night there.

Next day I planned our movement on the map and moved off. We moved down to another small stream and found some Japanese shaving using a large Burmese mirror. None saw us. We moved off and eventually recognised the Lancashire Fusiliers in a wired position with their weapons ready to shoot down aeroplanes. We were very thirsty by then and felt safe. We had been ordered not to drink from our water bottles without an officer's order. Before we reached the camp we had to cross a small stream and we started to drink that water. However, it was smelly and brown from the blood of Japanese casualties suffered upstream the previous day. We spat it out and rested. We still did not drink the fresh water from our water bottles.

At that time a man came up to us. He had no hat and his clothes were torn, no weapon and no equipment. I thought he was a Japanese

---

[41] 'Fire' and 'chilli'.

so undid my safety catch and aimed at him. But he was Kharu Pun who had been by himself for the past three days. As soon as he saw us he stood stock still, petrified, with his mouth wide open, thinking we were Japanese. When he saw we were Gurkhas he burst into tears. When the British soldiers saw us they thought we were Japanese and they took up fire positions. But I waved my cloth map at them and they saw who we were. They said "Come on Johnny. Sit down, sit down. Smoke, Johnny. Tea, Johnny, biscuit, Johnny, *bhabri wala*,[42] Johnny."

They saw the lance havildar, wounded now for three days, and said "Hospital, Johnny" and "Shaw, Shaw," the name of our CO, pointing out to us where he was. "Have you NCO?" they asked. "No." "Who is your senior?" One man was a day or so senior to me but I was the person who had done all the work so I said I was. The British soldiers made contact with 3/6 GR who had told them about the contact with Japanese tanks and that they were still eight men short. That would be our group. The British soldiers had been told to tell 3/6 GR immediately if the eight men turned up. One British soldier ran up to take us over to our people who were having tea prior to an attack and ready to move. We were told to hurry up and given some tea but salt had been put in instead of sugar. We just could not drink it.

Chhabe laughed at this.

We moved off to the attack and there was a great fight. Both sides finished their ammunition so there was no more firing. We were told to move back and the Japanese started shouting "halaha halaha" at us as they chased us back. By luck our aircraft came over and I was told to fire smoke to show them the Japanese position. The aircraft fired from front and rear of the Japanese and killed many of them. They broke off their attack and we retired safely. That would be about a day's walk from White City. The Japanese were in the middle of three hills but I don't know the name of that place. In all I fired 14 rounds at them then.

General Wingate came and asked who was the 3-inch mortar No 1. I said I was. We shook hands, he patted my back and made a note of my name, number and rank. He congratulated me for my good shooting. He then got into his aircraft, flew away, crashed and was killed. I never knew if he would have put my name in for a *bahaduri* or not.

We had fought for six months and were told we were going to be

---

[42] *Bhabri wala*, British soldiers' slang for an escaper or evader.

relieved by another unit. We had to go to Myitkyina to be flown out but we only got as far as Mogaung. It was monsoon time and we were exhausted. The country was difficult, wet and full of leeches. At Mogaung we had to fight the Japanese. Our rations were finished and we asked for an airdrop. One came but the parachutes lodged in the trees. A Japanese OP was on a hill overlooking the parachutes so we could not collect them. Lance Havildar Simbahadur Thakuri was sent to attack the OP up at the top of a hill. With Simbahadur, a PT instructor, was a new, young British officer who did not speak enough Khaskura. Simbahadur attacked the post and started hand-to-hand fighting with the Japanese who were weak from no rations. He pulled them out, one by one, from their position and threw them away. The new British officer threw a grenade into the post but it landed on Simbahadur and killed him as well as some Japanese.

The OP had warned their artillery to fire at us and a shell landed in our ammunition, blowing it up. There were many casualties, including all the officers, so a havildar was promoted there and then. Firing lasted for three days and three nights. On the fourth day we moved towards Mogaung. Two soldiers of the Lancashire Fusiliers appeared wearing no shirts. Japanese opened fire on them and killed both. Why they did not wear shirts I don't know but they may have been too hot.

When we got to Mogaung we crossed a small stream and the Japanese came the other way. There was a firefight and C Company took casualties, including a Bren gunner. By this time our 3-inch mortar team had joined up and we were the nearest to help C Company. We were told to send one man to act as LMG 1. Tulbahadur Pun was detailed as we could spare him. He had no ammunition on him so we gave him what we had and he went to join C Company which was a hundred yards away. I told him that I would give him covering fire on the Japanese position that had two LMGs that fired left and right at the same time. Tulbahadur was not seen by the Japanese who were about 200 yards away. At the same time as my bombs hit the position Tulbahadur aimed at the smoke above the Japanese position and, quite by chance, killed the Japanese in it. The position was destroyed.

Small arms fire continued from both sides but at no time did anyone close with the enemy for hand-to-hand or kukri fighting. After the firing Tulbahadur was congratulated by a British officer. I did not see what Captain Allmand did when he was winning his VC, but Tulbahadur deserved his for killing those Japanese.

Then enemy mortar bombs fell on Mogaung bazaar killing many people. The Japanese ran away. Our aircraft also attacked them when they were surrounded in a bend of the River Mogaung. We chased them and they jumped into the river to escape. We killed them, some drowned like dying fish. All died.

After one *Habsi* ambush they came across many Japanese wounded. I saw them kill some at point blank range and others by throwing them on a big fire to burn to death. I saw one *Habsi* carving up the meat from a Japanese soldier's thighs and eating the meat raw. "Chop, chop, good meat," he said then he let the Japanese die. That was the only time I have seen a man eat another man's flesh raw.

We went back to India, were re-equipped and did *pani patya* at Dehra Dun. The others were sent on 84 days' leave but I and Subedar Dikbahadur Gurung, MC, with two men from 3/4 GR, were sent back to bury our dead at Samu where a war cemetery was established. Fifty British troops from the Lancashire Fusiliers and the South Staffordshire Regiment were also sent. There were no Japanese there but the war had not finished. We worked for six months. We paid the Burmese three rupees a day to dig the graves. The British officers put lime powder on the corpses and our group buried them. The stink was dreadful. I was a storeman in charge of rations and items like blankets.

On our way back we went to Rangoon and arrived there during a Japanese attack. We were then detailed to go and guard captured Japanese in Bangkok. We flew there. I was due for leave after three years but I said I would not go as I would have to be by myself. We moved to Kuala Lumpur in Malaya.

When we got back to Calcutta I was asked why I was overdue leave. I said I did not want to go by myself so I refused to go. I would rather go on release. I was told I could not go on release and had to serve another three years. I was paid out 800 rupees and told I would have to go on leave the next day but that evening we were told that no specialist could leave the army although 3/6 GR was due to disband. Anyone not agreeing to this would be punished by 28 days' detention. I refused to accept this and was taken in front of the CO. I was threatened with 28 days' detention. I told the CO I was ready to go inside for 28 days. I was the only son and my parents were old so how could it be that I was not allowed to go home on release?[43] I had done enough for the battalion already, surely. I was told I would be excused

---

[43] At this point in the narrative the old man broke down in tears.

parades for that day and would work in the cookhouse preparing the rations and to think about my answer. On the next day I was told to go away and think out my answer and again on the day after that also. The CO was still the same who had commanded us in Burma. I refused and the CO said he would ask the general if I could go on discharge or not. Ten months later the answer came and I was told on roll call one night that I could go on discharge. I had not thought Chindit work was special or different from other Burma work but I was proud of what I had done and my morale had been high.

I left the army on 14 July 1947. I fathered six sons and two daughters. Two sons are dead and I have not much longer to go myself.

Main Force Actions, 1944–45

Bakansing Gurung, 1/6 GR. I was 16 when I went to Gorakhpur to enlist. I was the only potential recruit the *Galla Wala* took with him. It was a four-day walk to the railhead at Nautanwa. The journey was difficult, up and down steep hills before jungle in the Terai. There were still many wild animals in those days and no roads.

At Nautanwa I saw a train for the first time. The engine was stronger than five elephants. At the recruiting depot my head was shaved, all except for the *tupi,* and so I was bald. I was accepted and enlisted on 4 December 1933 in 6 GR. I went to Abbottabad with about 90 others. That took three days and three nights. It was all dream-like. We had been given a plate, a mug, chapplies [sandals], socks, two sets of underwear, shorts and a woollen cap.

We trained until the end of 1934. The training was hard and took place from 0700 hours to 1600 hours. We learnt drill, discipline and weapon training. I was surprised at seeing arms and ammunition. The NCOs swore at us. One treated us badly, beating and kicking us. Five men couldn't bear it and went back home. That man was a great bully and we could not report him. The Gurkha platoon commanders and the British officers did not know he was a bully. I will give an instance of his bullying. One day we were given the order to quick march and sent off in the direction of very steep ground that lay above a river that was the dividing line between 5 GR and 6 GR. If we had not stopped on the brink we would have fallen into the water below and been swept away. But the NCO did not give us the order to halt, and the men in front stopped of their own accord. Our punishment for halting without an order was to wear full equipment and stand outside our barrack for most of the night for a week.

Food was inadequate and the half mug of tea in the morning was not enough. The British officers appeared not to be concerned about our feeding arrangements; indeed, in those days and until we joined the British Army in 1948, British officers were not allowed inside our cookhouses. However, once we went to the war in 1944, they did show themselves concerned whether we had enough to eat or not.

After training finished we took an oath of loyalty to the regiment. In those days some of the officers spoke our language, the rest spoke only Urdu. From 1934 to 1937 we were in Waziristan, chiefly at Damdil. It was a bad place. I was an MMG gunner. When I was first in action it felt like advanced training!

Once 1/6 GR went up a mountain to relieve B Company where a captain, a subedar and a jemadar and 59 rank and file had been killed by Pathans. They had been forcibly circumcised while still alive and chillis rubbed into the cuts. We carried away the corpses till midnight and buried them, in 62 graves all the next day. The smell of the corpses was such that I lost my appetite. I felt we had lost military face and respect. Officers were posted away and new ones came but whether that was because of this defeat I never knew.

In 1938 we went back to Abbottabad and on to Malakand to peacetime duties and to relieve 1/4 GR. At the end of 1939 I went on leave after *pani patya* because a low-caste man had enlisted as a traditional martial class warrior so we were all contaminated. I had 7½ months' leave and took my new wife back to the battalion. She had to stay in Abbottabad when 1/6 GR went back to Waziristan.

In 1940 the Pathans made a big attack on us but there were no casualties. We were in Damdil, Razmak and Peshawar for two years, 1940–41. I went to A Company as a naik and was a havildar by the end of 1941. I was sent on an MMG course but was trained on 3-inch mortars so I went to Saugor for a conversion course. I was wanted as an instructor there but the battalion did not allow it. I was made 3-inch Mortar Platoon Commander.

At the end of 1942 we were warned we might have to go to Burma but we trained near Madras until 1944. I asked myself why the delay; the battalion had a good name and I might win a *bahaduri*. We had no trouble from any Indian activists during the training period. We moved from near Madras to Bangalore for final war preparation. One day we were ordered to dry out some 3-inch mortar ammunition and some of the shells started smoking so we hid but nothing happened and we took the ammunition back to the store. 3-inch mortar ammunition of local Indian units exploded but ours didn't.

The day before we left for Burma, 12 February 1944, we were inspected by Mountbatten. He did not address the rank and file. All our officers, less two, were new. OC D Company, Major Patterson, spoke our language well, the CO, Lieutenant Colonel Grove, not so well.

From Bangalore we went to near the Brahmaputra, by rail, vehicle and boat and on to the Tiddim road near where Gaje Ghale won the VC. It was from there we walked to Rangoon.

It took two days to cross the Irrawaddy, three men to a rubber boat by night. Some men were swept away only to return two or three days later. We went forward as reinforcements. We opened our rations and the fish smelt. All night it smelt but it was not fish in the rations but dead Japanese.

It took 15 days to Khampa [?], fighting all the way. The 3-inch Mortar Platoon jemadar died because of not clearing a field of fire through the trees. I became 3-inch Mortar Platoon commander as well as being CHM of HQ Company.

It was hilly country. One evening, at 2000 hours, the OC – Major Yates, I think he was called, he wore specs and was recently promoted – ordered us to fire all six mortars, giving the fire orders by megaphone from his slit trench. All was lit up. The Japanese OP saw us and started firing back with mortars. One bomb landed on our bombs which exploded. I was in the trench and got hit in the head and stomach. All my intestines fell out. My runner put them back with some leaves and dirt and bound me up with a first field dressing. I don't know how many of us died but only one other of my men remained alive. I think the disaster was the major's fault.

Later that night, around 0100 hours, I became conscious and could see the stars. I was deaf and completely disoriented. I had to stay there a week and my stomach stank as it became rotten. I was taken to an airstrip at Saiboo [?] and evacuated in a Dakota on a stretcher and flown to Comilla. I was a year in hospital.

Much later an IAMC Bengali lieutenant colonel and a Darjeeling nurse saw some metal still in my stomach in an X-Ray and I was warned for another operation. I demurred as I had no friends. However, there was a man from Tanahun[44] working there who helped kill between 200 and 400 fowl daily in the cookhouse and he was my friend for the operation. I was taken to be operated on and the metal was extracted. I woke up at 1800 hours. Fruit was brought to me in bed and the man from Tanahun asked me what I'd like to eat. I said nothing. I wanted to drink. I ate a little fruit. Ten days later I was able to be moved and the stitches were taken out. Scissors cut them and tubes were pulled out. That hurt.

I only rejoined my battalion after the war had finished.

Rewantbahadur Pradhan, MM, 4/10 GR, *gave another slant.*

I was posted to B Company. The Japanese moved by night and we moved by day. They moved in line and anyone firing straight could have killed three of them with one bullet. We moved in open formation. They refused to be taken prisoner. They would prefer to blow themselves up on grenades rather than be taken.

I was in an ambush on the Irrawaddy. I was armed with a rifle. We had been told that C Company would liaise with us. We took up positions on a rise in the ground in trenches we had dug. The platoon havildar, 5284 Chandrabahadur Rai, saw some men coming and said, "Here come the 'fathers'." It was not C Company but the Japanese coming over in boats. No order to fire was given as they landed but I opened fire, killing ten with ten bullets. Then the rest of the platoon opened fire, killing 30 to 40 more a short distance away. Later we were told that the brigade had killed around 500.

The platoon havildar appeared an hour later and threw a grenade, telling us to engage the enemy. There was another havildar, Thagbahadur '58, who was a section commander. "Why fire now?" he asked Chandrabahadur. "Where have you been for the last hour? You gave no orders before. Why give them now?" and the two men squared up as though they were going to fight but they only argued. I said, "Don't quarrel. We've opened fire already and killed the enemy. Why claim anything different? You are our commander."

---

[44] The adjacent district to Bakansing's in Nepal.

Then the CO came and asked who had killed the enemy. The platoon havildar said he had killed them with a grenade. The CO examined the corpses and saw that bullets, not a grenade, had killed them. "Havildar, why do you tell me lies? Who did kill these men?" The second havildar, Thagbahadur, pointed me out and said that I had killed them all.

The CO then told the platoon havildar it was wrong to tell lies and told Havildar Thagbahadur to make a note of my name and give it in to the office. The CO called me into his office the following day and said he'd give me a big *bahaduri*. "I can't give it you myself but I can give you promotion now."

I told him I did not want promotion but I'd rather have a *bahaduri*. The CO could not guarantee I got a big one but he could say I'd get an MM. I was satisfied and my morale went up. After that I was always in front of my section.

Once over the river we reached Taligon, Japanese position No 500. We were there for a week. One day three jemadars and seven soldiers were killed by our own artillery fire. One jemadar was looking through binoculars, one looking was looking at a map and the other was giving fire orders. Five days later we went and cleaned up the Japanese position. There were many dead.

As we advanced we heard that the Japanese had surrendered. We were sent to Saigon where we collected Japanese prisoners of war and acted as sentries to them. I was sent on leave but in Calcutta we were caught up in Hindu–Muslim violence and had to do duty there until it had finished.

I was then detailed to go to England, before I went on leave, to a Victory Parade, in 1947. I shook hands with the King and Queen and their daughters, the princesses. Happy! Very good! That made all our wartime *dukha* worthwhile.

We were shown round the place by veterans of the first war, shown their weapons and photographs. I knew no English but seven or eight of the men who did – all from Darjeeling – were taken away by the English memsahibs and never came back. The memsahibs loved us and one Gurkha had a queue of ten of them waiting for him.

In the barrack rooms the Fiji and *Habsi* soldiers tried to fight us with their fists because they were so jealous of the favours we Gurkhas were shown. I didn't fight. I spoke no English so I returned to my village to marry. England was wonderful; good food, water in taps, hot water for washing. We were taken around the rubber estates. And all of this for free!

Rewantbahadur was referring to the London parks!

Birbahadur Pun, MM, 4/8 GR, *fought till the end.*

We got to Taungdaw, where Lachhuman Gurung[45] won his VC. At first we could not manage to make our attacks effective. We withdrew and tried another way but fell into a Japanese ambush. There were casualties on both sides and we withdrew. One of my friends, a Gurung, came back with three Japanese heads. He won an IOM but only the gods know whether he cut off dead heads or live ones.[46] He was believed and got his *bahaduri* but I, who had never behaved that way, got nothing.

We had to stay in that place in defence. Six or seven times a day the Japanese attacked us; even more at night, seven or eight times. They always came using as much cover, tree trunks or boulders, as they could. They never came standing up. But we heard them shouting "Charge". They could not penetrate our position. All they did was to make us confused.

I'll tell you what happened. I was first sentry, Lachhuman, my *jori*, was second sentry. I told him I was very sleepy and I was going to rest in the trench which we had already dug. I also said to him, "Lo, younger brother, come and wake me up when you feel sleepy and I'll take over."

I woke up. I don't know what had happened, whether Lachhuman's grenade or a Japanese bomb exploded. He shouted that a bomb had exploded and dropped down into my trench beside me. I saw that his arm was badly smashed and blood was everywhere. I bandaged him with his and my first field dressings but could not staunch the blood. I took off his and my puttees and bound his arm but, although the bindings were as thick as a bridegroom's *pagri*,[47] it did not stop the bleeding. He was crying out in his pain and I told him not to as the Japanese might hear us and come in and bayonet us to death. He didn't obey me. I was scared as we were only two. The platoon havildar and

---

[45] The man enlisted as Lachhiman, not Lachhuman, as Gurkhas who know him call him.

[46] Ironic laughter.

[47] Swathes of cloth bound around the head of a bridegroom at a marriage ceremony.

a runner were in another trench and in yet another the officers. It was no good my sitting there on our own. I went to the platoon commander and told him I was in stress. The wounded man would not stop crying and the enemy might hear him. "I don't need ammunition," I told him, "I need a knife. Please make a decision; either send someone to help me or do something else." Before Lachhuman's arm was shattered that night, neither of us had killed a Japanese and he certainly didn't fire anything after he'd come down into the trench with his wound.[48]

Although it was night time, each post gave up one man to help dig another trench in the middle of the position. We put Lachhuman there. I stayed there with him all night and the Japanese made seven or eight more attacks. They used gas rattles that made a noise like rapid fire. That's how I spent that night. At dawn the enemy efforts slackened and they moved back. I was given a big *shabash* because I had managed to fire enough to keep them away. No other part of the platoon position was attacked. After that I went on a recce to see where the enemy were. I lost all my fear and really did think I would get a *bahaduri* now.

Next night I was sent on yet another recce patrol and I found out that the enemy had not moved very far, not as far as had been thought. I came back quickly and told the platoon commander where the enemy were. He congratulated me. We were surrounded there for another four days. There was water in a stream not far off but the Japanese did not let us get to it. An aeroplane came throbbing, "gananananananana", dropping rations but they did not fall into our positions. The Japanese ate our rations and then attacked us again. Very fatiguing.

The CO, I forget his name, published an order saying that anyone who could capture a live Japanese would get a 150 rupee reward, be sent on six months' leave and, if a rifleman, be promoted to immediate lance naik. If anyone could bring in a Japanese head, he would also get immediate promotion, be given a 100 rupee reward and be sent on six months' leave. I was upset; I felt a fire burning inside me. That meant anybody who could find a sick Japanese in a Burmese house would get a reward. I had done work but no one had seen me, so I got nothing.

I heard that my mother was ill. I was sent on leave and she died while I was at home.

---

[48] See also note 25, page 91.

Home Kami, Indian Pioneer Corps, *had a harrowing experience. His dates were awry but, as one of the illiterate under-class, he could not be expected to remember chapter and verse after 54 years. He wept as he told his tale, the grisly bits having to be prised out of him.*

My task was chiefly road building. After being in Chittagong for two months, we went on to Tamu Road and Hill 1444.

After the infantry left us behind, about a hundred of us were encircled by the Japanese in Ramree. There were no British officers with us, they were all in the rear. The Japanese gathered up the airdrops we had and only fed us a little. They made us work hard on general fatigues. I had my face slapped hard many times.

Eventually 12 American aircraft flew over and dropped bombs, causing most of the Japanese to run away and killing one of us, my friend. A captain came and took his corpse away. The *Habsis* came in and captured six Japanese. Having stripped them they crucified them, cutting their bodies with knives and putting salt and peppers into the wounds. They cut off their members and put them in their mouths, their testicles into their eye sockets, having blinded them and then pierced their ear drums. Most died within two hours and the *Habsis* cut the throats of the remaining. They then cut their thigh meat away and cooked it. I saw it all. We were offered to partake of their meal but we refused. We cleared up the remains of the corpses and buried them.

You ask me why they did that. Because, when the Japanese surrounded us they had done just that to five of our Gurkha soldiers.

The Japanese are a sinful race. No amount of money they now give to Nepal can ever repay the wrongs that they did to the Gurkhas.

Chandrabahadur Pun, 1/3 GR.   Eventually we reached the Sittang. There was no bridge to get us over and the men in the section asked me how we were going to cross it. I ordered them to bring two lengths of bamboo, measured off and cut into five cubit [about 8 ft] lengths. We tied our weapons and ammunition to our heads, put the pieces of bamboo under each arm and entered the river. The current and our own arm movements helped us over. Later Foster sahib asked me how I had crossed such a large stretch of water without losing any of my men and I told him. We got into position and started to have a rest. One of my men said he had seen someone moving in front of us as the long grass was waving. I told them to be careful. It turned out to be a Japanese patrol. Some hours later the air force came and bombed that Japanese position. One big bomb nearly hit us also. Many Japanese were killed there.

We captured a good-looking young Japanese and bound his hands behind his back. We took him to the acting OC, Subedar Birtasing Gurung, and asked him what to do with him. He told us to take him away and kill him otherwise there would have to be three men as sentries if we kept him and he would have to take a report about it to the CO. It was all too much *dukha*. I led him away, took out my kukri and took his head off in one stroke. Before he died he asked, in Khaskura, for a cigarette. I did not give him one. His dead body writhed a lot. I told the subedar what I'd done and was given a *shabash*.

After Sittang we advanced 12 miles when a young British officer who did not speak much Khaskura said that the battalion would soon be relieved. There was a dry stream bed and a hut. The Japanese were so hungry they were running away from us like chased dogs. We captured two from a Burmese house made of bamboo and told the young British officer how the Japanese had killed our men and would he let me kill these two my way. He said he would. I ordered my men to kill a goat out of sight and to cook it. I then took one Japanese and cut his head off in front of the other and my men took his guts out and cut his body into little bits and took them away. The other Japanese saw it all but did not see that the bits of body had been thrown into a trench.

Later the cooked goat was brought in. I offered some to the Japanese who refused it. I said if he did not eat any I'd cut his head off. We all sat round with the young officer and ate the goat meat. After the meal I detailed two men to take the second Japanese away to the jungle. He would think he was going to be killed. My men were to release him and let him go back to his unit. He would tell the others we were eating prisoners so they would not now attack us and instead leave us alone. The young British officer thought that a very good idea. So that is what happened. The Japanese ran away.

But the Japanese were under very strict army rules. They were to blow themselves up with grenades rather than surrender. The Japanese were brave soldiers but the cruelest in the world. Burning a captured man in kerosene or petrol was at least a quicker death than most others they inflicted.

Now our young people go to Japan to make money because money means so much to them. I have no comment to make on that. I have even met two young Nepalis, one a Gurung lad, married to Japanese women. When I see Japanese tourists come to Nepal I turn my eyes away from them.

As a tail piece, let **Ranbahadur Khatri, 1/3 GR,** *say it all.*

Then the war ended; how many attacks, how many, had there been? We were in Burma until 1947. The war was fought because the Japanese were greedy for the world and the British did not let them have it. The Japanese are like rats digging into the ground. It is wrong for our young to go to Japan and work for Japanese money as the Japanese are wicked people. I heard how they tortured prisoners by cutting their flesh and rubbing salt, chillis and spices into the wounds. I never saw that being done but came across dying bodies afterwards. We left them still alive because there was nothing we could do for them. God made us Gurkhas to withstand hardship. Without the Gurkhas the British and the Indians would have been beaten.

Force 136 – Malaya

Force 136, the Special Operations Executive organisation in the Far East, mounted three guerilla operations behind Japanese lines in Malaya. Gurkhas seem only to have been involved in one of them when 75 men each from 1 GR, 2 GR and 9 GR took part as a Gurkha Support Group. All members of Force 136 were awarded the Burma Star, not the Pacific Star, so this narrative has been put with the Burma section.

Dalbahadur Khatri, 9 GR. We went to Ceylon for six months' training which included jungle warfare, hand signals, swimming and basic Malay. I was never a good swimmer and I was helped to pass my test by the British officer in charge of us who saw I was in difficulties and dived in to rescue me from drowning. He said that when we dropped over Malaya he'd be around to help me out if I was in difficulties and, as it would be in the dark, I'd have to whistle for help.

The snakes in Ceylon were fearsome. They were not poisonous but our mosquito nets would be covered by them every morning and they also festooned themselves in the trees. One morning Captain Douglas-Kerr, a US captain training with us, shouted out "fucking snakes" and threw a boot at them. With that scores of them came and surrounded him. We couldn't stay there. I went to the nearest village for help and a man said we had committed a sin by throwing things at the snakes. He came back with me, lit joss sticks and sprinkled holy water over them and the snakes went away.

We went to 154 Parachute Battalion in Rawalpindi for ten days' training which included seven day-jumps and one night-jump. We were given our "butterfly" wings. After we had passed out we were given an extra 50 rupees [a month] and that, with our 16 rupees pay, made us really rich. Everybody envied us.

We were flown over to Malaya and one group parachuted into the Sungei Siput area and the other group into the Baling area. I was in the Sungei Siput group. The first night we went to make our descent there was a W sign and not the T sign that the pilots had been briefed about so we returned to Ceylon where we spent the next three days. No one knew why the W had been shown and messages passed. It was a mistake the Malaya end and, the next time we went, there was the T. Our group was in three platoons. I was batman to Captain Douglas-Kerr in 1 Platoon; 2 Platoon was commanded by Matthews sahib and 3 Platoon by Lackourdie [?] sahib. Lieutenant Colonel Young was the force commander and he jumped with us

It was a nine- or ten-hour flight and we were given rations on the aircraft. I forget what kind it was.[49] We had to leave it by a hole in the floor and I bumped my knee on my way out and that somehow delayed the opening of my parachute and it only deployed quite near the ground, though I did have time to lower the rope my kit was tied to and let the load swing below me. I saw a large river under me and I feared the worst. There was no one to help me out as none of the others had dropped nearer than two furlongs away. I carried a day's rations, a rifle, a pistol and an LMG. I was scared I'd land in water but I landed in a tree on a little island in the middle of the river. I got down to the

---

[49] Mk VI Liberators of 357 Sqn, RAF.

ground and and, as I was hungry, I ate my rations. I needed a cigarette and, cupping my hands so no one could see the flame, had one.

I was there all night and next morning a jemadar and a guerilla, whom I thought was a Japanese, came to the river. The guerilla pointed his finger at me and, as I still thought he was a Japanese, I aimed my rifle at him. At least I'd kill one Japanese before I was killed myself. But he shouted "*Shanta, shanta*, 136."[50] I still was not convinced. He looked like a Japanese and his uniform was not all that different. I stayed in the firing position. The jemadar waved a white handkerchief to tell me all was safe and they crossed over towards me using the stem of a banana plant as a boat.

I was still in the firing position when the guerilla came up to me. He shouted: "Rifle down, rifle down. Come to help you. Colonel Young commanding. A Company, Lackourdie, you Douglas-Kerr party." That convinced me. It was just as well I knew a bit of English.

I learnt that one of the first men to leave the aeroplane, Ranbahadur Thapa, got caught up in the tail and it was only after the aeroplane had gone round three times that the crew realized there was a man outside. He was hanging for quite some time before they managed to pull him in. He was excused dropping, taken back to India, sent back to 9 GRRC and went back home with a pension.

Once down and in a guerilla camp we met a major who commanded the stay-behind party. He was by himself and never wore many clothes, even at night. He had a beard and a moustache. We lived alongside the Chinese guerillas who looked after rations and administration as our work was at night and we rested by day.

My job was with a six-man demolition team and we had to break up the railway line. We would set up fuses at bridges, on information from secret sources, and wait for convoys. We set our watches and when the train was in the middle of the bridge we would set off our fuses and both train and bridge would fall into the river.

During the two months we were on operations, supplies would be dropped two or three times a week, according to the signals we sent. The free drops were the most dangerous and we were scared of being hit by them. Rice would be dropped in metal containers. Grenades would be dropped separately from the fuses. The Sakai aborigines and the Chinese helped locate the 'chutes. One three-week period we had nothing so lived on jungle produce, tapioca, yams, bamboo shoots and

---

[50] 'Peace, peace'.

sweet potato but no salt. We were often hungry. In Malaya there were no snakes like there were in Ceylon. We were only afraid of the enemy. We passed messages to each other by whispering as we had been taught during training. We managed; we didn't die.

We often clashed with the Japanese when in the open and always escaped back into the jungle. I killed around half a dozen or more of them with my LMG. I aimed at the engine of the train or the vehicle.

On 18 August 1945 we were due to blow up a 27-year-old power house and we were also told that the US Army, Navy and Air Force were all ready to attack it. On the 17th we put the detonators in place ready to blow the power house up the next day but, instead, we heard that an atom bomb had been dropped on Hiroshima, so blowing up the power house was cancelled. If the atom bomb had not been dropped the combined attack on the power house would have killed us.

The Japanese came to capture us but Captain Douglas-Kerr shouted "War surrender" three times and the Japanese left us alone. Each Japanese group we came across he would shout at them like that. It was very dangerous. The next day we were ordered by a senior officer to take charge of the Japanese and they came to surrender turn by turn, saluted and went to their appointed place. But one lot of Japanese refused to surrender as they were more remote than the others. They attacked us. A soldier named Kasiram had his ear shot off and Havildar Ranbahadur was killed. We all dispersed into the jungle and recharged the wireless batteries by pedalling. We eventually made contact and got a message through and the Japanese stopped attacking us.

We came out of the jungle and held a kit parade for the Japanese who gave up their Mark 3 rifles, their artillery, clothes, gold, silver, watches – everything. We were warned not to take any of these stores for ourselves. We took the bolts from the rifles, put them in sacks and buried them. We piled the rifles, poured petrol on them and burnt them. This made the barrels bend. That took a lot of time and we became very tired. 3/3 GR and a British battalion came and helped us and we eventually finished the job. Those two battalions then took responsibility for the stores.

After the Japanese had surrendered the villagers were very happy. They had had enough of the Japanese. The guerrillas came out of the jungle and joined in celebrations in the villages. The civilians were also pleased with the work we had done. After some time we went to Kuala Lumpur for a parade and from 0800 till 1100 hours we had to present arms for the Japanese surrender. Some of our men keeled over. After disarming the Japanese we put them in three lots, VIPs, officers and soldiers. Pairs of us guarded them for a week at a time. For the first day or so they were given no water or food as a punishment. Later on we handed those duties over to 3/3 GR and to the British battalion.

The Japanese wrought much damage by cutting down the rubber trees and destroying the plantations. They also acted unlawfully and wickedly to the civil population, especially to the girls. They sent some to Tokyo and gang-raped others, the last man to use her killing her. We were told that by two British soldiers who turned on one Japanese, kicking him and punching him, shouting "Bloody, fucking Japanese".

However, now the Japanese are not the most cruel people in the world. They have learnt how to behave and they give Nepal aid worth much money. The most cruel are the Muslims as they have not learnt how to behave and they are as they were then. They do not understand the meaning of the word kindness.

We were warned for return to India and embarked in Singapore. Our destination should have been Calcutta but because of troubles there we disembarked in Madras. We had been given five golden Straits dollars as a reserve for use in emergencies which we had to give up when we reached Delhi. On the boat one western naik was found to have stolen S$2000 and was put into the jail at the bottom of the boat. He gave back the money so was excused and rejoined us at Madras. Another man said he'd lost his and we all gave him a bit of ours. It was only after we had left 9 GRRC going home did he let on that he had fooled us. He laughed at us when he showed what we had given him and gave nothing back.

At Dehra Dun we were treated as heroes. Who but heroes could earn 50 rupees extra a month? I went back home with three GORs. I joined the police when trouble broke out in 1950. I served for a dozen or so years as a havildar clerk. I have a welfare pension. I have wanted to talk to a British officer about my wartime activities since 1947 and am delighted to be able to do so after so long. I am old now and get giddy spells. My other sadness is that I never got the medals for the war service I did.

I presented him with a set of mint medals on 9 February 2000, nearly 55 years later.

CHAPTER 6

War with Germany

Iraq, Persia and Syria assumed great importance in 1941 because the Germans had overrun the Balkans and might well move on from there into Persia and Iraq then on to Cairo and the Suez Canal, a vital Allied supply and communications artery. Persia and Iraq were rich in oil and, apart from the grave fear of the Germans driving a wedge between the European theatre and India, had the Allies been deprived of vital oil supplies, matters could have become terminally serious. Thus it was that the British, who had started the war for democracy, invaded three neutral countries against the wishes of their governments.

Axis money had bought support in Iraq and Persia; the Vichy French in Syria had promised collaboration but Britain had treaty rights with Iraq allowing the use of ports and passage of troops. A British battalion was flown to Shaiba from India and, on 2 May 1941, the Iraqi Government was informed that an Indian brigade was on its way. Iraq declared war on Great Britain.

Control of Basra was assumed after some skirmishing. Thereafter there were three separate and more significant series of combats. The first involved a 'running scuffle' from Basra to Lake Habbaniya where an RAF treaty-held aerodrome was under threat. After Vichy French and local Iraqi forces had been driven off, troops continued on to Mosul in the extreme north of Iraq to quieten the place down.

The second advance was to Syria in late June, almost as far as Aleppo and the Mediterranean, to prevent the Vichy French governor from allowing German infiltration and so ease pressure on Turkey to join the Axis. The third was to the northeast into Persia. Over 3,000 Germans were in Persia, disguised as diplomats, technical advisers, engineers and businessmen, and this fifth column had to be expelled.

In mid-August the British and USSR Governments presented a joint demand that Persia expel these Germans. The reply was evasive enough to justify a combined Anglo-Soviet invasion. A line was drawn across Persia, the USSR being responsible for the north and Great Britain the south. A brief campaign ensued and on 28 August 1941 all resistance ceased. On 17 September British and Soviet forces entered Teheran.

A number of Gurkha battalions were involved in these operations. Many were moved around with seemingly gay abandon; the situation became confused and, to the Gurkhas, almost aimless. Iraqis, Persians and Syrians all looked alike, as did Germans, Poles and Vichy French – fertile ground for bewilderment!

The desert campaigns in North Africa were of sterner stuff. There was fighting in Egypt, Libya and Tunisia from June 1940 to May 1943. In the first campaign the Italians were defeated. The second, in which Gurkhas were involved, was a seesaw affair dominated by the struggle for air and sea superiority in the battle for control of the Mediterranean and by the logistics of supplying both armies through inadequate ports and then over hundreds of miles of desert, mostly along a single coastal road. At soldier level much was confused and confusing, with the Gurkhas' main memories centred on the defeat at Tobruk, which fell on 20 June 1942, and their subsequent experiences as POWs.

In an effort to exploit the Axis collapse in North Africa in 1943 the war was carried into Italy. Allied progress north was patchy, with severe and protracted fighting much of the way. Whatever else, it drew in German troops as reinforcements that might have held up the Soviet advance, been used against the Allies in north-west Europe, or both. Many cases of heroic bravery were shown on both sides. One of the most famed battles was around Cassino and this, rather than other aspects of fighting, is vividly remembered by 1/2 GR, 2/7 GR and 1/9 GR men. The veterans of 43rd Gurkha Lorried Brigade, comprised of 2/6 GR, 2/8 GR and 2/10 GR, remember the fighting to the east of the country.

Bilbahadur Thapa, 2/8 GR, *had a great story.*

At Karachi we embarked in a very big ship and after nine days we reached Basra. The locals were hostile and we disembarked waving a white flag. We told them we were not there to fight but to train for a week or so. Four German aeroplanes fled from the airport which we defended by digging trenches around it.

A week later 2/4 GR reached Basra. As they disembarked the Iraqis opened fire on them and killed up to a platoon's worth. This is because the Iraqis were on the side of Germany and against the British.

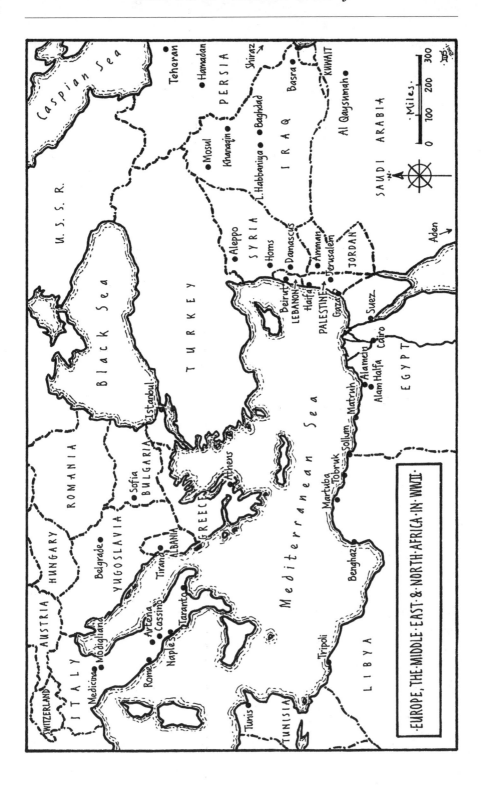

·EUROPE, THE·MIDDLE·EAST·&·NORTH·AFRICA·IN·WWII·

From there we went to Baghdad where we spent about two years. To keep out enemy tanks a 40–50 mile-long obstacle was constructed. At that time there was a great battle between the Russians and the Germans at somewhere called the Crimea. Then the Germans got to within 20 miles of Moscow, so we heard. We were put onto half rations to help the Russians.

The Russians drove the Germans out of their country and the Germans advanced towards Libya. We were ordered to leave Iraq at night to go to Cairo and we drove through Palestine and on to Libya. That was in 1942.

We reached Tobruk at around 0400 hours. The Germans dropped flares and bombs but only four vehicles were damaged. We took up defensive positions. About fifteen days after that the Germans, who were very strong, put on British Army military police uniforms and attacked us from a different direction. I was at brigade HQ and was told to escape. Two of us tried to get away at night by ourselves. We met a British officers' mess vehicle which took us, but wherever we went we were fired on. At dawn we saw our battalion transport so we approached it but found all the vehicles driven by Germans. We drove into their camp and the Germans were surprised at seeing us. "What men are you?" "Nepali." They didn't understand. I threw away my arms and ammunition without them seeing me do so. They made us POWs.

They took us to Benghazi where we were made to labour under difficult conditions and without much food. Eighteen months later I saw a Red Cross ship in Benghazi harbour. I hid in a trench, thinking that the British had returned. The Germans started burning the camp and I was forced out of my trench.

In Tripoli two British submarines came from Malta and forced a stand to. We waited four hours. If we had come 25 minutes earlier we would have been killed.

Eighteen months later, as the British advanced, we were sent to Sicily from where we reached Italy and went to a POW camp in Naples. We stayed for eight to nine months there, then we were sent to another at Abijyana for five to six months. Escape was always in my mind.

I managed to escape with three British soldiers into wooded country and went to a village called Samben Detta where we met a woman driving a horse and cart. She asked us if we were Germans and I said no, Indians. We introduced ourselves and sat in the cart. At her village we introduced ourselves to the senior man who gave us civilian clothes and tried to put us individually in separate houses, to hide in cupboards if necessary. The British soldiers did not want that because of the language problem. I was the only one who spoke Italian. I don't know where my three friends went. By day I hid in the woods.

In Detta village was a Mrs Pastolina Martina. One son, one daughter and her husband were British spies so they were prisoners. In the woods I met up with a Lance Naik Kharakbahadur Sunwar of 2/7 GR. Mrs Pastolina Martina said she would hide both of us. One day two Germans, one a sergeant major, came to the house looking for us but couldn't find us as we had gone to the woods to hide that night because someone, a German, probably an undercover agent, had earlier on tried to make us talk to him. We decided that if we met one or two Germans we would kill them and take their weapons and ammunition.

One winter's night at about 2130 hours we two were hiding in a hut when three Germans came in. They surprised us. They had pistols and told us to put our hands up. We refused and when one put a pistol to my neck I snatched it with both hands. The German fired eight shots and when Kharakbahadur Sunwar came to help me he was unexpectedly shot and killed.

When the German had finished firing his pistol I ran away to the woods and was fired on repeatedly by automatic fire but was not hit as I jinked, weaved and ducked as I ran away. I crossed a chest-high stream which the Germans didn't cross. They lit flares and fired three or four magazines rapid in my direction. Much later I heard that the Germans thought I'd been wounded in the back.

My fingers were so cold I thought they had fallen off. I had ice up to my chest as it was freezing and I was sad and uncomfortable. I found a haystack and spent the rest of the night in it. Next morning a girl came to dig tubers and saw me. She told me to come and I told her to speak softly. We decided on silence. At the house she took me to I was given bread, jam and wine but I had fever by then and couldn't face the food. My boots had frozen onto my feet and I could not get them off.

I crawled away and managed to walk for six or seven hours. I came across a field of sugar beet and saw an old man smoking a pipe. He cooked some beet and I dried my boots. I stayed there two or three days. One night I dreamt I escaped in a British jeep and was waved away by the villagers.

The old man told me he had some work to do and left me. He told me to stay there alone. I was worried that he would tell the Germans where I was. Twelve Germans did come, threw two or three grenades and ordered the door to be opened. I refused and they broke it down.

They came inside and made me put my hands up. I was lying down and refused so they fired a burst over my head. I stayed down, happy to die there. I had thrown away my identity discs but not my pay book which I had stitched into my clothes. As they searched me I told them I was Italian but my pay book was discovered so the Germans knew I wasn't. I was asked if I knew who was the man who had fought the three Germans in the other house. They said he was a very brave man. They did not know I was that man.

They marched me away for three or four hours to a village called Benerdi where next morning they put me in a vehicle under escort of two men armed with pistols aimed at me. A German sergeant major sat with the driver. British aircraft made occasional bombing raids. I was taken to a British officers' POW camp where there were Africans, Gurkhas and Indians also. As we reached the camp at 0600 hours British aeroplanes attacked it and the prisoners scattered. Three POWs were killed.

British aeroplanes made more attacks and we Gurkhas were taken away for two to three hours to an African soldiers' camp. Before then I had tried to escape again but failed to. We were given only a little bread and gruel each day. Later on we Gurkhas were taken away for another three hours to a railway where we were put into goods waggons. We were in them for three or four days. We were told we were going to Berlin. It was dark in the waggons and there were no windows. We were locked in, packed together. We had to relieve ourselves where we stood. We called to the sentries who told us we could only go to the lavatory once we were in Germany.

In Germany we were taken to a large barracks and met many other Gurkha POWs. There was provision for games. The Germans separated POWs by nationality. Feeding arrangements were very poor – no hot food – but we were given new clothing. In 1944 we got Red Cross parcels from many countries, some even sent from Nepal and some returned from Japan.

One day seven fatigue men went six or seven hours by train to Darmstadt and seven miles on we came across a small camp containing Muslims. We were given war-scale rations and clothing and worked there for six to seven months, chiefly shifting stores underground, three storeys deep. At that time we were told that British aeroplanes bombarded a harbour [*sic*] called Mannheim. At times the British POWs stopped working at ammunition dumps, petrol tanks, railway stations and such places as the Germans had been warned by leaflets. Leaflets were also dropped saying ground forces were coming that way. Three days later there was a heavy British raid. We went into trenches. Our camp was covered in soot from factories destroyed by fire. Seven POWs in one bunker were killed. On another day Darmstadt was destroyed by fire bombs and I saw many civilian corpses. There were many raids and roofs of houses were blown away.

Thereafter the POWs marched for a week to another military camp. About 10,000 of us POWs were collected and sent towards advancing US forces. We hid by day and moved by night. On the way we collected vegetables to eat and raided a large store of wheat. Next morning only the straw remained; much of what we found to eat we ate raw. Ten or so days later the Germans handed us over to the Americans at 1400 hours. The American commander told us we were no longer POWs. About fifty of us then collected Germans and their weapons and made them POWs. We reported those who had been cruel to us.

We stayed a week in the US camp and were sent to Paris by air. We had been issued with full kit, mess tins and three blankets. After about four days in Paris we went to England where we POWs had a tremendous welcome from the public. We were in England for a month and visited many places, travelling on the underground train and to a university, Parliament House, churches, London Bridge and the king's palace. After a big parade I shook hands with King George VI, Queen Mary and Mr. Churchill. I remember it as though it were yesterday.

We were sent back to India with a great send-off. We travelled through the Red Sea and reached Bombay 18 days later. At Aden we heard that the Japanese had surrendered.

I rejoined my battalion in Quetta and was sent on 84 days' leave in Nepal after seven years. Once home I learnt that my mother, grandfather and young brother had died. My father had died earlier. I was in great sorrow that I could not meet them. I returned to Quetta and found many of my juniors had been promoted over me. I was not promoted. As there was no one else at home I reported to Major Mackenzie I wanted to go home. I was told I'd get five or six medals when I left but I got none. After serving with much *dukha* I reached home on 13 June 1946.

By 1999 Bilbahadur was a cripple, a recently converted Christian and obviously a man of stature in his community. He showed us three photographs of the British royal family. He was extraordinarily happy to be able to talk about his military life and proud he had been able to meet the king and queen.

Gaganbahadur Thapa, IDSM, 1/9 GR, *was frank and fearless.*

We were loaded in a ship and, at 1445 hours, started off for Basra. We went via Ceylon. At Basra we unloaded in small boats. Basra had nothing but flies, not even kite hawks. It was very hot and the vehicles overheated. We could not start them with the handle.

We went on a column to Khanaqin, on to Baghdad, to Homs and to Cairo which we reached at 1900 hours. A British officer showed us an attacking German aircraft which was shot down. He said that the Germans were a cruel race who shot people out of hand. The British didn't necessarily kill on sight.

We were sent to Tripoli. The Germans were there already, in defensive posts. A British officer shot down a low-flying German aeroplane with his rifle. We thought he'd get a VC but he went back to England and we never saw him again. We went on to Tunis. We had a new CO who marched us in threes on the plain below the high ground where the Germans were. The enemy were in ambush. Not far away Subedar Lalbahadur Thapa won the VC on the left flank. We were on the right flank. At 0500 hours the hill was taken and we were ordered up onto it.

We went on to Tunis, got drunk on grape wine and felt so full of vigour that the Germans seemed smaller than before. We took the German positions. After aerial bomb attacks we went in for hand-to-hand fighting. I cut down four or five men with my kukri.

On to Taranto. We moved by bounds and taking up firing positions. The Germans fought well and silently for as long as possible. When there was no hope they surrendered to us by putting up their hands and not talking as we knew no German.

I was a section commander. We got to Cassino. The Germans had stores in caves with 14 years' rations. The Americans bombed the position severely. We could do nothing. Eventually Cassino was taken by being burnt with petrol bombs and we got to the top.

When Sherbahadur Thapa of A Company won his VC, his company commander had a double MC and 14 wounds. I thought it would be me or Sherbahadur who would get the VC. At around 0800 hours the Germans attacked us and there was more hand-to-hand fighting. I killed several of them, using a Tommy gun or my kukri. Only two of my section were left by then. I was wounded. My own brother had his arm cut off and that sent me mad. The Germans withdrew. I went forward and found a large cave where some Italian civilians were hiding. They put their hands up when I entered. There was a fat woman with a long skirt with her legs apart. I was suspicious and went and lifted her skirt and underneath was a German officer between her legs. I caught him and pulled him out. A wounded British battalion officer was there. We could not talk to each other. I sent him back. It was he who saw what I did that day against the Germans and got me my IDSM.

When we reached the edge of Italy the war finished. We were told we were going to Germany but the subedar major said why waste money going there. "The war's over. Let's get back." We went to Poona and were visited by the Viceroy, Lord Wavell, and his daughter. We held a big parade for him. He was very pleased with us. He gave me my IDSM and shook my hand. I was so sad when the British left. They did very well for us all. If the Germans had beaten us we'd have been made to clean the latrines. The Japanese and Germans were equally wicked.

Kulman Pun, 2/3 GR, *spoke at length.*

We moved to Bombay and on to Iraq, later to Iran. The Germans had gone to Iran. There were British and Indian battalions as well as Gurkha battalions. The CO told us to be on our guard when we moved forward. There was a swamp one side and an armoured division and artillery firing on the other. We advanced as far as Mosul, erected tank obstacles and guarded them. There were flocks of sheep and German spies were hiding under them, wearing the fleece of those they had killed. They came to reconnoitre the tank obstacles. We saw that some of the sheep had different feet and we caught them only to find out that they were men. We dug more tank obstacles because we heard that more enemy were on their way. The British officers exercised their brains on how better to keep the enemy away. In the end nothing happened.

We first went to Martuba [?] and then on to Alamein. The Germans had left for Matruh before we got there. So what were we to do? We were meant to go to Megnas [Benghazi?] and we were all put into goods waggons but there was not enough space so we went by company groups. On the ration trucks we had Bren guns on their bipods and tripods. We received information that we were cut off and we had to get back as best we could in groups of twos and threes. We were told to move off to the left to start with and to go back to Alamein. We had no maps and no compass. On and on we walked and eventually found the battalion on a stony hill feature.[1] We made defensive positions using gun cotton with engineer help. We stayed there with our mortars dug in. 2/3 GR was between a British and a Sikh battalion.

We stood to, waiting for the attack. We had laid mines in front of us. The Germans advanced on us like hornets. Water was in short supply and we were told we could drink it or wash in it but once it was used up we could get no more. German tanks were on our left and British light, medium and heavy tanks counter-attacked. Our artillery was 6-pounders and 25-pounders. For every one shot we fired the Germans fired five back at us. We hung on for one night then the firing ceased. We were told to take a water bottle, our pay book and our weapons and make our own way back. Tanks had surrounded us and the enemy dropped parachute flares. In my group with me were a cook and three British soldiers. We threw away our rifles, filled up our water bottles and off we went.

We saw a tank and thought it was a German one. We heard its wireless and its engine was still running. A BOR said to go and have a look so we went up to it and found it one of ours with all the crew dead. It was then that we met up with our battalion vehicles, including the ambulance. The BOR waved to them and shouted "Johnny, will you take us?" The vehicles stopped but they were filled with Germans who got out, pointed their weapons at our chests and told us to put our hands up. We surrendered. We could not understand what they said. They took our water bottles and kukris off us and made us get into the vehicles. They took the five of us away to a place where many men were, Africans, British, Indians and Gurkhas, brought in from every direction. The Germans fired pistols around our heads to threaten us. Whenever our artillery shells came over we were told to sit in the area being shelled. We thought we would be killed.

Later the shelling ceased and we prisoners were put into an old truck and taken away over very bumpy ground which was very uncomfortable as we were thrown about. We were taken to Matruh and

---

[1] The escarpment in the Alam Halfa region.

separated into national groups. We found some British rations most of which we did not eat. We threw most of them away[2] but Indians picked them up and ate them. We were given some inedible bread but no proper rations for five days. Water was scarce. A British officer who spoke our language came over to us and called us "sons" and told us not to grieve. He had not shaved for five days. On the fifth day a major, from D Company 2/8 GR, wearing a Gurkha hat, came to us. He saw that British rations were not for us so, besides bringing water, he brought us some bread and jam instead, telling the subedar major to distribute it.

Fifty of us were called forward, to bring more rations we thought. I was the fiftieth. The youngest was aged 16. We had been detailed as a fatigue party to go and unload a big ship carrying ammunition and take it to trucks to load it. At the end we were offered food cooked by the Germans. A naik writer and an older man told us not to eat what the Germans had cooked for religious reasons so we did not eat it. The Germans beat us. "No worry, if we die, we die," we said. The Germans then put us in a long line, and pointing pistols and rifles at us, said they would kill us if we did not eat the rations. We said no once more and three men were shot dead. That did not change our views: "We are ready to eat your bullets, not your food," we said.

The writer shouted out in English asking how many Germans the British had captured? "The British will kill as many of you as you kill of us. We won't eat your food." They then gave us a packet of biscuits, a tin of fish and some coffee between every two men and we started eating that but a British aeroplane came over just at that moment, bombed everywhere and set all alight. We hid in the trenches we ourselves had dug, trembling with fear. We felt we were rootless.

We stayed there till dark when a British officer took us back to where we had been earlier. Next day the strong men, including the Africans, took picks and shovels and went back to the airfield where the bombing had been. Things were still smoking and we were very afraid to touch them. A British officer who spoke a little Urdu told us what to do and the writer translated it for us. We were made to fill in the trenches, just to give us *dukha*, under German sentries. The next job was to unload German bombs from hand trolleys brought from a store. The Germans showed us how to fix DB[3] pins and firing pins into the

---

[2] Probably because they contained bully beef.
[3] The full name of these pins was not known at time of publication.

bombs before they were put into aeroplanes. They were to be dropped on our troops, so, when the Germans were not looking, we took out the DB pins and the firing pins, put the DB pins into where the firing pins should have been and dropped the firing pins into the sand and trod them in before loading the bombs into the aircraft. We hoped that they would not explode on our troops.

We were taken to Tobruk which the British recaptured. After six months as a prisoner I was set free.

I was sent to the reinforcement unit for retraining after which we were warned for more active service. We were sent to Italy. I was the CO's runner and we went with an artillery major and a sergeant to an OP. Fire orders were given and heavy fire was opened on various targets. As soon as we stopped firing the enemy opened up on us and killed the gunner officer who was already in the OP and the major. The CO was looking through his binoculars and I saw him fall down the slope before I lost consciousness and fell down on top of him. The CO called us young men "grandsons". I was promoted to unpaid lance naik. Patchett sub-machine guns were issued about then.

We tried to break the German defences at Artuna [?] for three months. Other defensive positions that the Germans held on to were Cassino and Monte Grande. We had a British battalion on one side of us. To trap the Germans a group of us took a Red Cross flag and moved towards them. Fire was stopped as we went forward. I fixed my machine guns to fire on them when we lowered the flag but the Germans had been observing us through binoculars and immediately opened fire on us, killing my two men. Some of the others hid in trenches and a big fire-fight broke out. It was pandemonium. I was not touched but as I tried to lift up the dead men I got covered in blood. With great difficulty I was rescued by someone who came my way, otherwise I'd have been finished off that night.

On our way back to a rest area the Germans fired on us. I fired a PIAT which was good against tanks but no good against men and which broke one's shoulder if not fired properly. I was firing at German tanks but, however low I fired, my bombs went high. I had to fire it even if I were to hold it badly and break my shoulder. The Germans had a seven-barrel weapon which caused many casualties, burying some of our men. We tried to dig them out. Some were alive, others dead.

Even so we went on and on and on till we reached Frentino [?]. The battalion to our flank was badly hit by air and artillery, as were we. My section of five men went ahead and our aircraft fired at the Germans in front. It was still dark. We encircled one German post and told them to put their hands up as we brandished our kukris at them, with our guns in our other hands. We captured the post and brought the five Germans back to company HQ. We got a big *shabash*.

That same day we were sent on a recce patrol before a night attack. I took two grenades and an SMG with two magazines. A major sahib went with us. There was a hill feature and a large German cookhouse the other side. We found that artillery had already smashed it. We saw some camouflaged clothing. I crawled up to see what was what and beckoned the others forward. We found we had gone beyond the Germans. In one large house all the Germans had slung arms and we, covered in mud, were not sure what to do. We crawled ahead and heard a great noise in the cookhouse. I got my SMG ready. I went ahead, down a small incline and the Germans fired at me. The bullets splashed all around me and covered me in mud but I was not hit. I got back. The major sahib asked me why I had not gone the whole way and I showed him where exactly the house was. "Where, where?" he asked. "There, there." I said. I took him to the rise in the ground and he kept on asking "Where, where?" loudly. I told him to lower his voice and showed him once more. I fired a burst at the house and smoke rose from the inside. From the window heavy fire was opened at us.

That evening a British air attack came in on the enemy but our artillery fell on us as well to left and right so we were pinned down. I had three grenades which I threw at the Germans who only then stopped firing. I found myself on my own. I started bleeding in the leg and I knew I'd been hit but it didn't hurt. I threw away my equipment and ran back. I was a D Company man but I found myself in A Company. The acting OC, a subedar, questioned me and sent me to the doctor who gave me an injection. I was told I was not to have any water to drink but I was so thirsty I told the medical orderly I didn't care if I died so I had a drink.

It was daylight by now and I asked where D Company was. I was carried away on a stretcher but we were fired on by the enemy. The stretcher bearers ran away and left me there all night. Next morning early I saw a medical orderly and told him to kill me or rescue me. I met up with the doctor again and he told me not to worry. I was taken to some docks, put on a boat and delivered to a hospital, full of wounded men. I was operated on there and had a bullet that had lodged in my body taken out. I was asked what I wanted and I said to go back to India. Two sisters and one driver took me to Rome, a journey that took a day. I had two more operations and was put into plaster. After a week the war ended.

There was a German in the hospital. I told him the war and my suffering was all his fault and I wanted to chop him with my kukri. I was restrained from jumping on him by others and a sister told me he was a POW, knew nothing of what it was all about and I was not to do anything to him. But *was* I angry!

I was sent to Taranto and the CO came to see me with some senior warrant officers I did not recognise. I was told I'd get a *bahaduri*. I went back to India and got no *bahaduri*, no promotion and no pension.

I left the army in March 1947, "bare-footed".

Gumansing Thapa, 2/4 GR, *was pleased to tell his story.*

We went to Basra to fight the Iraqis. We were told only to fire if we were fired on which no one did as we disembarked. We were sent forward, along a canal and advanced. We were fired on from the other side and the navy fired back. Those who could swim jumped into the canal and were safe, those who could not swim stayed on the road and some of them were wounded. No one was killed.

The Iraqis surrendered after some of them were killed and others wounded. We went on to Syria and were bombed by German aircraft for three days. Two of our men shot down one German aeroplane each and were both put in for a *bahaduri*. After some spasmodic firing the Syrians surrendered. We went to Iran as they were supplying Germans with rations. Our forces bombarded a hill with aircraft and artillery and the two sides fired at each other. Enemy were killed but we suffered no casualties. The British told the Iranians that they had to surrender within a week and, if they did not, their capital city would be bombed. We remained in defence. Then bugles blew and we knew that Iran had capitulated. They came to shake our hands and we had a big feast with them because there was no more worry about a German attack.

After a week there we were warned to go to Turkey but the CO ordered us to retire and we had three to four months' training before being ordered to go to Libya. We went by way of Haifa, by train to the Suez Canal and on to Cairo. There they were all black people. We went on to Alamein which the Germans couldn't take and farther on west to Sollum to take over from 2/8 GR. That was on 15 April 1942.

Rumour had it that the British had captured a German division but the truth was that the Germans captured the British and we were taken prisoner. German aircraft bombed us and the Germans came on us from the rear and said "Hands up!" We had finished our ammunition.

The Germans put us to work but we were given no rations for four days nor did they give us anything to sleep on. That was a difficult place, wind from all directions and sand storms. The Germans are not men; it is better to die than be a prisoner of the Germans. Only hill men could cope. Indians and Gurkha "line boys" couldn't be relied on. The CO and other officers argued that we had to be given something to eat and drink and at last we were given food and water.

We were in Tobruk seven months. Then we were taken, first to Sicily and later to Naples, where we were put to work loading bombs from a factory onto vehicles. Without the Germans seeing, we'd take the fuses out and hide them in the mud. This meant that our friends would not be killed when the bombs were dropped on them. That was how we obeyed our oath on enlistment. When the Germans found out we were spoiling their bombs they punished us severely. We dug a 12-foot deep trench and had to climb up step ladders to throw away the soil. At night they would take away the ladders and make us stay there in the cold at the bottom. Some of the older soldiers died of cold.

They took us to another place and tried to cajole us into joining their army by offering promotion and women. "If you work for us we will not give you any more trouble," they said. "British are foreign to you, as are Germans, so work for us." A few of our men fell for this and said they would work for the Germans but most of us stayed true to our salt. Italy surrendered and we only saw women, no men. We were taken to Austria.

After being POWs for so long American aircraft bombed all round us and the Germans surrendered. After the war we were set free and joined up and paraded in national groups under our national flags, with bands. Hands were shaken all round and after the parade we went back to our own camp. We emplaned and were told we were going to France but after circling around a town for an hour we went on to Belgium. We were three days in Belgium and given a great welcome. We were given many feasts and some men were lost there because we POWs had no commander and no unit.

We were told to emplane once more and when in flight I looked out and saw water! Where was I? We landed in England to a tremendous welcome. We were kept separately from the British. Those who had volunteered for Germany were taken away. I have no idea what happened to them. I did hear that they were sent back home without any end-of-war reward. We were in England for three months. We went to the king's palace and to his church where there was much gold. I shook hands with all the royal family, including the present queen. We were taken everywhere. London is so big we could walk all day and not get to the edge. Wonderful!

Bhaktabahadur Limbu, 2/7 GR, *was another unfortunate.*

After three months in Iraq the battalion moved to Benghazi and to Tobruk. On one side was the sea and the other side land communications. I think our defensive positions were bad as the Germans surrounded and captured us. We had not been able to fight much. A British officer of HQ Company said it was better to die than to be captured. He pulled out his pistol and pointed it at his orderly. But he turned the weapon onto himself, shot himself in the stomach three times and died in front of us. We buried him as well as his pistol, binoculars and watch. I don't know his name.

I did not think it was all over for me so I just waited to see what happened. We were taken to Benghazi. There were many POWs, four lots of 2,000 men. We were 15 days there, five of them without food or water. Our mouths dried and there was no need to empty our bladders. After five days water was at last brought but, so many were we, there was a great scrimmage and men were injured.

After being captured the GOs took off their badges of rank and mingled with us. There was no fear of being recognised as none had any documentation. In the prisoner of war camp in Italy we were visited by Subhas Chandra Bose who was dressed in German uniform as a general. With him were Sikhs, Madrassis and Dogras. He lectured us and said that we Nepalis knew nothing, had to rid ourselves of the British and join him. We refused, telling him that we had all taken an oath which we could not break.

Italy had had enough of the war and their king, 80 years old, said that the prisoners had to be made happy so we were to be let out at night to be able to escape if we wanted to. We could stay in the camp if we did not want to escape. I did escape and went to live in a village. I did not understand what they said but they fed me as I was hungry.

After I had been in the village for two months the Germans threatened reprisals against the villagers for shielding us and they became afraid. I was sent into the mountains to live with the shepherds. It snowed heavily. One shepherd gave me goat's milk. He caught hold of the animal and told me to kneel on the ground and suck the teats, not to bite them. The goat gave me a lot to drink and my belly swelled. The shepherds looked after me well. I was six weeks with them.

Then news was broadcast and leaflets dropped telling the villagers that the prisoners would be collected and to look after them till that happened. I was not far from Cassino and heard shooting and bombing. The Germans were beaten and withdrew, blowing up bridges as they went to delay the pursuit. Guerillas came to fetch me and I got back to my unit. I was sent back to Palampur by way of Cairo and Karachi.

I was sent on a month's leave and, on my return, offered a tape when made an instructor of recruits. I declined as by then so many who had joined after me had already been promoted so what was the point of having a tape? I stayed a rifleman until I went on release.

Patiram Thapa, 2/3 GR, *had some unusual experiences when he was in the Middle East.*

One day when I was on duty there was a conference of senior officers, a British brigadier whose name sounded like Wavell and two Germans. It seemed as if there had been a dispute. The brigadier came out by himself, got on his motorbike and drove away so rashly he crashed and killed himself.[4] We "reversed arms" when he was buried. Another man was ordered to drive the two Germans away but he refused and I was detailed. At 75mph I became afraid when I saw traffic in front of me. I put on the foot and the hand brake and the vehicle skidded to a halt and hit something, breaking a headlight. A motorcyclist despatch rider came up to me shouting "Return, return" and at the same time the Germans escaped.

---

[4] This fact is not remembered by surviving British officers. However, GOC 10 Indian Division was killed in an accident, details of which are not recorded, just before 2/3 GR moved to Italy in March 1944.

After that I was made LMG 1 in C Company. I said I was not a gunner so I was given a rifle and a grenade discharger cup instead. At Alamein I had an LMG once more. We had been ordered not to shoot. Why not, I do not know. Germans came and ordered "Hands up!" and I was captured. I was sent to Libya and was a prisoner for seven months. Other POWs were moved to Tobruk and Benghazi but I was sent elsewhere. Germans shouted "Hurrah, we've won," but I did not react and one German fired his rifle very near my ear which deafened me. At another place we saw ships which were struck by air attack and set on fire. One German went over the wire for something and was killed. We were pleased because he had been heavy-handed with us. My hands would often bleed from manual work but I was told they would get better.

We moved lower down to a place where we could play and read so I became wiser. We went on fatigues with about six or seven men. Once an aircraft came overhead and we signalled we were there. It circled once and opened fire on us. Every morning we were made to start the German vehicles with the starting handle. We had to salute the Germans with outstretched arms and say "Heil Hitler". For food we had a loaf of bread a day to share between four men. We had some tasteless black water called coffee. Was it the soot from the cooking pots?

After we had been rescued I went to Iran. On some high ground we had some machine guns and the CHM looked at me as though he hated me. From Iran we went to Syria where we fought for three days until the ruler abdicated. A British officer and I had to take a French women's army unit to Cyprus and away we went. There were no men in the unit. We had to show the women how to swim and how to do physical training. We had to cross a river and swim back as a demonstration. I was locked in a room with them for five days. What did I do?

In Cyprus I had to go to hospital as I had a throat problem from being a POW. I couldn't even drink water properly. I was afraid I'd be killed when I learnt that I was to be operated on. There was a Nepali nurse from Darjeeling and she called me "elder brother" and told me not to be afraid. I wept. She also told me I would have an unhappy life and that is why I am suffering now.

Above: Nk Maniratan Pun of 2/2 GR (*centre*) survived the retreat through Malaya to Singapore (*see page 39*). He was later commended for aiding wounded Gurkhas while under Japanese fire. Also pictured are the Area Welfare Officer for Beni, ex-Capt (QGO) Damarbahadur Gurung (left) and Lt Col J.P. Cross. (*Buddhiman Gurung*)

Below: Japanese troops overlooking the Sittang Bridge in Burma. The blowing of the bridge on 23 February 1942 left many men stranded on the far bank of the river, helplessly outnumbered by Japanese soldiers. (*The Gurkha Museum*)

Above: Rfn Chakrabahadur Tamang of 1/7 GR, pictured here with J.P. Cross, was taken prisoner by the Japanese after the blowing of the Sittang Bridge. Although in poor physical shape, Chakrabahadur managed to escape into the jungle with ten other POWs, finding refuge with Chinese troops fighting for the Allies (*pages 51–5*). (*Buddhiman Gurung*)

Left: Buddhibal Gurung of 3/8 GR, holding his Certificate of Gallantry. He took part in battles at the Yu River (17–20 January 1944; *page 101*) and at Wireless Hill (*page 104*). (*Alison Locke*)

Above: Gurkhas using kukris to sharpen stakes and dig themselves in on Burmese territory during World War II. This large, burnt-out patch of land is the product of spontaneous combustion due to the intense heat, and a frequent sight in the jungle. (*The Gurkha Museum*)

Left: A sortie from Imphal during June 1944. (*The Gurkha Museum*)

Below left: 3/1 GR cross the Irrawaddy Delta in 1944. See the account of Bakansing Gurung, 1/6 GR (*page 115*). (*The Gurkha Museum*)

Right: Dalbahadur Khatri, wearing a set of medals presented to him by Lt Col J.P. Cross in 2000 (*pages 122–6*). (*Alison Locke*)

Below: Tulbahadur Pun, VC, listens to a message from his old mortar detachment commander, Chhabe Thapa. Chhabe's account of the role played by his decorated rifleman appears on page 111. (*Zenith*)

Above: Lachiman Gurung of 4/8 GR, who was awarded his VC during action at Taungdaw. An account of the action appears on pages 118–9. (*Alison Locke*)

Above right: A rifleman of 2/7 GR street fighting in Italy, 1944. (*The Gurkha Museum*)

Right: The Victory Parade after the liberation of Tunis in May 1943. 1/9 GR lead, closely followed by 1/2 GR. (*The Gurkha Museum*)

152

Left: Java, 1946. In the aftermath of World War II, the Gurkhas were sent to quell civil unrest stirred up by nationalist fighters. The sentry in this photograph may be guarding prisoners. (*The Gurkha Museum*)

Right: Rambahadur Limbu, VC, 2/10 GR, rescued two wounded riflemen under Indonesian fire (*pages 248–53*). (*Alison Locke*)

Right: A Gurkha unit crosses a bamboo bridge while on patrol in Borneo. (*The Gurkha Museum*)

Left: Bhimraj Gurung, 2/6 GR, fought in Malaya in the mid-1950s and took part in border operations in Borneo (*pages 182–5, 247–8*). (*Alison Locke*)

Far left: LCpl Ojahang Limbu, 1/10 GR, describing his tour of duty in Borneo (*page 267*). (*Buddhiman Gurung*)

Far left, below: Rfn Manbahadur Gurung, 1/7 GR, recalls searching for a British officer who tried to join the Communists (*page 211*). (*Buddhiman Gurung*)

The changing face of the British military presence in Hong Kong: members of the Brigade of Gurkhas train for riots in the 1970s (*right*); and search for mines in the 1990s (*below*). (*The Gurkha Museum*)

Left: Cpl Aimansing Limbu of 1/7 GR (left) collects his Queen's Gallantry Medal from Buckingham Palace in 1979, following outstanding service in Hong Kong. The ribbon is already sewn into his jacket with a hook to enable the Queen to pin the medal to it – to date, he is the only Gurkha to receive the award. He is pictured with Cpl, acting Sgt, Dalbahadur Rai, 7 GR, who was at Buckingham Palace to receive the Queen's Commendation for Brave Conduct at the same time. (*British Army Gurkhas Crown Copyright*)

Above: Gurkhas of 10 GR were assigned to protect the British Sovereign Base Areas in Cyprus in 1974. The bases were under threat from displaced peoples fleeing the troubles between Greek and Turkish inhabitants. (*The Gurkha Museum*)

Left: Men of 1/7 GR search the hills above Port Stanley during the 1982 Falklands Campaign. (*The Gurkha Museum*)

Above: Members of 28 (Ambulance) Squadron GTR, who acted in support of 4th Armoured Brigade during Operation Granby – the prelude to Desert Storm in the Gulf, February 1991. (*The Gurkha Museum*)

Above: Men of 2 RGR on rural patrol in the hills overlooking Dili, East Timor, 1999. (*The Gurkha Museum*)

Above: Men of 1 RGR being airlifted to patrol during the deployment in Bosnia in 1999. (*The Gurkha Museum*)

Left: A *Galla Wala*, photographed in Danda Bazaar, Eastern Nepal, in 2000. Many of these recruiters have a long family history of service in the British Army; despite the casual attire, strict standards of selection always pertain. (*Alison Locke*)

Below: Lt Col J.P. Cross photographed with Buddhiman Gurung, in 2000. (*Alison Locke*)

CHAPTER 7

The Aftermath

In the aftermath of World War II, trouble in Greece, Palestine, South-east Asia and the tormented division of India needed the Gurkha Brigade to help restore order.

South-east Asia was never the same after the war as before; nationalist feelings were stirred irrevocably and the European diminished in Asian eyes. As soon after the Japanese surrender as possible the victorious allies had two tasks: one to disarm them in all the countries outside Japan and the other to return prewar colonies to their European masters. This latter proved controversial not only to the natives of the countries concerned – Burma, French Indo-China, Malaya and the Dutch East Indies – but also to the Congress Party in India who did not want Indian troops to be involved in pro-colonial activity when India was in ferment and aligned towards independence. Nepal was not concerned politically from a colonial point of view but Gurkhas were, from the incipient demise of British sub-continental authority.

Java

Pirthibahadur Tamang, 3/10 GR, *tells what happened to him after the war ended.*

We embarked at Madras and I remember waiting all night, standing in the rain with my wireless set on my back before my turn came.

It took nine days to get to Port Dickson, in Malaya. The Japanese were on the shore. Most of them surrendered but some ran away saying they were going to continue to fight. Once on land we saw where the Japanese had stolen cattle and food from hotels. A platoon was sent to arrest some Japanese in a hotel. One of them drew a pistol and the havildar killed them all with his Sten gun.

We marched off to Tampin where we collected the Japanese together and gathered their weapons. We were warned to go to Java. Garhwalis had gone bathing, believing the Javanese when they had said they would not fight. However, the Javanese had attacked them by advancing behind a screen of women, who lay flat shortly before reaching the Indian soldiers, who had thus been caused many casualties. We had been sent for in a hurry.

We were fired on by Javanese, not Japanese. We fired back and there were casualties on both sides. Firing went on half the night until 1100 hours the next day. We got off into smaller boats by groups the next night. We moved tactically, firing at targets and taking the prone position ourselves when necessary. I was the subedar major's wireless operator. I moved off to one side to relieve nature and heard firing. The subedar major asked what was happening. The other soldiers said that nothing was happening but I told the truth. He told us to stand to.

We started to cook our food but a message came through that two Gurkhas had been killed, one a wireless operator so a replacement was needed. A Darjeeling man hid so that he need not be sent and I was told to go. A vehicle was detailed and the driver was so frightened of being killed that he wept. I gathered up my half-cooked meal and got into the vehicle. "Why weep when we have to go and fetch a dead man?" I asked. As we left the subedar major told us to drive with all speed and fire our weapons if needs be.

Why look out for trouble when hungry, I asked myself as I bent low and ate my half-cooked meal. We saw nobody in the villages we passed through. We came to a governor's house where I was the relief for the dead operator. Our 3-inch mortars were there. One mortarman had shot off one of his fingers which he had inadvertently put over the barrel while he was firing on his own. There was not much firing although we were near a Javanese brigade HQ.

We were there for nine days, being fired on and firing back all the time. We had to move to Magelang, 30 miles away, but the Javanese had put up a road block so we had to turn round and find another way there, which we did, to the left. We reached Magelang safely where we stayed in a Dutch-run hotel that fed us for free and had mosquito nets on the beds. Two days later we were surrounded by the Javanese. I hid by a tree. They fired 2-inch mortars and I was nearly hit. They set fire to a vehicle and then disappeared. Next day our four rifle companies surrounded the area. The CO, adjutant and the signal officer with two operators stayed in a house. I helped put up 20 telephone lines. I was detailed to be with the CO for his wireless and telephone work.

One night an armed Javanese soldier came into the house and lit a cigarette. He walked backwards and forwards, smoking the whole time. He asked the CO what he was doing and the CO did not understand but told him to come closer. I realised that Javanese was like Malay, learnt when giving children sweets and biscuits in Tampin, so I interpreted for the CO. There was a conversation of sorts, "Where are you going?" "What are you doing?" and then the CO told him to stay the night. I asked the Javanese to let me see his rifle, which was heavier than ours. He had five rounds of ammunition. I asked him to swap his with mine but he declined. I told him to go away but he asked for another cigarette. He said that Gurkha cigarettes were better than Japanese ones.

When he said he was leaving the CO let him go. I said that he was a spy. I turned round but he had disappeared, how I don't know. About ten minutes later the Javanese opened fire on us from many directions. Telephone lines were cut and we had no proper reports from companies. D Company had no communications and C Company said they had been fired on.

By the morning the Javanese had withdrawn and as B Company had no communications I was sent to go and see what was what. A Japanese section was sent with me to open the road. While wading over a river we were fired on. We bent over so that our noses were almost in the water, which was very dirty. Eventually we got out on the other side but each man had to have one man pulling him and another pushing before he could get out. I needed two men to pull and two men to push me.

The Javanese threw grenades as we moved off. A Japanese soldier was hit. I tried to bandage him up, although he had been my enemy, but he refused. He was evacuated by vehicle.

We got to B Company with Dunkley sahib. A subedar from C Company had a walkie-talkie and he was fired on as he was talking into his set. He was not hit then but a bullet took his ear off later. He asked for a section, a havildar and nine men, to help him. I went with them and we captured a Javanese lieutenant colonel, a big black man armed with a rifle and two pistols, one on his belt, the other inside. We also captured two men with him, his underling and a writer. Dunkley sahib put him in a vehicle with a Javanese flag upside down. The Javanese put it the right way up and we turned it upside down again.

I said to Dunkley that we had to search the Javanese officer's body. Dunkley aimed his rifle at him I searched him, getting rid of the little pistol inside his belt. I took it off him and he was so angry he nearly hit me in the chest. We took him to the CO, with the flag upside down to prevent our men firing at the vehicle. The CO ordered him to cease fire and the Javanese lieutenant colonel gave orders for this and for his men to gather at battalion HQ.

There was no firing that night. Next day I went to C Company on a hill. There was a rum shop there and I took two bottles, putting one in each pocket. We had been told we could use any transport we came across and so I took a bicycle. As I rode down the hill I passed the Javanese who were withdrawing. They waved their hands at me, saying "Goodbye, goodbye." I turned to say "Goodbye" but fell off my bike and went into the river, breaking one of the bottles of rum. I got out, returned to my friends, and we all got drunk on that one bottle.

Later we moved back to the telephone exchange and, that night, it started blinking to show a message was coming through. It was about a Javanese battalion that had entered into a position where we had been. I told the CO and the artillery commander who alerted seven pieces. All fired at the same time and then again. I could see the fall of the shells so I could direct fire to the correct target. When the company said cease fire I told the artillery commander. But the Javanese were seen bringing up stores on mules so more fire was directed on that target. By day we saw that only three mules were left alive and all the Javanese had been killed.

We had to evacuate Magelang and go back to Semarong as we were only one battalion and they had many men. At 1900 hours we left, having loaded all that we could take and burnt those expendable stores, such as kerosene and rice, that we could not take with us. We thought that the Javanese would only come back after dark but they approached in daylight and ambushed us. Our front two vehicles were destroyed. The rest of the company debussed quickly, reformed in the jungle and shouting "*Ayo Gorkhali*, chaaaaarge"[1] attacked them. The Javanese threw away their weapons and pretended to be dead. We bayonetted them. Some of them asked us not to bayonet them so we killed them with kukris instead. We eventually reached Semarong.

---

[1] Loosely, 'Here come the Gurkhas, charge.'

I can remember being afraid of Javanese fire for the first week. We then lost our fear of bullets but not of bombs, although they fired a lot. We remained there in a defensive position with artillery nearby. The Javanese surrounded us at 1900 hours and opened fire. We, in our two-man trenches, held our fire to conserve our ammunition and to let them finish theirs. We were only to fire if we were attacked. At dawn they withdrew. We climbed up trees and observed them through our binoculars. When it was fully light their artillery fired for half an hour. We fired back and they stopped and opened up from another direction, then another, and yet a fourth.

One shell cut the telephone line so I was sent to re-lay the line to the guns with a Limbu from Darjeeling called Chandrabahadur. We went on bikes and I had a puncture. I called him back and we both moved off on the one bike. Chandrabahadur said "A son either has to die in battle or in the jungle."[2] Then he also had a puncture so we went ahead on foot. I was on the left and he on the right of the road. A shell exploded between us. I jumped into a ditch and, as taught, put my fingers in my ears to protect them against any more noise. Shells knocked down the branches of trees and had we not hidden we'd have been hit. In fact we each thought the other was dead. We repaired the line and ran back but soon decided to move slowly so no one could see us. We regained contact with B Company on some higher ground. One round had destroyed a bunker but no one was hurt. We went on back and had to pass the message about the shelling to brigade in Batavia.

A Japanese aeroplane had been captured and it flew overhead with our men inside to see the situation for themselves. I was told to go outside and make a signal with my flag to make sure who was flying it. The aircraft showed a flag out of the window so I knew it contained our men. I laid out cloth strips to tell the men in the aeroplane which unit we were, give them news of casualties and of ammunition and ration states. It flew around and waggled its wings to show the pilot understood. It flew away and I collected the cloth strips. I rolled my way out of the open space then, moving by bounds to avoid being hit, and regained battalion HQ.

That evening I, being the dumbest of all the signallers, was again detailed to go out. The others had made themselves scarce. Something had been seen dropped from the aircraft. I also had seen it so I was sent

---

[2] A Nepali proverb meaning that a man has to die in battle or defending his land against enemies.

to fetch it. I was afraid it might be a bomb and explode when I picked it up but it was a message in a metal container. We were told to wait for one more night, not to surrender, and that full supplies would be sent up on the morrow.

The Javanese did not attack that night but fired on us from a distance. The Signal Platoon subedar had gone to the main set but was hit by a Javanese mortar bomb. Two of their 3-inch mortar bombs fell on our mortar platoon. Only six men were left alive. Their bombs fell to left and right so we had to disperse for safety. As more fire fell, I moved back to the main set where the subedar was still asking for help.

The signal officer sahib came in. With eyes wide open he looked at me and smiled. He went into the exchange and made a phone call. Another bomb came and he disappeared. Yet another bomb exploded and a havildar hid under the table. I was in a corner. The table was hit but the havildar escaped. I smiled and was angry: smiled to see him under the table, but was angry that a senior NCO hid.

The next day we were reinforced by infantry and supplies were dropped by air, some into our area and some to the Javanese. The aircraft that did the dropping was escorted by fighters. We stayed in Semarong quite a while. We were relieved by a parachute unit and went back to Batavia by aeroplane. 3/5 GR was there. In Batavia we carried haversack rations and tea as we patrolled defensively. The Japanese had captured the place during the war. We had beaten the Japanese so the place should have belonged to us.

India

The end of all wars sees much upheaval and few places more so than in India. The Gurkha Brigade's problems were demobilisation of unwanted soldiers, and anxiety over its future and the status of its British officers. Everywhere was in a state of flux. The glass curtain of rumour and prejudice clouded, coloured and distorted all. Everyone was unsettled and a feeling of helplessness persisted. There was massive civic unrest throughout northern India wherever Muslim and Hindu lived in close proximity and finally the maladroit and politically charged courts-martial of the INA inflamed tempers even more, making mock heroes out of actual traitors and mock traitors out of actual heroes.

I can give one revealing example from my own experience. I cannot tell you the man's name as I never knew it but, in thick snow, a week after I had arrived in 1 GRRC, Dharmsala, a soldier of 2/1 GR, clad in rags and nearly dead, staggered into the adjutant's office, saluted, gave his number, rank and name – and fell into a dead faint. The doctor allowed him to be interviewed a week later. The adjutant took his copy of 2/1 GR's nominal roll and, one by one, the whereabouts of each and every man was elicited. He also gave valuable information about many INA members who were to be court-martialled and was seen as an important witness for the prosecution.

POWs were graded into 'white', 'grey' and 'black'. 'Whites' were those who had not joined the INA, 'greys' were those who had joined but who had nothing known else against them, and 'blacks' were those who had something against them. The evidence of the 2/1 GR man was rejected as he was grey. He was so disheartened at all the *dukha* he had undergone escaping and finding his own way back that he wrote a note – a lamentation of broken trust – and hanged himself.

Thousands of Gurkha soldiers, hastily enrolled for wartime units, found themselves no longer needed. Facilities for a quick and speedy release were swamped. In the war the mediocrity of others was stripped bare in most Gurkhas' presence; peace was too sudden and shallow to be quickly and adequately assimilated and something had to give. In a few cases, standards dropped. Not only that; men to be 'demobbed' had started military life as bucolic peasant lads and were now seasoned soldiers. Their outlook was different: mature, materialistic and less malleable. Even those who wanted to serve on generally found they couldn't and many of those who were asked to serve on didn't.

There are four reasons why a full military career normally cannot be realised: death, dishonour, disability and disillusion. After the war there were four more for Gurkhas: disruption, disbelief, destabilisation and disintegration. Disruption of the whole of normal conditions occurred throughout the northern reaches of the sub-continent, which became volatile at best, untenable at worst. Normal army organisation creaked drastically. Logistical shortages of clothing, transport, equipment, fuel and rations were a commonplace and could be got used to; lack of any directions about the future was more insidious.

Most of the soldiers of the twenty regular battalions had to stay put, apart from a few men sent on release and leave at the end of the fighting, until the future of the Gurkha Brigade had been decided. For them there were two factors that caused gathering gloom over the months. One was that British behaviour was seen as unbelievable folly: fight a devastating war to regain Burma and defend India – then give them both up! This was the great source of disbelief. Who could trust the British any more, especially when, even after independence was granted in August 1947, no terms of service for those wishing to transfer to the British Army were announced for some months so no comparisons of such matters as pay, allowances, leave and family facilities could be made?

Disintegration was the rupture of the 'extended family' ethos that had prevailed since the man was enlisted. 'You are good enough to fight and die for us,' had been the cry. Now it was 'We don't want you any longer.' To many, undecorated and mostly still humble riflemen, that seemed inadequate recompense for risks run – often beyond the call of duty – let alone, in many cases, bodily and mental damage caused by war. Being no longer wanted by any elite group is not far short of being detribalized.

Destabilizing factors for hill Gurkhas were, first, the constant, vicious and virulent anti-British propaganda that emanated from Indians and Indian-domiciled Nepalis and threats against the proposed British Gurkhas that worked at two levels – unabashed, unsubtle and unending outside a unit, but insidious, sly and full of half truths within. Some battalions had Indian chief clerks, not Gurkhas, and such men were not slow in spreading anti-British poison and pro-Congress propaganda. Small wonder that, when the 'opt' – the declaration of which army to serve in or not to serve at all – was made, fewer men volunteered for the British the nearer the unit was to Delhi.

Secondly, enormous pressures were put on hill men by 'line boys' or Darjeeling men not to join the British Army. Those were allied to blatant anti-British proselytizing by Indian rowdies who so blurred the distinctions of fact and fantasy they wilfully worsened an already inherently unstable situation, while the 'short-stroke' speed towards the end of the British raj played into the hands of those who wished to influence minds already confused by war.

In the months leading up to independence, the nobodies and nonentities of limited education and less intelligence who had a grudge against those more successful than themselves found a cause and ran riot. Likewise their political masters. When any clique of people at the top of any pile has a sense of superiority so dense as to be impenetrable, it engenders over-riding folly and mind-boggling arrogance which increase tension. Never mind what the real situation was; let it be as it was wanted to be. Impartiality, objectivity and balance were nowhere to be seen, were in no one's vocabulary. Strong prejudices in an ill-formed mind are hazardous and when combined with a position of power and an absence of law and order, even more so.

Every moon has its dark side; Gurkhas' darkness does exist and cannot be gainsaid. However, apart from individual cases of bad behaviour and occasional lapses through anger or drunkenness, individual disobedience, let alone mass protest, had always been rare. I expect the first time that British officers were almost stupefied by what they perceived as cases of inexplicably blatant disloyalty was in 1946–47.

Apart from anything else, it has to be remembered that, up till then, no Gurkha had ever been asked to serve permanently outside the sub-continent and never with his family. Hindus living in Nepal, a Hindu kingdom, were in danger of being contaminated at second hand by those who had been contaminated by having been 'over the black water'. Each person had to undergo *pani patya* before being allowed back over the border into Nepal. This caused many tensions.

Indeed, it was only a day or so before independence was announced on 15 August 1947 that the fate of the Gurkha Brigade became known. Negotiations between the three governments, Great Britain, Nepal and India, had been fraught and tedious. Before the announcement rumours were prolific and, as it turned out, inaccurate. When the announcement was made, GHQ Delhi was adamant that no British officer was to offer any advice on whether the soldier was better with a sub-continental devil he thought he knew rather than the British one he knew already. In other words, in the eyes of the Gurkhas chosen for the British Army, the Guardians of the Extended Family had again failed, as never before, to give guidance when needed. To us who were there it was hateful to have no knowledge of the future and have to be tongue-tied.

But, amazingly, although the chilling British arrogance in believing themselves always to be the obvious choice of the Gurkhas was cruelly proven wrong in many cases, many, many more Gurkhas – and Indian soldiers – stayed true to their 'oath of salt' than those who had 'an eye to the main chance' and who opted for India, where, later, many were sadly disappointed. Once 15 August had passed the mind-set of the masses changed. The British were no longer seen as enemies in a way that had

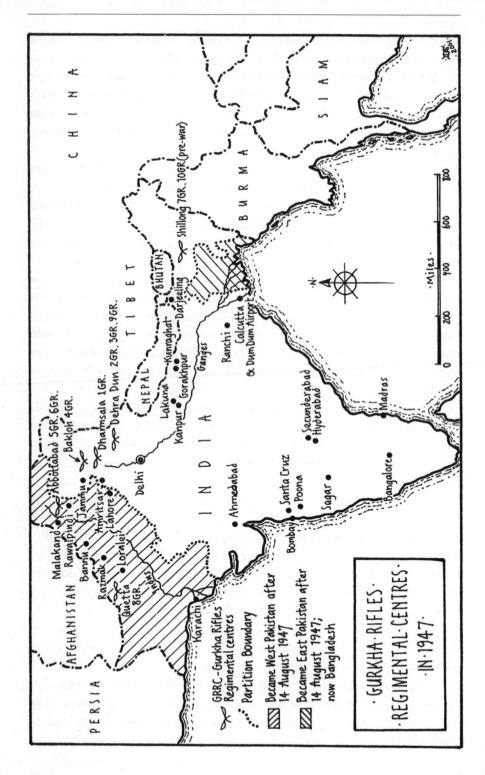

CHINA

PERSIA

AFGHANISTAN

Malakand
Rawalpindi
Bannu
Razmak
Loralai
Quetta
8 GR.
Abbottabad 5 GR. 6 GR.
Bakloh 4 GR.
Jammu
Amritsar
Lahore
Indus
Karachi

Dhamsala 1 GR.

Delhi

TIBET

NEPAL
Lakuna
Kanpur
Gorakhpur
Kunraghat
Dehra Dun 2 GR. 3 GR. 9 GR.
Darjeeling
Ganges

BHUTAN

Shillong 7 GR. 10 GR.(pre-war)

BURMA

SIAM

INDIA
Ahmedabad
Bombay
Santa Cruz
Poona
Sagar
Bangalore
Ranchi
Calcutta
& Dum Dum Airport
Secunderabad
Hyderabad
Madras

·N·

·Miles·
0   200   400   600   800

GRRC - Gurkha Rifles
Regimental centres
Partition Boundary

Became West Pakistan after
14 August 1947

Became East Pakistan after
14 August 1947;
now Bangladesh

·GURKHA·RIFLES·
·REGIMENTAL·CENTRES·
·IN·1947·

bound most communities together; now neighbours of another religion became the target and so communities broke apart.

2/9 GR, whose men had suffered under the INA as POWs, was not to be part of the British Army but the men had positive ideas to the contrary. One morning in late 1947 the C-in-C Pakistan Army, General Sir Douglas Gracey, ex-1 GR, woke to see a company of 2/9 GR, who had marched across the border from Amritsar during the night, sitting on his lawn in Rawalpindi, with a petition asking to continue service under the British, as service under Indian officers could not be contemplated.

The men had to be sent back. This story was confirmed to me by General Gracey in July 1959 and again, in March 2000, by Lance Naik Lekhbahadur Khatri of 2/9 GR. He said that, although details were now hazy, the hope in Rawalpindi that morning and the despair that followed still disturbed his dreams.

Our final orders to leave our battalions were precipitate. Having waited for something definite and not having had any firm news for so long, I was suddenly ordered to hand my company over to my 2IC because no Indian officer had arrived as announced. I walked the five miles over the Indian border to where C Company, 1/1 GR, was, in Jammu – where I had no right to be – on 15 November 1947.

At the end, my 2IC, Subedar Dhanbahadur Gurung, turned and made a remark that I can never forget: 'Sahib,' he said sadly, 'you British have been with us since 1815. Surely you can wait a few more days to hand over properly?' I am still ashamed that the answer had to be no.

Birbahadur Pun, 2/10 GR.   Muslims are bigger sinners than Hindus. I saw them disembowel a baby then let it crawl away, shrieking, to die. I saw Hindus with their testicles in their eye sockets and their vaginas split by knives. What bigger sins are there than these?

Maitaraj Limbu, 2/10 GR, *was a young soldier.*

In 1947 I joined the battalion in Hyderabad. There was much communal violence which we had to try and prevent but we were not allowed to use rifles. The Muslims had arrows and were persecuting the Hindus. In one brawl I cut the heads off three Muslims and we had no trouble at all after that. The Hindus came to us in streams, like a column of ants, trying to grasp us, so happy were they to be relieved of persecution.

From there we went to the Lahore area after it had become Pakistan. Hindus and Muslims massacred one another with atrocious cruelty. There was no one to look after affairs, no one to collect dead bodies and the corpses rotted with such a stench that none of us had any appetite left. There were uncountable deaths. The worst killers were the Sikhs – they were the most dangerous of all, killing any non-Sikh they met. They took notice of nobody but themselves and observed no laws but their own. If it had not been for the Gurkhas, they would have taken the whole country over. India owes that not happening to us Gurkhas. How can India and Pakistan work together after such happenings? I was young then and none of that affected me personally.

On my way back from leave by train to Calcutta the crowds threw stones at those trains they thought were carrying British Gurkhas.

Sherbahadur Rana, 2/2 GR. In 1946 and 1947 Hindus and Muslims killed each other. It was like war. I was a driver and it was dangerous to drive around then and the situation was tense. But they were killing each other so it was not my business.

Then, reflecting the common rumour, he continued:

Jawaharlal Nehru let the country be Pakistan and India to keep the population balanced. He did not want the Gurkhas to go to the British Army but the British government complained to the government in Kathmandu and the Ranas let four regiments go to the British Army but only if they volunteered. Nehru kept the British Gurkhas' pensions down and ordered the allowance for Malaya to be cut when our men came back to Nepal. That is my complaint. The CO and the subedar major told us to volunteer for the British Army; if they said "Go", we also said "Go". Mostly only the "line boys" went to India. There was no friction between those going to the Indian Army and those going to the British Army because we were volunteers.[3]

Harkabahadur Thapa, 1/1 GR, *recalled one difficulty.*

Before our British officers left we were asked if we wanted to go over

---

[3] No other person gave this positive version.

to the British Army or to stay in the battalion in the Indian Army. We all wanted to go, but although our names went forward nothing happened. It was never explained to us why we had been stopped although the British officers had quoted an official letter from GHQ saying that everybody in the Gurkha Brigade had a free choice: go to the British Army, stay in the Indian Army, or go on discharge.[4] In fact no one was allowed to go on leave for the next four years in case we deserted and tried to join the British Army. There was no meeting of minds between us and the Indian officers. The first one in, a Captain Mehta, was court-martialled after four months but I didn't gather what the reason was.

Barnabahadur Rai, 2/7 GR, *explained the pressures of going to the British Army.*

We were in Ahmedabad. Subedar Major Ishorman Rai, a Darjeeling man, wanted to stay in the Indian Army as he thought 2/7 GR would also stay in the Indian Army if enough men volunteered not to go to the British Army and he would be the battalion commander after the British had left. He therefore tried to make us take an oath not to go to the British Army. Many wanted to go over to the British but we were all scared that he would have us beaten up. I was unpopular and my bed was thrown out of the barrack room and put under a tree. The education jemadar, Naradman Rai, was so fed up with what was happening, he took off his uniform and badges of rank and took them to the CO and told him he was doing no more soldiering and was going back home to start an English language school. He wanted us to go to the British Army, learn English and then teach in his school. He said he did not want to comment on what the subedar major was up to.

---

[4] 'With regard to the Gurkha Officers and men. As you know, every single one is being given the choice of whether he wishes to serve under the War Office, under the new Government of India, or either, or neither, so there is no question of forcing them to serve under one or the other. Whatever they do will be of their own free will.' Extract of a letter, signed by the Adjutant General in India, in person, dated 14 August 1947. This just did not happen for those in units detailed to stay in the Indian Army.

Kharkadhoj Gurung, 1/2 GR. I joined the battalion in Santa Cruz, near Bombay, and after a year we moved to Poona to take over from 2/9 GR, having handed over to 3/5 GR. We were asked if we wanted to go to the British Army. Nobody wanted to go. We were then asked to sign our willingness to go but the man who brought the paper said it was not a proper form, only a temporary one. Then a quarrel arose. 1/2 GR had an Indian education jemadar in the "school-master party". He and his Gurkha NCOs came and told us not to go to the British Army and on a certain day not to parade but to assemble at the Quarter Guard. Only D Company which was on duty did not go. There was a row. We opened the cells and let the prisoners out. Then we opened the stores, took out many clothes and waved them around on poles like flags, shouting "Hooray". We listened to nobody.

The British officers came and reminded us about the good name of the battalion made so by our fathers and grandfathers but we took no notice of them. The GOC punished all the companies. Some spent all night "playing in the water",[5] some with route marches and some by going onto the ranges, for a week. Then it was *Diwali* so we were allowed to return to the camp to celebrate the festival.

We were fallen in and each one of us was asked what we did on 6 November and some of us said we were told by our NCOs to clap our hands and shout "Hooray, hooray" and the NCOs then congratulated us. We were told to say which NCOs had ordered the men to do that and to give their numbers, names and ranks. The "school-master party" was sent off to Dehra Dun immediately and then those NCOs whose names had been given were also sent away, but in dribs and drabs.

After the trouble makers had left the battalion we were lectured on Malaya and given the terms of service in the British Army. At the opt were the CO, the subedar major, Major Padma Thapa of the Nepalese Artillery and an Indian captain of 5 GR. Those who opted for India fell in separately from those who opted for the British Army. In front of me were four who opted for India. I opted for the British and was given a big *shabash*. "You are the first to volunteer for the British," I was told.

---

[5] When asked what this meant, a Gurkha officer who was present at the time said he did not understand and that the whole description of punishment was exaggerated.

Bakansing Gurung, 1/6 GR, *recovered from the wounds he had received in Burma.*

After I was better I was detailed as draft commander of 500 reinforcements. The war ended and the draft was cancelled so I took the men back to Abbottabad. In 1946 I rejoined the battalion which was still in Burma, at Mingladon.

I was posted to Holding Company as company havildar major and a fellow villager of mine was the jemadar platoon commander. We had known each other from early Abbottabad days. We had in our company men who were being sent back to Nepal. My name was not on any list of those being sent home and I was to stay on in the army. I was again due leave although I was still medically graded category C by the hospital. The adjutant said I was no longer in that category. By the time I came back from seven and half months' leave it was opt time for service in the British or Indian Armies. The battalion havildar major was a friend and we with the "white sticks" – CHMs or BHM – decided to stick together and opt for India, in other words leave our battalion. The senior GO recommended me for commissioning to GO. He didn't speak to me for a week as he had opted for the British Army and so he was angry with me and my decision. The CO, Anderson, called all the havildars together one evening and asked us why we had opted for the Indian Army. I thought that over and realised that the Indians did not know enough about us so I rethought my position and volunteered for the British Army. At the first opt only 45 men volunteered to go to the British Army. All the rest of the battalion were dismayed with us 45 men.

I had thought it over and finally plumped for the British Army. My record was good wherever I had been. I thought of promotion. The BHM, Dharmaraj Ghale, went to India and I was promoted to BHM for the British Army. There were no British officers or Gurkha officers around for most of the time. One evening at the canteen the men came my way to talk to me because they knew I played it straight and trusted me. That was in November 1947. After that hundreds of men volunteered to go to the British Army, that is to say, stay with 1/6 GR.

Bakansing Gurung left the army as a Captain (QGO).

Part Three

GURKHAS OF THE BRITISH ARMY

DEPLOYMENT OF BRITISH ARMY GURKHAS

The deployment, tasks and training of the Brigade of Gurkhas since its inception on 1 January 1948 are strictly in accordance with British Army and hence British Government policy. This is that all units are fit to be deployed successfully in whatever role Government policy so requires. Since 1 January 1948 this has involved Gurkhas in such diverse activities as disaster relief work in Nepal itself as well as other locations, peace-keeping duties with various UN forces, counter-terrorist operations in several countries or former colonies, and larger-scale conflicts in the South Atlantic and the Gulf.

Recollections of the Malayan Emergency, Brunei Rebellion, Confrontation with Indonesia in Borneo, Hong Kong, Cyprus, Falklands, the Gulf, Bosnia, Kosovo and East Timor are all featured in the pages that follow, but even this wide range only tells part of the Gurkha story.

CHAPTER 8

Malayan Emergency

In January 1948 British Army Gurkha battalions, all under-strength, starting arriving in Malaya and Singapore. The Malayan Communist Party had reactivated its guerilla wing and its civil counterpart. Accurate reports about this reorganization and the threat of revolutionary warfare it posed were not believed by 'higher authority' so nothing was done to counter it at first. In June 1948 an Emergency was declared and a purely guerilla campaign started. Defeating this did not depend primarily on the high command but on the man on the spot whose initiative, resourcefulness and self-reliance in remote situations counted for far more than in conventional campaigns. Junior leaders and riflemen bore the brunt.

Initially the guerillas were known as 'bandits' but this was soon changed to Communist Terrorists, or CTs. With the lawlessness of recently evacuated India still fresh in everyone's minds, the Gurkhas called the guerillas 'Congress' but this changed to and remained as *daku* – short for *dacoit* – for the duration of the Emergency. This word, or 'enemy', has been used in the narratives that follow.

Initially there were some negative factors militating against efficiency in and out of camp. Apart from a completely new system of administration, 2/2 GR still suffered from so many of its men having been POWs. It was taking about twelve years to become a lance corporal and most of the battalion had had no battle experience since early 1942. 2/6 GR and 2/7 GR, badly hit by the 'Congress factor', went over to Malaya at strengths of about fifty. Recruits were sent to guard vital points before they knew how to use a rifle safely or shoot straight. In one case orders for operational guard duties were 'to refrain from loading rifles but to use the kukri or bayonet instead'. At this critical moment 7 GR were made gunners. The only common language between British gunner instructors in 2/7 GR and the senior Gurkha ranks was Italian!

It bordered on the miraculous that the Roll of Honour was not longer than it was. Gurkha renown was amply maintained. At the first investiture

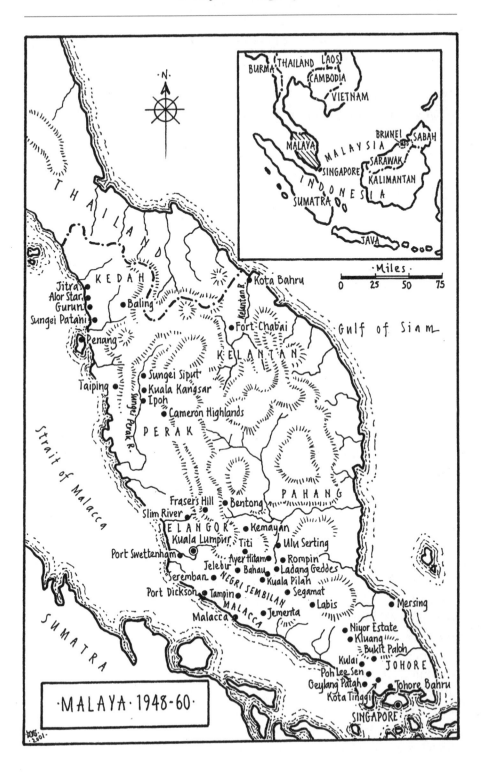

·MALAYA·1948-60·

to be held in Kuala Lumpur in 1950, 37 out of 51 recipients were from the Brigade of Gurkhas.

Malaya achieved independence in 1957 and operations, for the British Army, eventually petered out in 1962. Just one statistic: in the mid-1950s I calculated that a million man hours of security work were needed for one contact and the average time a soldier had a target in his sights was 20 seconds. British battalions only had one three-year tour, which was seen as enough; Gurkha battalions, except for a two-year break in Hong Kong, were at it the whole time. And, by and large, standards never fell.

Sukdeo Pun, 1/2 GR, *was living in the past when he told his story.*

I was enlisted on 20 October 1948 in Lehra[1] and went to Malaya by boat. I was seasick, the food did not agree with me and I had a headache. I cannot remember how long the voyage took. We went to Ipoh. I can't tell you much about that place as we were kept inside a camp that had wire around it like a lot of sheep during our basic recruit training. Anyway, we were not all that interested and couldn't speak the language.

We trained on a treeless hill that had much bracken on it and from one side we could see the jail. Occasionally we heard rifle shots from the prison. The training lasted nine to ten months and then I was sent to 1/2 GR. Life was easier there than as a recruit except that we had to go on operations, day or night, rain or fine. Around that time our work was mostly on rubber estates. There were traps for wild pig that were covered over and sometimes the leading scout fell into them, during the day and at night. We would get him out by joining our rifle slings as a rope. Even when there were spikes on the floor of the trap the man was never impaled. When we got tired we fell asleep on the ground, using our packs as pillows. Even when it rained we did not notice. One time we woke to find our packs had shifted in some water and they took a lot of finding.

We met *daku* many times. We would go out on patrol and shots would be fired at us. By night keeping contact with the man in front was hard. The *daku* would come out of the jungle to get their rations from rubber estate labour lines or villages. On one occasion we saw four of them who ran away back towards the jungle. They were armed.

---

[1] Recruiting depots were still in India, only moving into Nepal in 1959.

I carried a rifle that was fixed with a grenade discharger cup on the muzzle, an EY rifle. I felt that if I killed the *daku* I'd get a *bahaduri* which meant everything to me. I ran ahead, outstripping the others. I could not fire bullets when the discharger cup was on so, as I ran, I worked it off and loaded bullets. I cocked my rifle, ready to fire.

By now the four *daku* had split into two pairs. The men behind me were firing but not hitting anyone. I and one other, Devilal Rana, were nearing the jungle edge and, as the section commander was far behind, I shouted out that we had to kill or capture them. I opened fire twice as I ran forward and missed. I realized that I could only drop either man by taking an aimed shot. I was worried that the *daku* would escape. I came to a small hillock, lay down and took an aimed shot. I could see that the *daku* were out of breath as much as I was. They disappeared into dead ground and as they emerged I shot one, very near the jungle edge. I also shot the other.

By now the others had joined us and all claimed that it was their bullets that had killed the *daku*. I asked them where their bullets had hit but none could say. I told them where I had aimed and when we went to see the corpses I could prove I had killed them.

It is natural for soldiers to gather around the corpses to see what souvenirs are worth their taking, such as, say, a watch. They crowded around, bunching dangerously. Although I was only a young soldier I told them not to bunch as I knew the other two *daku* could not be far off. I wanted to warn them of the danger of the other *daku* but, as a junior rifleman, who would have listened to me?

I acted as an NCO should have acted. I shouted out that I could see the enemy was about to open fire and that dispersed them. Devilal and I moved off to a flank and about 60 yards off saw a third *daku*. Devilal, also a good shot, killed him in one. The dead man had a grenade in his hand and we did not know if it would explode. We took off our toggle ropes, joined them, tied one end to the corpse's feet, took the other end off as far as possible and pulled the body towards us. As the grenade did not explode we went back and took it out of his hand. We did not find the fourth man.

We sent a message by radio to the camp asking for transport and carried the three corpses over our shoulders for an hour. We returned to camp and reported to the OC about the incident. He asked who had killed the *daku* and I told him I had killed two and Devilal had killed one. He gave us a *shabash* and told us to go to the canteen and have a bottle of beer on him. We soldiers had a great talk about who would get a *bahaduri* for that action and I was sure I would.

I then went on leave to Nepal and on my return the company clerk told me that in the modern age one kills the enemy but another gets the reward. So, although a *bahaduri* had come to the company, the oldest soldier of us all, one who had not been out with us that time, had got it. I do not know if he killed any *daku* during his service or not.

I felt that I was an unlucky man – winning a medal had not been written in the inside of my forehead. But it was *my* chasing the enemy and *my* tactics in killing them. *I* had saved the bunched soldiers from being a target of the enemy. Then I was strong, now I am not, but, even today as a man at the end of his time, that event seems very recent. No, I could not act like that now. I am delighted to get this heaven-sent opportunity to get that sadness off my chest today.[2] No other officer has ever bothered to ask me such questions.

Another interesting incident was when I was in an ambush. One enemy walked into it and we all opened fire. No one knows whose bullets felled him. We went up to him and he put his hands together in supplication and said something we did not understand but obviously asking for help. The NCO in charge said that we had hit him so badly that it was kinder to put him out of his misery as he would never be good for anything again. So I shot him dead on the section commander's order. That was a sin.

Bhimraj Gurung, 2/6 GR, *enlisted in October 1951.*

After about a year's training we were sworn in as full soldiers. I was sent to Kluang and posted to A Company. The Chinese in the south of Malaya were different from those in the north in looks and habits. The place was on the warm side but was cooled down by daily showers. However, we were not there very often, being deployed on operations after two weeks settling in. We were in the jungle almost all the time, in various places in Malaya: Labis, Titi and Pahang. We took seven days' rations with us and were re-supplied by air. When we were short of rations we picked bamboo shoots and carilla.[3]

---

[2] On 2 June 1999, 48 years later. He appeared shriven after his talk, so pent up had he been.

[3] A bitter vegetable, *Momordica pharantia.*

I had no idea why we were fighting the *daku* or anything about them. It was not our job to know about such matters. We were there to fight. We were there for the money and the *bahaduris*. It was only the commanders who had to know what it was all about. The *daku* were chiefly Chinese with the occasional Madrassi. We never saw any Malays. The Chinese were better than the Malays, much less lazy. The *daku* gave villagers much *dukha* asking for rations and supplies.

I was either the leading scout, when I carried an SMG, or the LMG 1. There was no talking and we communicated by hand signals, for instance a "thumbs up" for no *daku* seen and a "thumbs down" for *daku* seen, other signals for move, halt and calling the leader. Unless there was a head-on contact, we would take all round positions until a plan for attack had been fixed. For over a year my platoon did not have a contact. My first contact was in 1954 and I was LMG 1. It was raining, not very heavily, when we heard a sound like the cutting of coconuts. I was the first to see who was making the noise, six or seven *daku* about 200 yards away. The leading scout then gave the sign that he had seen them. We closed in on them and we could see they wore khaki, had a red star in their caps and carried shotguns. Two of them were women. They did not have any sentry out and we opened fire with all we had, killing them all. I fired three magazines. I think the two men armed with SMGs actually killed them as they were in front. Certainly that was what they thought. One man was Kamansing from the far west of Nepal and the other, Tulbahadur, the son of a subedar major in the Indian Army.

Until fire was opened we were always on the cautious side but once we had opened fire it was good fun. Our one hope was to win a *bahaduri*, especially so this first time for me. It was about 1600 hours when we killed them and it was too late to do anything else that night but to make camp. The orders then were to carry out the corpses and it was always much easier to kill a person than to carry the corpse out. On this occasion it took us all the next day to get to the main road. We cut branches and wrapped the corpses in our poncho capes. These we exchanged when we had finished our job.

The platoon sergeant and one other went and made the report to the police station. The CO, Lieutenant Colonel Powell-Jones, not a Nepali speaker having come from an Indian unit but a Hindi speaker, and three others came out in an armoured vehicle to meet us. He was very happy with what we had done. It seems that, when at the police station, the platoon sergeant gave the impression that he was responsible for the killing. At any rate, he was awarded an MM in the next honours list as was another man who told me he had never seen the *daku*. He was, in fact, a friend of the platoon sergeant. Kamansing was so disappointed he did not get a *bahaduri* he never returned from leave but Tulbahadur did.

One unfortunate incident related to a colour sergeant who had made a mess of the accounts and was being court-martialled. He went with the platoon to make up numbers. The CO told him he was so pleased with the platoon's work that he would be a lieutenant (QGO). Naturally he was delighted and on the night we got back to base he threw a party to celebrate his promotion. It came as a great shock to be told, the very next day, that his court-martial had pronounced his dismissal from the army and he had to leave the unit immediately.

Our rations were tinned and not very appetizing. In those days we did not have fresh vegetables or live chickens in our airdrops and we were always glad to get back to camp to have a good meal, a wash and a change of clothes, and to see the sun.

The hardest operation we ever did was under Major G.H. Walsh against the strong *daku* 3 Platoon. That lasted for 15 days. Although we saw many of them on a distant hill the OC thought that his company was too small to take them on. He requested a battalion attack but that never happened. Major Walsh and, later, OC GIPC when I was his batman, were the only two officers I met who had a high standard in the jungle, movement and tactics. Why neither of them was ever awarded a *bahaduri* I could never understand, especially having seen some of the officers who did and what they had done to get it. I never had any faith in the British Government after I saw the way those two officers were given nothing.

We were ambushed by the *daku* in the Mersing road area and three of our men were killed. I managed to take cover behind a large tree and would have been killed had I not done so as, after the battle was over, I saw that the tree was riddled with bullets. We drove them off and had to return to camp with our dead and to get more rations. We were told we had to destroy the band that had attacked us but, although we followed up tracks for a week and did see them once, we lost them.

It was also in the Mersing road area that we ambushed and killed four *daku* as they were drawing rations from a loggers' camp. We had had the tip-off from a villager. We put down a linear ambush and waited till the lead man was at the end and the others were in the killing zone. We killed them all. I opened fire but cannot say if it was my bullets which did the damage. The platoon commander was awarded an MC.

In all I was involved in about half a dozen contacts. We would often move out of camp at night and lie up in the jungle till it was light enough to move forward. An operation would normally last between seven and ten days. The longest operation I did lasted for 30 days. All I ever knew about the enemy's tactics was that they would kill us if we did not kill them first. The hardest place to operate was in the Cameron Highlands. The intense cold and steep terrain made it hard work and the road with all those bends made it a dangerous ride in a vehicle. The hardest job was to be the leading scout. After my leave in 1955 we continued operating until 1958.

Jasbahadur Limbu, MM, 1/10 GR, *joined the British Army in February 1948.*

On being sent to my active battalion I was posted to D Company. We drew our bedding from the stores but before we had time to make up our beds we were called out on operations to the Bukit Paloh area. Once there we were given a guide – a man in plain clothes without a weapon – to go to another place. We went into the jungle and did not take our boots off for the next 13 days during which time we did not meet any enemy although we saw a lot of fresh tracks of many men.

The next day a patrol came across some enemy eating their meal and reported back asking for instructions. Our orders were to engage them as quickly as possible. That evening, while the overnight camp was being prepared, my section commander sent two of us as OPs some way from the camp. The other man was the LMG 1 and I, as LMG 2, carried four magazines. The section commander gave me his Sten gun and took my rifle. The other sentry had something else to do and left me for a while. My post was a very big tree with a thick trunk. I was told that the *daku* could come either way along a track in front of me. I was to keep alert. I could see for about 30 yards in front of me. It was raining and it was muddy underfoot. I had some biscuits in my pocket which I nibbled. I was not allowed to smoke although I had some cigarettes in my pocket. I didn't disobey orders. I wondered if I could find my way back to the company if I was not relieved.

I then saw movement to my front. Branches moving. I hadn't seen a *daku* so was it the rain or the wind making the movement? I had never met a *daku* before nor had I fired at any. I had been told what to expect: khaki dress, puttees and a peaked hat with a red star as a badge. So different from ours that it would be easy to recognize. As I waited a man came into view, then two more to make three in all. I waited behind the tree and the leading man came to take up his position on the other side of that same tree. I aimed at him and he saw me. We looked at each other. He did not have his weapon ready but mine was. He smiled at me and I smiled at him. I then shot him dead with a short burst.

That was why I had enlisted, I thought, to kill the government's enemies. He fell. The second man had taken up a position to fire at me but, before he fired, I shot and killed him. The third man ran away and I shot him dead also.

The people in the overnight base camp heard the firing and came running up, just as they were, some with full uniform on, others not so. The rest of the enemy opened fire from a little way off with seven machine guns and, as I had four magazines with me, I fired back with the LMG. All the undergrowth around my position was shot away as was the bark of the tree I was behind. I didn't know whether I'd stay alive or not, in fact I had no hope of living. All I did was stay where I was. My position was very strong and I still had the LMG and some rounds so I could deal with any enemy who came my way.

The platoon commander, Lieutenant (KGO) Manbahadur Rai, came up to me. He was armed with a pistol. He asked me what was happening and I told him I had killed three men but hadn't seen any others. He told me that the track was also used by A Company and was I sure I had not killed our own troops? I told him of the uniform and he was assured. I showed him where the men I had killed were.

First he gave me a *shabash* then he rocketed me for not collecting their weapons as they might not be dead and could kill us. All that time other *daku* were firing at us so it was not possible to go and collect the weapons. But the platoon commander insisted that I did, so I went forward and collected them. I was given two men to give me covering fire. In fact I had not thought about collecting the weapons as it was the first time I had been in a contact.

It was quite dark by then. *Daku* were still firing. The platoon commander ordered me to throw a smoke grenade towards the firing.

I was very strong then and I threw it as far as I could. By good luck it landed in the middle of the *daku*. The platoon commander ordered us to charge. We shouted "Chaaaaarge" as we went in and killed another six of them. The rest of them ran away so the firing stopped.

Two men set an ambush beside the dead *daku* all night but no one came back for them. We had suffered no casualties and returned to base. We set up our radio and made contact with the battalion and were told to stay where we were, in all-round defence. I had forgotten all thoughts of hunger then but back in camp I felt hungry once more. However, there were no rations there then so we all stayed hungry and thirsty. It was a long night. We had no idea if the *daku* were trying to encircle us.

Next morning, when it was light we reported again and were withdrawn with A Company taking over from us. 1/7 GR was alerted but was not needed. We were also dropped rations so we had a meal. We were very happy. We were told to wash the faces of the dead men, take their photographs and collect all their watches, rings and trinkets, then to bring the corpses back with us. This we did. It took us all that day and until about 0930 hours on the second day to get to Bukit Paloh. The brigadier and the CO, C.C. Graham, the adjutant and the Gurkha Major came to meet us. They were told I was the main killer and I was told I'd get a *bahaduri*. "I'll tell you tomorrow," said the brigadier.

The company was given seven sheep and seven gallons of rum for a party and we stayed up all night. We were also given seven days' leave. We were all happy. Next morning I was called to the phone and asked who I was. I told the caller. It was the brigadier. He said that I had been awarded the MM and the king would give it to me. Another man was awarded the MM and two an m-i-d. The company 2IC sent for us and told us that he had heard about our *bahaduris* and we would have to treat the company to a feast. I said I would but I would need to draw two or three months' pay in advance.

As we all walked back to the lines a runner came and told the 2IC sahib that he had been awarded an MC. We told him he would have to pay for the party instead. He looked at me and said we had been given a *bahaduri* and so had been recognized and, really, there was no need for a party. So we didn't have one.

Gundabahadur Rai, MM, 1/10 GR.   After 30 days' leave in early 1948, I rejoined my battalion, now in Kuala Lumpur, after which we went to Johore Bahru. There we were told about the communists. We had no idea what it was all about but we were told they were as good fighters as the Japanese. I went on many jungle operations. I remember one of them: A Company had to go up the Mersing road. We left camp at 0330 hours and, at dawn, debussed near a village to our right. 3 Platoon was in front with 2 Platoon in the rear. We entered the rubber and were fired on heavily. It was like Burma all over again. My section commander was shot in the foot. There were many enemy in a valley, thick as fleas. We couldn't do much about it. We went back to Johore Bahru. As we were having a meal we were told to go to a lecture by the CO, Lieutenant Colonel C.C. Graham, straightaway. The NCOs had said we hadn't charged them but had taken up lying positions because we thought they were as hard as Japanese. He told us we were no good. The *daku* were thieves and not like the Japanese. "Call them *daku*, not communists." He was very angry. "I want *josh*," he cried out, in English.

He was so angry that he jumped up and down, "brrrk, brrrk", and, throwing his arms about wildly, knocked over a blackboard that fell on his head and knocked him out. We said nothing and sat quietly. It was something none of us could ever forget. After he had regained consciousness he ordered us, there and then, out to MS 18 on the Mersing road and not to come back until we had shown we could kill *daku*.

A Company went out. I was in 9 Section, 3 Platoon, on the left. A village was nearby. I was told to check it. We were fired on. I didn't know where the firing came from so I jumped up to see. I saw some enemy running away in the rubber estate towards the jungle so I immediately charged after them, by myself. I killed two of them with my Sten gun. The enemy dropped their weapons. The other platoon did not come up to the sound of the firing. I did not know where the enemy had disappeared to into the jungle and I did not think it wise to go looking for them by myself. I picked up the two weapons and decided to rejoin my platoon.

I told the platoon sergeant I had killed two men. "Tell me a lie? Don't lie to me. What's this all about?" he asked angrily. I showed him the two captured weapons and felt snubbed. Another man saw a *daku* crawling away about 60 yards distant. I told the platoon sergeant that he was one of the men I had floored. "And you tell me I'd lied to you?" There was an argument and I went to kill the *daku*.

The CO then appeared. "Ho! I wanted *josh*!" he cried. There were 13 or 14 enemy but the others got away. "Go and attack them NOW," he ordered. He said they were not like Japanese and, once they had fired, they ran away. That is what he taught us so we went after them straight away.

Later that day the CO told us to go to Kulai estate where the manager had some information from informers that the enemy were coming to collect rations that night. We surrounded the labour lines in ambush from 2000 hours. It was dark. My section was near the dumped rations. Two enemy came at 0330 hours. I fired my carbine in the dark, on automatic. I heard a shout of pain but it was so dark I stayed where I was. When it was light I found I had killed two men.

Another time the manager gave similar news to another company which killed three. The enemy had tried to kill the manager three times. In all, during those operations, A Company killed nine enemy.

Later on A and D Companies went to Pahang. We were told to go and investigate a suspected enemy camp but one of the map sheets we were given only had rivers marked on it, all the rest was blank. There were no other details! How could we manage? Major Castle was our OC. We entered the jungle and found navigation very difficult. The OC told us only to use the compass. We were four map squares[4] below the point we had to check. No one wanted to go all that way on a compass bearing but I told the OC I would go with my section and he said he'd go with me. After four map squares we were only 150 yards from the camp. We were fired on by two enemy sentries. Shouting "Chaaarge" I chased them and shot them both. I found myself in the middle of the enemy camp. I suppose there had been 14 or 15 of them. They had run away. I followed one and shot him dead and took his pistol and also two rifles and shouted for the section to come up to me. No one came and I was by myself. At last they did come.

It was dark by then and I was afraid we would be ambushed if we went back the same way. I wanted to go back another route but that was not possible so I led the section back the same way by compass bearing in the dark. We got back to the overnight camp and the OC gave me a big *shabash*.

By now it was 1955. After a month with no contacts we moved to

---

[4] 4,000 yards.

Bentong. Our task was to prevent the enemy ambushing the road convoys. This was not easy and I suggested that we ambush the ambushers. The ambushes happened by day so we would have to go out at night and catch the enemy as they moved to take up their ambush positions. In that way we managed to kill five or six of them and the road became safe to drive along.

Tulbahadur Rai, DCM, 1/7 GR, *was over 20 years old, illiterate and unmarried, when he joined the army in December 1941.*

In 1947, when the regiment was chosen for the British Army, I was on 60 days' leave. I was posted to 7 GRTW in Paroi, near Seremban, Malaya. I was put in charge of education and when the Lieutenant (KGO) in charge, Rajman Rai, went mad, I was put in charge of it all, as a sergeant. I was sent on a three-month education course but I learnt that my mother had died and the house had fallen down so I could not concentrate properly.

Then the Emergency against the communist *daku* started. To start with, when I bicycled around Paroi, I could see them and would wave to them but they would never wave back. One of our first tasks was guarding vital points in the town – I remember the railway station and the bank – and, as post commander, I had to speak Malay and English. I was also sent to Kuala Lumpur on a guard for the MGBG, Major General Boucher. My soldiers were completely untrained and life was hard for us all. We did not even dare to load their rifles they knew so little.

Jungle operations began. On one very early operation 1/6 GR had been in the Pahang area and there had been bombing by the RAF. One bomb was known to have been dropped unfused. An engineer officer was sent out several times to look for it with one lot or another. That last time I was his squad commander. It was only after I had a good look at the map that I realized that one of the rivers had been shown to be flowing the wrong way. After that we knew where we were and did find it. The engineer officer was so pleased with me he gave me a double-bladed pen-knife, which I still have.

On my return from leave in 1953 I was on SS *Sangola* when it ran aground in the River Hooghley near Calcutta and was in grave danger of breaking up. I was in charge of the families who panicked. There were about 180 families including many children. I shut the door of the cabin where they had been assembled and prevented them from escaping, which would probably have meant their death.[5]

The *daku* still intimidated and killed civilians even after they had been put into New Village resettlement centres. We would move out of our camp at night to avoid being ambushed and to prevent *daku* agents from reporting our movements. We had to move in single file, like a long procession of ants. On really dark nights men had to hold on to the man in front. We had large battalion-sized operations in those days and on one in the Titi area one of the men in the middle of the column fell asleep on a halt and, when we started off, the man behind him went the wrong way leading half the battalion after him. The operation was, therefore, a failure. The man was punished.

I commanded 2 Platoon, A Company, and Major J.P. Cross was my company commander for three years and was responsible for my *bahaduris*.[6] Only he knew how hard I worked as a platoon commander. Even he could not get me promoted to Lieutenant (QGO). I was always lucky with my jungle work. Apart from having a Chinese JCLO for interpreting, the company commander spoke Malay and Chinese. He always trusted me to do my best. There were many times we went out together on operations and some of them I have forgotten. Not all our work was in the jungle. We had to partake in food denial operations along the roads, erecting "knife rests" and searching cars, bicycles (letters were even hidden in the handlebars) and people. These operations later took us into the jungle. One time we were not all that far from a rubber estate that had a bad reputation for helping the *daku*. One morning in the jungle we stopped for a ten-minute break. The OC's golden rule was that no one be allowed to smoke until five minutes had

---

[5] A letter was subsequently received by the Commander, British Gurkhas in India, from the pilot of the vessel in which he expressed, on behalf of the captain and himself, the highest praise of the behaviour of all ranks of the Brigade of Gurkhas during the incident. Their conduct, he wrote, in the emergency, when panic threatened amongst the civilian passengers, undoubtedly averted what might well have been a serious disaster. Both he and the captain wished to express their admiration and thanks.

[6] Tulbahadur Rai won a DCM and an m-i-d during this time and was also recommended for the BEM when on a spell as Demonstration Platoon Sergeant in the FARELF (Far East Land Forces) Training Centre (FTC) which later became known as the Jungle Warfare School. Instead of the BEM, he was awarded a C-in-C's Certificate. He finished up with two m-i-ds.

elapsed and that would mean that any *daku* near enough to smell our smoke would not escape.

That morning a *daku* did walk into us and was shot. The OC went to help him and had his hands on his flesh, binding up the wound as he was dying. His soul went into the OC who had to be exorcized but that took place several days later.[7] We recovered the *daku*'s rifle and ammunition and some fresh tapioca he was carrying along with some rice, clothing, 52 exercise books, nine maps, five letters, a saw and many diaries. The OC took his photo and finger prints, then we buried him. The brigade commander, a new one I gather, ordered the CO to get the body fetched out and the CO passed this order on. The OC tried to refuse, saying that apart from security of our operation being broken if the estate workforce saw the corpse, the soldiers did not like the idea of any dead body being disturbed by exhumation. The OC had to give way, the body was exhumed and taken to where he had started from. And, of course, all security was broken.

We would take airdrops every five days. Once when we were expecting one the OC said that in his dream that the airdrop would be a bad one and that we had British rations containing beef dropped in on us.[8] The airdrop was bad with it being dropped on some *daku* smoke the pilot saw 10,000 yards to our south and when another lot was sent it did contain British beef! On our way out of the jungle we came across a pile of porcupine quills which showed us that that was the type of meat the *daku* managed to eat. That was the time we found no running water to drink or cook with for 12 days. When we did get back to our company base something had gone wrong with the local water supply so there was none to wash in.

When we suspected that we had discovered an enemy camp the drill was to surround it. That was harder to do than it sounds as we had to know the size of the perimeter, the sentry posts and defensive positions to say nothing of correct navigation and stealthy movement to prevent our presence being discovered, all within a given time. Although we practised it many times we never managed to surround one when it was

---

[7] The excorcism took place travelling to battallion HQ in a scout car. Luckily the driver was a shaman. The stress caused to me was exactly as would have been expected in a Christian excorcism ceremony.

[8] Gurkhas put a lot of faith in dreams. If, however, a dream is described before an event, as indeed happened in this case, the opposite is supposed to happen. Tulbahadur remembered the incident because it had bucked the trend.

actually occupied. I remember when the OC and I heard what we thought was the enemy preparing a new camp. We surrounded it, one platoon going round on one flank, the second on the other and the third, with the OC, to attack it. We all felt sure we were in for a big kill so it was most disappointing to find nothing at all when the third platoon went to attack the camp. It was only when the OC had called us in to give us more orders that we realized that the noise we had thought was the enemy was made by monkeys in the trees beating the branches with sticks! That taught us never to take anything for granted.

Map reading was never easy. Once we were baffled until I realized one of the rivers we should have found was, in fact, flowing underground and, in another place, instead of three hills on the map to match three hills on the ground, there were only two hills shown.

The standard of the Malay Police Field Force was very low. We came across one of their groups ambushing a *daku* ration dump it had found. The police were talking and smoking only 20 yards from the ambush site. No wonder the people at the top wanted us Gurkhas in the jungle.

Many operations did not result in contacts. One time we were following up a gang of *daku* who were so exhausted even their faeces were green. They moved very cautiously and tracking them was difficult. I saw proof that we were on their tracks. I looked at what the lead scout had thought was a tiger's pug mark. As there had been a tiger calling out ahead of us he took it that the mark was of that tiger. I looked at it and realized that it had to be made by a man because otherwise the tiger would have been walking backwards. The end man of the *daku* group had been turning round and making the pug mark with his hand and another man, skilled in imitating a tiger, was calling out like one. I had to convince the OC that that was so!

That evening we really did think we had found them. Shortly before dusk we had reached a hollow between two spurs. It was thick jungle and a storm was abating. Suddenly a thin trail of smoke came round a spur to our east and we knew it had to be *daku* trying to cook an evening meal. The OC immediately ordered that the area be surrounded but, despite all our efforts, we found nothing. Very dispirited we spent an uncomfortable night. The next morning we searched and found that the *daku* had indeed cooked up something to eat but to our west. The currents of air generated by the storm had taken the smoke over to the east and curled it back as though it had started off there. We were fooled and the *daku* got away, leaving our company area so we could not follow them up. Another company contacted them.

I was good at tracking but the OC had the edge on me when it came to making bird and monkey calls. He would whistle to call his platoon commanders for orders and to move off after a halt. Sometimes the birds would answer him. He used monkey calls to keep in contact when platoons were separated. I couldn't make either noise!

One day, early in the morning, the OC and I were moving through the jungle when we saw some ash in front of us. We knew that another company had had a contact a couple of days before some distance away but all our patrolling efforts had found nothing and any signs of movement we did find were a couple of days old. Nothing fresh. I bent down to see if the ash was warm and, as my hand touched it finding it was so, out of the corner of my eye I saw a *daku* hiding in the undergrowth. I pulled him out and disarmed him. He had been wounded and the maggots were eating him. The OC ordered the CSM to give him a tot of rum and, to prove it was not poison, told him to drink a tot himself in front of the *daku*. The OC said something in Chinese to the *daku* – which later he told me was not to be afraid as it was ordinary rum – when the *daku* looked up at us and, in English, asked us if it was whisky.

On another occasion, when I was on my own with my platoon, I wanted to know who were the *daku* sympathizers among the rubber tappers as we could never get any success in that area. I decided to pretend I was a *daku* myself so I took off my green shirt, put on a white one and, covering my mouth with a handkerchief, approached a group of them in a latex shed. In Malay, I demanded money and arrested those who gave me some and praised those who had not given me anything. I called in the rest of my platoon and handed over those who had tried to give me the money, and the money itself, to the police. I had to go in front of the OC to be censured.[9]

The OC was very skilled and keen on this sort of warfare and when he went ahead we all followed him with enthusiasm. We got information from the police one day about *daku* coming in to collect food from the villagers. We went out in vehicles. The OC was in the front vehicle and I was in the rear one. After debussing, half of the men

---

[9] When the brigade commander, Brig M.C.A. Henniker, CBE, DSO, MC, heard of this he told the CO that 'this is a *ruse de guerre* unbecoming to civilised warfare and will not happen again.'

went with the OC and half with me. It was my lucky day as I had an extra LMG with me. On my way to the point I'd been told to go to I saw seven or eight *daku*. Under covering fire I went into the attack and got my hat shot off and bullets through my pouch. I wounded two and killed one. Once fire was opened it was like being drunk; I had no fear at all. I was almost on top of the *daku* when the supporting gunner shouted out that one of the wounded enemy was on the point of throwing a grenade at me. The men with me went to ground on hearing the gunner but I went on and captured him before he could throw it. In the event the grenade did not explode.

The OC asked me on the radio for a situation report and I was told to bring out the corpse and the wounded and take them to the police station. The OC gave us a feast he was so happy. I have forgotten much else of what I did but it all added up to my winning the DCM.

At Labis there was a *daku* camp not far from a village. Other companies had not been able to stop the villagers from helping them. I was sent into the area and I found myself on top of one of the *daku* whom I captured. Unfortunately one of my men shot and killed him and there was a police case. However, the OC explained it away properly and no action was taken against me.

I managed to do correctly everything I was ordered to. I was decorated because of the work I did. None of the officers I met were as sincere as OC A Company. People will say anything but people who do things are rare.

I was promoted lieutenant (QGO) and was sent to the UK on the mortar course and made the Mortar Platoon commander. I worked with the Australian Army in Borneo. Later I was promoted to captain (QGO) and was sent to the UK on another course and to be QGOO, which I did for 14 months. It was almost unbelievable that I, one time so poor I had no shoes and was illiterate, should find myself as QGOO. I was awarded the MVO. One time Field Marshal Slim and I had our photographs taken together.

All the jobs I did in the army had their own difficulties but I think the hardest job was being in Boys Company in Sungei Patani. Luckily I had had experience of Boys Company in Palampur. The hardest single thing I had to do was when I had to stop the families panicking on SS *Sangola*.

After I returned to my home on pension I became a Christian, being jailed for my beliefs. I can't tell you how happy I am to meet my old

OC after 20 years to tell him what I remember of those days over 40 years ago.

Tulbahadur Rai died a few months after recounting these memories.

✂

Khayalman Rai, MC, 1/7 GR, *joined the army on 29 November 1939. After service on the North-West Frontier in 4/7 GR he was posted to 1/7 GR at Pegu in Burma at the end of the war.*

After Pegu, where Japanese POWs were put to work, we were posted to Insein then to Victoria Lake in Rangoon. There we were joined by about nine officers from the Indian Army battalion, 1/1 GR. I was in HQ Company, acting as CQMH. It was a most difficult time as those who did not want to serve with the British caused endless trouble, messing up the stores. Most of the senior ranks opted for India. I had no storemen so I had to be responsible for rations, stores, arms and ammunition, and no fatigue party to draw rations. Most of the senior GOs kept their heads down for fear of reprisals. Those who wanted to go to India would take off the tent ropes and after dark go around looking for those going to the British Army, "who would have to use knives and forks to eat with",[10] so that they could beat them. We, certainly in HQ Company, had to hide; there was less fear of trouble in rifle companies as more people had opted for the British Army than for the Indian Army. I was a special target. The British officers' batmen found it easier to hide. I still do not know why they behaved like that or got so angry. In December 1947 contingents separated for service in the Indian or British Army. I have not met any of them since.

We went over to Seremban, in Malaya, to be made into gunners. We were short of many senior ranks and I was made acting CQMS and then acting RSM although I was only a sergeant. Matters gradually improved. I learnt that my father had died and I went on leave. When I reported in at the Darjeeling depot after leave with my family I was told I was a Lieutenant (KGO). I missed the time that the battalion trained to become gunners as I was in HQ before going on leave. I was sent to B Company and did some jungle training under Lieutenant Colonel W.C. Walker.[11]

---

[10] Before then only spoons were issued for rice, and hence knives and forks would signify a departure from accepted norms.

[11] Later Gen Sir Walter Walker, KCB, CBE, DSO (with 2 Bars).

Training included snap shooting Figure 2 targets that were hard to see. In the final test I hit seven out of ten and thought I'd failed but was passed. Back in the battalion in B Company I worked very closely with Major P.R. Richards. He was good and won his MC in B Company. I had no idea I would ever get an MC, though as long as I had been a soldier I had always tried my best.

One day we were started off through Pertang estate and the OC was with me and my 4 Platoon. Once in the jungle we contacted four *daku* on a re-supply mission and I shot three of them. Snap shooting in the jungle is not easy. The OC's policy was not to chase them as it was not easy to kill them that way. We picked up four packs. As one had escaped I wondered if the OC would be angry with me but he was not.

We went back to our base, re-rationed for five days' operations and left camp at night in an armoured lorry to look for the main camp. We even had an Air OP flying to try and help us pinpoint a target. We found nothing that time. So we tried again in the Durian Tipus area. We were looking for a *daku* called Ten Foot Long.[12] Bombing was used and we found many food dumps. One day the OC was with 5 Platoon and I was on my own. I was ambushing a ration dump. 5 Platoon moved off to the right, *daku* were heard and the *daku* fired on 5 Platoon. They ran away, leaving their packs behind them once more.

Next morning my platoon searched to see if there were any dead *daku*. We met up with Ten Foot Long's camp that still had *panjis*[13] around it. There had not been time for them to be uprooted and carried off. I told the OC on the radio about this and he came to see the camp. The next day I went on another recce but found nothing. On the third day, more by guesswork than anything, I went to explore a river that ran through steep-sided hills making it difficult to move along but it was more likely to produce results than walking along ridge lines. We went uphill and took a rest. I sent off some men to collect water for a brew of tea and took three men to look for *daku*. I went back down to the river, and saw a wooden ladder with vines to help climb up on the other side. There were tracks that *had* to be *daku*. I went back up to the platoon and took them into an ambush position. I put the LMG group with a rifle group on the left, five men in all, and ordered them to open fire at any *daku*. I went farther on up the hill. The ambush opened fire and killed three of the four *daku* who fell into the river

---

[12] Nickname of Tang Fook Leong, a brave soldier and a good commander.
[13] Sharpened and hardened bamboo stakes.

where I saw three dead bodies. The fourth escaped but we did recover an LMG, a pistol, packs and documents. I reported this to the OC and he came down the hill by himself. Had the fourth *daku* fallen into the river? he asked. The OC took photos of the bodies and also their fingerprints. The documents were taken out and looked at by the police. They showed that they had belonged to Ten Foot Long's group and they contained so much information that a brigade operation was launched. We got a *shabash* from brigade.

We were relieved by another company at that point. Was it for what I had done then that I won an MC? I think probably it was. In all I had killed *daku* before in ones and twos but with the OC I first killed three myself then four with a lot of trouble. My platoon killed 21 *daku*.

In 1951 I had been posted to the TDBG for two and a half years, training two intakes of recruits. In 1955 we had Major J. Davis as OC. We took an airdrop in the Langkap area and I guessed that *daku* were in a certain map square and asked if I could go and look for them. He did not let me go first of all but later on he did. I did meet up with *daku* but did not manage to kill any though we came across a large ration dump. This we carried out to the main road and back-loaded.

Once again I asked to be allowed to operate on my own with my platoon rather than be with the OC as part of a larger company operation. This was not allowed. I met another three *daku* and again missed them but the documents left behind showed that one of them had been a district committee member. The group had been collecting money. There was not as much money in their packs as they had written down in their accounts and we only gave in what we actually found.

I was transferred to C Company which was not as well trained as was B. They drank more and went out at night more. Their jungle work was not up to the standard of my old company. Near Seremban, around the 1,360-foot hill there, an old *daku* camp was found and I said I'd take my platoon in to look for *daku*. We came across three and I shot them all myself. I smelt smoke and came across another camp which I ambushed. More *daku* came from an unexpected angle, along steep country. I heard them coming and held my fire. One of my men coughed and frightened them away. They kept contact with each other by whimpering like small dogs. I signalled to my men that another *daku* was in the vicinity. I was hidden in the roots of a fallen tree. I slowly turned my head and saw yet another *daku*. So there was one in front of me and one behind me. I fired at the nearest and killed him. I saw the first also run away and killed him. Then I came under fire from below; it was one of my soldiers who thought that it was the *daku* firing at him not me firing at the *daku*. The low standard of C Company was the reason for this bad soldiering.

I had a spell up in the Grik area of Perak without any contact and after that went to Brunei where I killed two and captured one of Azahari's gang[14] who were hiding up near our camp. I finished my service as Gurkha Major of the battalion.

Chandrabahadur Rai, 2/7 GR, *had his share of action.*

I was born in 1931 and enlisted on 1 November 1949, going on discharge after 12 years' service in 1961. The sea journey over to Malaya took a week and I felt a bit seasick. Initially I was sent as a boy soldier to Sungei Patani but as 2/7 GR was so short of men I was moved on to recruit training three months later. That took nine months and took place in Paroi, outside Seremban. After the passing out parade I was happy to be a trained soldier. Work was not as hard as it was as a recruit and the pay was better.

The first job in 2/7 GR was to go on a six-day operation in the Bentong area as part of 3 Platoon, A Company. We had many contacts in those early years. At times it rained all night and there were leeches in profusion. I wore wet jungle boots without taking them off for a week, going on and on with my feet so sore that it was not easy to walk. The jungle boots made the feet very hot. When I did take my boots off my skin was in ribbons. We had to keep alert all day and patrol continuously.

We were based on Paroi Camp and one Saturday the OC, Major Gopsill, told us to play football. Captain (KGO) Danbahadur Gurung's platoon had gone to investigate some suspected *daku* not so far from the camp in an overgrown rubber estate when they were attacked by *daku* who had three LMGs with them and fired them on fixed lines. The OC, sitting in the mess at about 1300 hours, heard the firing and, jumping up, went and drew an LMG and some spare ammunition. With one man he ran towards the sound of the shooting. My platoon was also alerted to get ready instantly and go out to relieve the platoon under fire. Not so very far from the shooting, so I was told later, the OC felt

---

[14] See Chapter 9, pages 224 and 228.

he had to give supporting fire but as the undergrowth was too thick to fire from a lying position and as the LMG could not be fired from the shoulder, he ordered the man with him to bend down and, placing the bipod on the man's pack, fired that way. That alerted the platoon under fire that help was coming.

By the time the OC reached the platoon Gurkha casualties were two dead and two wounded, including the signaller. The platoon was out of ammunition and Danbahadur Gurung was walking up and down in front of his men, ready with his kukri, cursing the enemy for all he was worth and encouraging the soldiers. The battle had gone on for two hours and some of the enemy had got very near. They must also have become short of ammunition. One of them, armed with a Sten gun, got in front of a tree that Hastabahadur Rai was behind. Hastabahadur caught hold of the man who struggled but Hastabahadur killed him with his kukri.[15] Hastabahadur was awarded an MM. Danbahadur Gurung was as brave as Mahisa[16] and he won an MC for that,[17] later winning a bar to it.

My platoon arrived at 1500 hours and stayed there the night. Our wounded were evacuated and we stacked the six enemy corpses which were to be taken away the next day. We remained alert all night in case the *daku* returned to gather their dead. Aircraft bombed the nearby jungle next day and strafed it from both directions. Both times the bullets came so close to us we thought we were going to be killed. After the strike we patrolled the jungle and found around 60 enemy packs but no enemy. We destroyed the food in them and buried the ammunition.

Another time the company was being led by an SEP we came under fire and had no time to take off our packs or get into a firing position. That's how it was. My weapon was not ready and bullets zinged around my head. I was scared. Bullets were everywhere. One went through my pack. I could not see the enemy and did not want to fire blindly as I did not know where the rest of our men were. Two of our men were killed and two were wounded. One of the wounded was the company 2IC, Captain (KGO) Bhaktabahadur Rai. From what I gather the enemy were wearing a type of army uniform, even some of them wearing the recognition mark of 2/7 GR in their hats. Bhaktabahadur went forward,

---

[15] That was the only recorded occasion during the whole Emergency of a CT being killed with a kurki.

[16] The king of the demons whom only Durga could kill.

[17] His OC, Maj (later Lt Col) E. Gopsill, felt he had earned a higher award.

not sure whether the men were *daku* or ours and got shot in the knee by the *daku*. He had to have his leg amputated.[18]

Once a European estate manager came in to tell us that *daku* were planning to collect rations from his rubber estate the next day. We left at 0300 hours by MT and after debussing walked for half an hour. As we were trying to surround where we thought about 15 *daku* were, still in the dark, they opened fire and wounded the 2IC's batman. My platoon went forward, crossed a small river and went up the hill on the other side. The *daku* ran away but when it was light enough to see properly we saw blood trails on the ground. We followed them up and found a wounded *daku*. We captured him and found he was carrying a lot of money. Later we counted S$10,000. We saw another and shot and killed him. I saw a third man and aimed at him then saw he was unarmed so I did not shoot him. He was a Malay villager looking for bananas to cut and take back to his house.

On our return to our lines the OC was so pleased with us he gave each of us a bottle of beer.

In 1952 I was posted to the MT platoon. It was an easier life than in Gopsill sahib's company as he was a very strict man. I was only ambushed twice as a driver and was not wounded.

Chandrabahadur Rana, MM, 2/2 GR. I joined the army on 27 November 1947 as a boy soldier, aged around 15. I was posted to Dehra Dun but shortly afterwards we all went to Malaya. On the way I became ill and was in Ranchi hospital for three weeks. I crossed over to Malaya with 10 GR rear party.

We boys were happy to go to Malaya. Pay in India was 9 rupees a month for a boy and 25 a month for a trained soldier but in Malaya it was worth 60. I finished boys' training in January 1949 and then started on recruit training proper. That was only for six weeks, with 20 rounds fired on the range, as we were wanted in the jungle against the *daku*.

I was involved in section, platoon and company operations until 1954 when the battalion went to Hong Kong. I never did see an enemy nor had anything but a chance contact when they fled. In other platoons there were battles but never in mine.

---

[18] He was given a bar to his MC. He became the first Capt (QGO) to be promoted Hon Capt (GCO).

After two years in Hong Kong we returned to Malaya in 1956. One day a man surrendered in the Seremban area and told Special Branch that there were seven *daku* whose job was with money and without arms somewhere up in the high hills who wanted to surrender. Head of Special Branch with three policemen and the SEP, the OC[19] with a radio operator and 14 GORs commanded by me as a lance corporal set off to capture them. The CO gave orders to bring back the seven alive. It was planned to approach the camp from an unexpected direction and this entailed travelling over most precipitous terrain. We carried rifles, 50 rounds and a grenade, and wore skeleton equipment with only a water bottle. We had a meal before we set off from the camp at 0600 hours.

The approach march took all day and we reached their camp before midnight. I went forward with my men and the *daku* were moving around near us. We could have been seen at any moment. The *daku* were talking and singing until after midnight and we waited until 0200 hours before attacking them. The *daku* camp was well sited and we had to move most cautiously. I went into the camp and, fumbling around, caught hold of a man's head. He shouted in alarm and woke up all the others. In front was Chandrabahadur and the SEP who also shouted out an alarm to the sleeping *daku*.

Fire broke out from automatic weapons and it was only later that we found out that there were 30 armed *daku* in the camp and that the SEP had tricked us. I saw flashes of bullets being fired at me from about 15 yards in front. Chandrabahadur had gone to ground behind me in a prone fire position and I was standing by myself. In my carelessness I dropped my magazine on the ground and felt around for it to put it back on. I could not find it so went ahead to where the Bren gun was firing at me, took it out of the *daku*'s hands and routed the rest of them. I killed two, wounded two who escaped and, so we were told, later died. We were also told that another three wounded men were captured and that the *daku* had five rifles, two Sten guns, pistols and grenades as well as the Bren gun.[20]

The OC called to me from behind to ask what had happened and I told him. We finished the operation at 0330 hours, very hungry and tired. Next morning we found four or five more camps in the area, some of which were full of rations. We found a rifle and three pistols and

---

[19] Maj J.E.G. Vivian, MC.

[20] 2/6 GR followed up and, in all, eight CT were killed, four captured and 15 surrendered.

some ammunition and many packs. We burnt the packs, destroyed the rations and brought the weapons back with us when we finally left. We also discovered S$5000 with one of the dead who was dressed as though he was a senior man. A message came from HQ asking us if we had captured the *daku* alive and ordering us to take the dead *daku* out to the road. That took four hours. As there were only 14 of us we were all very tired when we reached the road. We were met by the CO, who asked who had done the killing and shook my hand, and the police who took the bodies away. The company was given S$300 to have a party. I got an MM and the OC a bar to his MC.

I was posted to the TDBG as a corporal and trained three lots of recruits. I went on leave and was on my way to rejoin the battalion as a sergeant when I was once again posted to the recruit company. I was not happy about that as I was fed up with instructing and wanted to rejoin my company. I then learnt that someone junior to me had been promoted over me and I asked to go on pension. This was allowed although Parks sahib, the adjutant, tried to dissuade me.

Thambahadur Gurung, MM, 1/2 GR, *was in action early.*

I enlisted on 4 November 1947 and went to Malaya soon afterwards. We had been told we'd be in brick buildings but we were all in tents, including the British officers' families, at Ulu Pandan in Singapore. Apart from the many fatigues we were used on to establish the camp, we had very little training, only shooting five practices on the range. We moved out on what we were told was to be a three-month operation but we were back after one month. We had many operations around the Poh Lee Sen area of Johore. Some operations were to surround where suspected *daku* were while the air force bombed it. The first time this happened nothing was found, nor on the second time.

The third time there was no air support and I was in a platoon that met up with *daku* tracks. We followed them for a week. That day I was in front and the platoon commander, Jemadar[21] Ganeshbahadur Gurung, was behind me. He had a rifle and I had an LMG. We came across an enemy camp with trenches around it and saw the sentry. He was asleep. We crawled up as near to him as possible and the platoon

---

[21] King's Gurkha Officers' ranks were named as they had been in India until 1949.

commander said he would shoot the sentry and I was to spray the camp with bursts. The jemadar killed the sentry and I sprayed the camp with fire. No one shot back as the camp had been emptied of men. Neither of us saw anyone leave though there could have been up to 40 people in the camp. The platoon came up and we searched the camp, finding a workshop and all the arms, ammunition and kit the enemy had left behind. It took a day to carry the corpse and the kit from the workshop back to the main road. In the workshop were three rifles and 12 hand bombs. The sentry was dressed in khaki and had a red star in his hat. Ganeshbahadur won an MC for that action.[22]

In another action I was with Lieutenant (KGO) Dalbir Ghale, IDSM, on Niyor Estate. There were many *daku* in the area. We were some three hours' walk into the jungle from the nearest rubber estate. We heard fire to a flank. As there were none of our troops in that area it had to be *daku* firing. Aircraft were bombing yet another area. Dalbir and I, both with LMGs, set up an ambush. Two men walked about ten yards in front of us, carrying sickles, wearing packs but with no headgear. They wore rubber shoes. As I did not see any weapons I did not open fire but Dalbir did, killing them both. The rest of the platoon came up to where we were and we carried the bodies out and gave them to the police.

There must have been a complaint from somewhere as I was arrested and put in prison. Wood sahib told me what to say when my case came up and that I had to stick to my story. I repeated my story in the High Court in Johore Bahru. An Englishman with false hair on his head sat in the middle with Malays sitting on either side of him. I stuck to my story and was acquitted so I did not have to go back to jail.

Another operation I went out on after that was when Lieutenant (KGO) Partap Gurung was platoon commander. This time it was in the Geylang Patah area, near a swamp and not far away was a river that had crocodiles in it. The company base was in a rubber estate factory that had been made empty for us. News came about *daku* coming in to pick up some rations and stores at a certain place. We had to ambush them and we stayed there for a week, 11 Platoon across the river and my 10

---

[22] *A Pride Of Gurkhas* by Harold James and Denis Sheil-Small, quotes from the citation on page 20. The story given there is that the enemy fired an LMG at Jem Ganeshbahadur Gurung from close range and he was lucky to escape death as the bullets passed between his open legs. The discrepancy only surfaced half a century later.

Platoon this side of it. I was No 1 on the LMG. The *daku* RV was in the middle. The rubber tappers were in that area milling around and seven *daku* came into our killing zone with them, talking loudly. One had an LMG and the others rifles and grenades, all weapons at the ready.

Partap was dozing by his LMG when the *daku* came into view so I nudged him awake and told him that some of the people to our front were tappers and some had weapons. He said that he would aim at one man and kill him and I was to open rapid fire on the rest of them. I was afraid I might kill some of the rubber tappers when I killed the *daku* but that couldn't be helped if they were mixed up. Partap killed one and I opened fire. The *daku* returned fire and wounded Partap who slumped down. They scattered and tried to escape. I killed some and then chased a couple of them as they ran away, firing as I did. Once in the jungle I killed one of them.

The other *daku* had an LMG and he turned and fired at me but his bullets went high. He then went into dead ground up a ravine. I swore at him, "Run away would you?" and chased him. I went ahead, saw him, selected a lying position and fired at him. I killed him also. I found myself alone then. I made my way back and heard Partap shouting at me, "*Shabash, shabash.*" We joined up and he said he would recommend me for a *bahaduri.*

I got an MM.

❦

Dhanbahadur Rana, MM, 1/6 GR, *was glad to be able to tell his story.*

I joined the army in 1948 and after our training in 1949 heard news of an ambush by the *daku* that had killed a British major and a number of soldiers. Thirteen bodies were brought to the quarter guard. The ambush took place in Sentok, Kedah.

On one operation we were in the region of a 7,162-foot high mountain, not far from Ipoh. We came from uphill without the enemy knowing. We brewed up in ten minutes and charged the enemy, who were in a hut, with our battle cry, "*Ayo Gorkhali*". I fell into the guerilla latrine, up to the navel in shit. The camp *daku* doctor fell wounded. I got out of the latrine and joined LMG 1. I smelled so badly no one would let me be near him. The OC gave the order to charge across the river but no one moved. I went forward, to wash the shit off in the river, and the others thought I was charging the enemy by myself so all rallied behind me. I stayed behind in the river, washing off the shit behind a large rock. The others thought I was missing.

On the OC's order I killed the doctor as the OC, Major Harkasing Rai, feared he would use his pistol against us.

In 1950 I was on an operation that went to a camp for 300 *daku* which had just been evacuated. This was in the Cameron Highlands area. I went on a patrol to get more information on the enemy. Our own 5.5-inch artillery gave us covering fire in front of the *daku*. We followed them up all day and, at dusk, were a thousand yards from them. Our four days' rations were finished. Next day we took an airdrop. The *daku* ambushed our previous night's base. 9 Platoon patrolled ahead, 7 Platoon behind and 8 Platoon circled the camp.

The *daku* plan was to encircle us in our camp. They opened fire, from above, on Aitaman's section and shot Aitaman's hat off his head. Our own casualties were one killed and three wounded. We jumped out of the way. Our packs were stacked in one place and our wireless was broken We pulled the wounded to safety. 9 and 7 Platoons attacked but there were no enemy casualties. The one corpse and the three wounded were evacuated to the road and we returned to follow up the enemy.

In a later operation, with a new OC, Major Gopsill, we had recced a *daku* camp for about 300 *daku*. I had been the leading scout. The OC ordered a dawn attack on the camp so, at 0300 hours, we got up in our overnight camp. We were told to brew up and I kicked over my mess tin of tea by mistake. The OC spoke to me in a way that made me angry so I set off, without the others, there and then to go and attack the camp by myself.

After about a thousand yards I saw two sentries of the *daku* camp. I went into the camp without seeing any other *daku* and without the *daku* seeing me. I saw stacks of rations and their rifles. I took out a grenade and took the pin out. I realized that I might kill a whole lot of them but then the others would kill me. I put the pin back in the grenade. I heard the two sentries talking. I thought I'd just kill those two and run away back. I shot at them with my silent Sten and they ran off. I took their two rifles and packs, and a bugle.

When I returned to the camp the OC asked me where I'd been and I told him, showing him what I had brought back with me. We moved off and, with an added platoon of 1/10 GR, made a dawn assault. I went with the OC who fired the LMG but no *daku* was killed. Later on we accounted for seven of them. The OC killed one wounded sentry with a machete. I found some of the *daku* commander's cake in their camp and ate it. I was awarded an MM.

Later I came in from a patrol, washed and was enjoying a beer in the mess when a party of those leaving the unit started a fracas. I was accused of being involved and was taken in front of the CO. He said that as I had an MM he would take no other action other than cancel the papers already prepared to make me into a QGO. I was not interested in serving on under those circumstances when those above me were junior in service to me so I volunteered to be sent on pension.

Dhanrup Rai, 1/7 GR, *had two major contacts and another, unusual, aspect to his soldiering.*

I joined the army on 3 February 1948. We flew to Ranchi. I was afraid as it was the first time I had been in the air. From Ranchi we went by train to Madras where we embarked on the *Sirdhana* for Malaya. We all felt seasick and could not eat without wanting to bring it up. On deck we saw flying fishes and the noses of sea horses.

Our camp at Paroi, near Seremban, was poor and we had to do a lot of work on it. After training, as I was strong, I was made LMG 1 in 9 Platoon C, Company, 1/7 GR. The LMG weighed 23½lbs. We often met *daku*. We had one three-month operation in the Durian Tipus area. On the last day my section was told to draw seven days' rations and go back out as an Auster pilot had thought he had seen a *daku* camp. We were only eight, one of us being a signaller, armed with a pistol. We took two Bren guns and many magazines. At that area we did meet a *daku* camp. Three trees were felled in the middle leaving a large stump, eaten by white ants, that looked like a man. There was an open space in the middle.

The section commander told the other six to stay where they were and he took me to make a recce of the camp. From a little distance we saw things coloured red, white and yellow which we did not understand until we saw that they were ration boxes. There were many items: rice, pulse, cooking oil, tinned fish, tinned meat and much more. The camp was empty of men. Before we two went back to the others we took as many tins we could carry.

We sent a message to HQ and were told that men of 10 GR would be sent to relieve us and we were to stay there till they came. It was swampy country and we recced in full and found out that, apart from the path we had taken, there was another entrance over a felled log in the swamp acting as a bridge.

We put one LMG with two men at one end of the bridge and set up two more positions, one of two men with the other LMG and a third whose weapons included a Patchett gun. As the signaller only had a pistol he was not counted for fighting. There were so many rations in the camp we expected about a battalion's worth of *daku* to come.

Many *daku* did come and one of the LMG groups opened fire in three bursts. At that we all opened fire and the second gun group shouted "Charge". This was to give the impression that we were more than we were in fact. Three *daku* were killed outright and a wounded man died a little later. None of us was touched. We picked up eight rifles and waited for a counter-attack. One of the dead was a Chinese major who was carrying a lot of money and lists.

We were told that 10 GR would reach us during the night and, as a password, they would break three sticks and as a counter-sign we would also break three. Come they did and as we heard them advance we were scared until we heard sticks being snapped. We then snapped our three and met up with them.

For that operation, the man in charge of the gun group that opened fire was awarded an MM and the patrol commander an m-i-d.

On another occasion we were out with Captain (QGO) Narbahadur Rai, the company 2IC, looking for a *daku* camp in the area of Lenggeng. When we thought we had reached the place where the police had told us to go, the captain sahib, armed with a carbine, told the others to wait and me to go with him with my LMG. We advanced cautiously and saw that mosquito nets had been put up. So we were at the camp. Something moved and the captain sahib flapped, firing one round. His hands then trembled and he did not fire again. I fired a burst and killed three of the enemy. We collected nine weapons and had to take them and the bodies to the nearest police station.

Those two were my major contacts.

One day, sitting by a stream as sentry for an airdrop I smelled tiger, more and more strongly. I saw the top of its body but it did not know I was there. I could have shot it. But we did capture a female tiger cub we named Nepti due to the shape of her nose. We took her to the lines and detailed a handler for her. We fed her with a pound of meat and a pound of milk a day. She was very tame and played with the men. One day she jumped on an officer's dog which voided itself with fear but the handler called her off and the dog ran away unscathed. We kept pigs in the lines, looked after by an old rifleman. One kept on trying to get out by burrowing under the wooden slats of its pen. One day, in the middle of such an attempted escape, Nepti saw it and jumped on it. Again her handler called her off and the pig, unhurt, retreated back into its pen. It never tried to escape again!

Nepti grew so big it was thought she'd be a danger so she was sent to the London zoo. When she gave birth it was in the papers.

We also kept a wild pig which wandered around the lines. We named it Raté, "the red one". One day it went into the CO's office and hit his leg with its snout. That evening's Part 1 orders had that either the pig was to be killed or taken back to the jungle. We killed it for its meat; it weighed 90 kilos.

My father died leaving my mother and my wife alone at home. Both my elder brothers were serving so I, as the youngest, asked for discharge to go and look after my mother. That was granted and I left the army after 7 years and 156 days' service.

⚔

Dilbahadur Thapa, MM, 1/10 GR, *had his share of ups and downs.*

I joined the army on 4 December 1948 and after six months' training in Kluang was posted to 11 Platoon, D Company. We did not have the full training because there were not enough men in the battalion for operations against the *daku*. It was hard work on operations in the jungle. We'd start off with a week's rations which made our load heavy. I began operations in the Kuala Pilah area then we moved north to Bentong. Sometimes we were in swamp which was difficult terrain. We would go out for periods of up to a month and rations and kit would be dropped by air. There were no helicopters in those days.

We had to patrol the rubber estates as the tappers were in touch with the *daku* and gave us *dukha*[23] by giving away our positions to them as well as provisioning them. On one occasion we were sent on a day patrol and we contacted eight or nine armed and uniformed *daku* as they emerged from the jungle. That was at about 0800 hours. I had only been in a contact with the *daku* once before but had taken no part in

---

[23] At that stage of the Emergency tappers would refuse to go tapping without a military escort, thus tying down troops as well as making them an easier target.

the action. This time they ran away and our platoon chased them, headlong, for about two hours. Somehow I became separated from the others and found myself alone. I was armed with a rifle. The *daku* saw me, turned and came towards me. I took up a firing position as they approached me. I shot the first one dead. Another took his place and I shot him dead. A third took his place, quite near by now, and I shot him dead also.

The fourth shot me in the left hand and the bullet ran up my arm into my shoulder. I fell, losing consciousness. I came round very soon after but could not stand up. I thought I'd throw a grenade but stupidly I threw it unfused. It was, however, my lucky day. I remembered I had a smoke grenade and I threw that. Fortunately it exploded in the middle of the other *daku*, who were very near me by this time. The *daku* ran away and I managed to move off.

I thought my platoon would be near me so I shouted out that I had been hit but I was not heard. My left hand was useless. I had six rounds in my rifle which I loaded by cocking it with a piece of wood I had picked up. With my right hand I managed to put it into a position so that I could fire it with my foot. I let off one round and I thought I heard shouting in the distance. But nobody turned up so I let off the other five rounds at regular intervals.

I heard my name shouted and I shouted back. I did not see the others so I took my hat off and, placing it on the end of my kukri, waved it above my head. My friends eventually saw it and reached me, an hour after I'd been hit. They had been tracking some of the *daku* who had run off in another direction.

The platoon sergeant asked me what it was all about and I told him I had killed some and been wounded. "Where and how many?" he asked. I told him I had killed three. I had my hand bound up by the man carrying the medical pack. It hurt a good deal. It was lucky that my chasing the *daku* had brought me to a place not far from the road leading to our company base and a vehicle was sent for. I and the corpses were loaded into it. I was sent to Bentong hospital then evacuated to Kuala Lumpur. I was there for six months and it was during that time that I heard I had been awarded the MM.

The brigadier doctor who spoke Hindi told me I was no good for any more soldiering, but there were no medical pensions awarded at that time so I was allowed to stay on doing light duties. I was in the provost section for a while then made battalion ration storeman.

Unfortunately the GCO company commander didn't like me being in fatigue dress when I was suddenly called to his office and I was discharged after 12 years' service without a pension.

Dilbahadur finally said that he would much rather have no bravery award than an arm that had hurt him for the next fifty years.

Manbahadur Gurung, 1/7 GR, *was not used to conditions he found.*

I was 15 years old when I went to join the army and was lucky to be enlisted as a boy soldier. That was on 19 October 1948. I was also ignorant and fearful of the train we went to Calcutta in. When we did get to Malaya we were told we always had to relieve ourselves in the building made for that purpose and nowhere else. This was a surprise and there were many others. We had to write home and to a friend to tell them we had got safely to Sungei Patani, Boys Company. I was fit for man's service in 1950 and started training on 1 April.

On completion of recruit training I was posted to 1/7 GR and underwent basic signal training. I was also sent on a PT course and learnt to be a boxer. Back in the battalion I would be attached to various rifle companies for operations. The 62 wireless set and dry batteries I had to carry weighed 35lbs. One time I went out to the Titi area at night and surrounded *daku* in long grass. It was during that engagement that a bullet went through my pouch. It was lucky I did not have a grenade in it otherwise there would have been many casualties on our side.

Manbahadur had another experience he never forgot.

Another time we were very excited when, in Support Company at Ladang Geddes estate one of our British officers ran away to try and join the *daku*. We all went in search of him but did not find him. In the event he came out by himself some days later, very thin and hungry, not having met the *daku* nor having had much to eat. He was quickly posted out of the battalion.[24]

I left the army on 12 October 1962.

---

[24] Lt F.V. Joyce. To this day this case is shrouded in mystery.

Tejbahadur Gurung, MM, 1/2 GR, *had a good grounding in the Emergency for work later on.*

I joined the army on 10 October 1949 and, once I got to Malaya, went to 2 GRTW in Ipoh. After staying there for four months I went to Sungei Patani for nine months' recruit training. I was posted to 7 Section, 3 Platoon, A Company, 1/2 GR. Major MacDonald was my OC. One month after joining the company I was sent on jungle operations but initially had no contact. News came in about some *daku* and as we went up a winding *nullah* the second day we were ambushed by about 15 of them on some high ground. We were moving in single file and were fired on from in front. We lost four wounded and two killed. Two of the wounded were hit in the leg and one was hit in the stomach. What with evacuating them and making a plan we did not move forward for nearly an hour by which time the *daku* had withdrawn.

That was the first time I had been under fire. My section was at the rear and I was not involved. The commander of the lead section won an MM. We came across one dead *daku* then and another corpse later when we had been reinforced by another platoon. When my platoon had men killed I found extra strength and courage to chase and deal with the *daku*.

Thorny lantana and swamp made movement difficult and there was always a danger of wildlife in one form or another. One man was attacked by a 20-foot long python which wrapped itself twice around his body. The man became unconscious and was only saved by his elder brother's quick action with a kukri. A helicopter pad was constructed that evening and the man was lifted out on the morrow. He still has white marks on his body where he was crushed, even though he was fully clothed at the time.

There were many small incidents. Once one man went out from the camp without his weapon to relieve nature and bumped into a *daku* who was similarly unarmed. We had to move camp otherwise the *daku* could have attacked us. Another danger was falling branches. One man had his leg broken that way.

In all I was in three contacts before my first leave. The next time we went out to a tin mine not far off the Mersing road, acting on information that there would be *daku* there. The second day we found a camp for about 50 and the *daku* were moving off as we got there. The lead scout saw two of them, whether sentries or those on a recce patrol was not established, and killed them both. The rest ran away.

Another time we came across a ration collecting party near a rubber estate. I did not kill any *daku* myself.

Singbahadur Gurung, 1/6 GR.   I had wanted to enlist ever since I had seen the village men coming on leave and I joined the army in October 1955. I could write in Nepali and the Roman alphabet and knew how to count. I went to Paklihawa and on to Lehra. After enlistment we were taken to Calcutta, at the Transit Camp at Barrackpore, then went by boat to Malaya. We trained in Sungei Patani and, on passing out, I was posted to 1/6 GR which was operating in the Cameron Highlands region.

I was with B Company for about four months. In the Cameron Highlands it rained a lot and was very wet. We would go out with seven days' rations. The leading scout would be changed every three hours. He was usually armed with a shotgun. When I was not in that position, I carried an SLR. In that mountainous terrain 1,000 yards an hour was too fast. There was a *daku* presence and we kept off the ridge lines, moving athwart the slopes. The job of a leading scout was to notice dangerous places and look for tell-tale signs of enemy movement such as broken twigs, foot prints, bent leaves and cut branches. We could tell how long before such signs had been made by the speed we knew that leaves dried and that rain made a difference to footprints. It was sometimes difficult to tell bear prints from men's but bears have toes more in a straight line then men's as well as having a claw at the end of their heels. Later, in Brunei, we once wasted two hours looking for enemy after seeing prints which were, in fact, a bear's. Depending, of course, on the state of the undergrowth, it would be normal to be able to see about 30 yards in front of us, seldom as far as 75. The worst type of terrain was swamp, then thorny plants. Not even a hundred yards an hour was possible.

We would have hot tea first thing and be off between 0630 hours and 0700 hours. Our magazines carried 28 rounds and we had one full bandolier in our packs or round our waists. We also carried machetes or kukris. In the late afternoon we would make camp, always making sure there was no hostile presence in the area first. We could tell where water for cooking was from the shape of the ground and from the map. Camp consisted of tying poncho capes on poles for shelter, flattening the ground underneath and laying leaves and another poncho on top for sleeping. We cooked in sections.

I was out with three others on patrol once on steep ground and saw some Sakai[25] coming towards us. We took cover behind the roots of a buttress tree and they passed by without seeing us. We waited. The commander knew that the *daku* would make the Sakai move in front of them as a screen. Nobody came after them and we returned to our overnight camp. Next day, when I was leading scout, I saw 14 enemy 30 yards in front. They wore khaki uniform and had red stars in their caps. I took cover and made a hand signal for the commander to come up. The *daku* also stopped where they were. My commander was a little slow in getting forward. We attacked, shouting "*Ayo Gorkhali*, charge", and killed four of them. They fired back but not heavily. That was the first time I had fired at men. I don't know if any of my bullets hit them or not. I found it hard to shoot another man that first time. I have found out that before any shooting starts we feel fear but after the bullets start flying fear leaves us. We photographed the corpses and buried them. We also found five packs and documents which we took back, along with the four dead men's weapons. Those who ran away took their weapons with them. The road was a day's walk away. The corporal in charge was congratulated. I was on many other patrols but had no other contacts. As an example, we went to investigate where the *daku* had stolen food from a village but we came away empty-handed.

Indrabahadur Rai, 1/7 GR.   In Malaya I acted as CQMS, CSM and RSM at various times and went to Hong Kong on a tactics course. In 1952 I was platoon sergeant of 2 Platoon, A Company. The company commander was Major J.P. Cross. I vividly remember when he and four of us went on a recce of a *daku* camp in an area we had been given as an extension to our original area. Any one we contacted there had to be enemy. After we had inspected it we waited on a small knoll and heard enemy on the other side of a swamp. The OC decided to cross over and investigate but, when we were half way over, the enemy crossed over to our side. They had a red blob in their jungle hats, like the communist red star badge. We all came to the aim and the OC quietly ordered us to shoot but when he did I recognized the man

---

[25] Aborigines.

leading them as my cousin, a sergeant in 2/7 GR. I whispered to the OC not to fire as they were Gurkhas in front of us. The OC immediately stepped forward, taking his hat off and lowering his rifle. He shouted out not to shoot.

It eventually transpired that the troops to the north had not been told that their boundary had been changed. It was very lucky that we had not had a severe fire-fight and killed each other.

Shamsherbahadur Rai, 1/7 GR. I was 15½ years old when I joined up on 21 October 1954. I enjoyed my recruit training, especially playing basketball and volleyball. As I was small I was given extra milk and fish oil. I also suffered from prickly heat and had to be treated for it.

I was posted to 1/7 GR in September 1955 and sent to the Pipes and Drums but I did not like that so asked to be sent to a rifle company instead. I ended up in A Company in Labis. The OC was Major J.P. Cross. I was in awe of him and the way he looked after us. He was never angry and kept us amused. We soldiers found that the days sped by because our efforts were appreciated and he understood us. One morning, on operations, he came to me and asked me if I knew that I talked in my sleep? No, I said, I didn't. I was told that the previous night I had shouted out in a loud voice, "The NCOs send me out on patrol," and "In the jungle the rice isn't cooked properly."

He used animal and bird noises instead of his voice when he wanted to call the platoon commanders for orders or to halt when on the march or to start after a rest. They were so realistic that monkeys and birds would answer him.

We had one month-long operation, having to move by night from Labis to Segamat and then farther north into Negri Sembilan. It was only afterwards were we told that our target was Chin Peng's[26] deputy, Yong Kwoh. I can remember, at the very start of the journey, we had to drive from our camp through Labis village. In those days villages were surrounded by barbed wire with locked gates on the roads. The OC had warned the police to open the gates at a certain time but both gates were shut, locked and unmanned. After a short delay the OC got out of the truck, told the driver to take a heavy tool from the tool box and give it to him so that he could smash the lock open. That made us late. The

---

[26] Chin Peng was Secretary General of the Malayan Communist Party.

gate at the other end of the village was treated in the same way. The CO was furious we were late to arrive in Segamat as the order of march was awry and there was no room or light for vehicles to change places in the battalion column. When the operation was over the OC told us that the person he had told to have the gates open, a Chinese inspector, was no longer there.

On another operation I can remember moving out in civilian vehicles with the hoods pulled tight so that the civilians could not see the troops inside. We were in the jungle for 18 days on that operation but we were not successful in contacting the *daku*.

On another occasion the OC had gone forward with two men and had heard the sounds of the *daku* making camp. He returned and, taking a marker balloon, went back to near the camp to inflate it so that it showed above the jungle canopy so that bombers could see where to bomb. He was not keen on bombing but the brigade commander had given the order so it was obeyed. We moved back quite a way for the night and that evening aeroplanes came over, bombing and machine gunning the area. Next morning we made an early start, moving off in the dark. Much of the target area had been flattened. We all went searching for dead bodies but found nothing. The OC was called to the radio and the CO told him that he had had a report that one of the aircraft had dropped its bombs without being fused. That was why we did not find any corpses.

We had to re-ration and search in an area a bit to the north. The area had not been surveyed so that map sheet was white except for a river marked in one corner. We set out in our patrols, three or four men in each, and shortly afterwards fire was opened. It resounded through the jungle, a burst then a single shot, another burst and another single shot, then again like that. As we had not gone far we all heard the noise and thought maybe that the party of *daku* we were chasing had ambushed one of our patrols. I reached the scene of the firing just as the OC came with the two men he had been patrolling with. We were all relieved to see no damage had been caused to our men.

Corporal Dhanbahadur Rai, who had been firing, was immediately quizzed by the OC. "How many have you killed?" he asked and we were all astonished to be told only one. What had happened was that Dhanbahadur had seen two *daku* and opened fire with his SMG. The one in the rear had escaped but the one in front, momentarily checked, came on at him with renewed vigour. So he fired another burst at him.

The *daku* fell backwards but once more sprang back at Dhanbahadur who once more opened fire on him. That happened again and it was only then that Dhanbahadur understood why the *daku* had refused to die and had three times sprung back at him. A piece of thorny rattan had clung to his clothing and had been stretched to its full limit as the man had been hurled back by the force of the bullets fired from close range. Once that pressure was off it sprung back, dragging the by then very dead man with it. I think over 70 bullet holes were counted before he was finger-printed, photographed and buried. Another time we captured all the printing press, papers and inks of a propaganda unit.

A new OC came in 1956, Captain (GCO) Nandaman Rai. That was in Kluang. Special Branch brought in news that a hut belonging to a Malay, only 500 yards from the Gurkha family lines, had been visited by the *daku* who had demanded rations for up to 20 men. An alarm buzzer was fixed up in the hut so when the *daku* came Nandaman's group could be easily alerted. About a month later we were called out and contact was made. Only five people came and one was killed and one wounded. Next morning on our search we found a girl, hit in the thigh and covered in blood, holding on to a lychee tree with one hand and with a pistol aimed at the search with the other. We told her to put her hands up but she refused. One of our men crept up behind her and knocked the pistol out of her hand. She was taken to the BMH in Kluang where she was looked after for one month.

Narbahadur Limbu, 1/7 GR. I joined the army on 28 May 1942 and was involved in training until the war was over. I was awarded an m-i-d but I never wore it. I then joined 1/7 GR in Burma and in 1948 went to Malaya. I have forgotten much of what happened as I am an old man.[27] In February 1952 we were based in Seremban and I was in A Company. My OC was Major J.P. Cross and he briefed us one evening. He told us that a tapper had come in to the police station to tell about four *daku* who were based on his tapping task and who were demanding money. He volunteered to lead us to where they were so we could kill them. He said it would take about three hours to walk there from the main road about ten or so miles down the Port Dickson road. The *daku* would be on top of a small hill.

---

[27] It took Narbahadur Limbu three days' walk to come to tell his story.

The plan was to go by truck and debus at the place nearest the tasking area but away from any labour lines just in case an agent ran ahead of us and told the *daku* that security forces were in the area. The guide would lead us to the *daku*. Once in the danger area one platoon would move to the right and another to the left to surround the hill while the third platoon would be the assault platoon, moving up the hill to the *daku*.

We debussed on a lonely part of the road and moved off into the rubber. It was not a moonlit night so we kept closed up by moving slowly. After an hour the ground started to slope and the OC queried the position with the guide. He answered in a quiet voice and told him that the *daku* were only a very short way ahead. Later we found that they were about ten yards from us. It was about 0200 hours then and the OC called his platoon commanders and told them not to try and surround the hill but to go back a little way, stay there till dawn and await any orders that he might give.

The OC then went forward with a very few of us, very slowly. It came as a shock to find that we very nearly trod on a sleeping *daku*. The man to my left crawled up to a rubber tree but got a tickle in his throat and tried to stifle a cough. Imagine our surprise when, from the other side of that same tree, a cough answered! It was a *daku*! The OC crawled over to the man and whispered in his ear. The man crawled back far enough for the *daku* not to hear his cough.

We waited impatiently. One man suggested to the OC that he throw a grenade into the sleeping men but they were so close that more of us were in danger of dying than the four *daku* in front of us, although they still had not been counted. After another wait another man whispered that he should go and bayonet the whole lot but again that was vetoed.

Eventually, shortly before dawn, the *daku* started to make early-morning-getting-up noises and we heard, rather than saw, movement. I suppose the OC felt that they might wander out of sight, hear us and so escape. He therefore gave the order for our assault group to fire. This we did, killing them all – there were four of them – though one of them managed to get one round off before he was killed.

We waited till full light before we cut four branches to use as poles for carrying the bodies, wrapped up in oil cloth, down to the main road. We got there at about 0800 hours and had to wait by the side of the road until our transport came to take us back. A number of early morning travelers looked at the four long bundles, still tied to the branches, and moved off again in a hurry!

I only remembered that story after all these years when the OC of those days reminded me of the times we'd been together.

Pahalman Rai, 1/10 GR, *had one most unusual experience, otherwise it was a case of 'more of the same'.*

I joined the army on 13 January 1950. During my initial training of ten months I was champion shot of the rifle and the Bren gun. After joining C Company I went on a lot of jungle operations, especially in the Bentong area of Pahang. Some operations lasted for two weeks, some for three and the longest I went on was for 35 days.

My company commander was Major McGurk and one day, towards evening, we were walking along a railway track. I was not far behind him and, at a mile stone at the side of the track, I saw him turn round and talk to somebody. I saw nobody there. The major sahib spoke severely, turned round to look at me then turned back again. He seemed visibly moved. I did not know why but learnt that he had seen a BOR corporal, without any weapon, in the area that was ours. He had wanted to know who he was and why he was there. After he had turned to look behind him he looked back but the man had vanished. That is why he looked the way he did. It so happened that, only a few days before, that a British company had been attacked in that area and a corporal was shot and killed by the *daku* but our OC had no means of knowing that.

The most *daku* killed at one time was when our 7 Platoon surrounded and ambushed them, on information. A Chinese girl who was a ration supplier was also killed at that time although she was not with the group. She was taking supplies to them and one of our bullets hit her. There was no trouble about her death as she was helping the *daku*. We killed *daku* in ones, twos and threes all through my time in the jungle.

One time when I was on the side of the road leading up to the Cameron Highlands a convoy of British troops drove up the road. The platoon commander was a corporal and he waved his hat at the BORs but they fired back with rifles and LMGs. Luckily none of us were hurt.

I also remember an estate manager whose house was raided by

daku. They castrated him and did dreadful things to him afterwards. We had JCLOs with us. A year after the JCLO who had been with our company left and had gone to live in Singapore, his house was burnt down by *daku* supporters.

I left the army in October 1964.

Ratbahadur Rai, 1/7 GR, GMP. I joined the army on 6 September 1950 and was posted to C Company, 1/7 GR, on completion of training. Our company went on many, many, jungle operations but only once did the CO and the OC both go together. It was in the Labis area and we had to ambush a building on a rubber estate where *daku* were going to come for a big food lift. Special Branch had arranged for the food to be brought to the building and our job was to ambush the group but not to shoot at the one man who was wearing a white shirt. We had been warned that the one man who would be wearing a white shirt was a police agent who was acting as a *daku* leader. We were warned that there would be many *daku* and we were cleverly sited at some short distance from the building and only to fire when we heard the sound of firing. That was to allow the agent to get clear of the others.

From where I was I saw the *daku* but they all seemed to be wearing white shirts. After some delay firing opened and the *daku* ran away. One *daku* was killed and the agent was rescued. The reason why we did not kill the *daku* when we so easily could have done was that all the sacks containing rations were white ones and the agent, who was on the point of going back to the police officer who was waiting for him, had been caught hold of by a *daku* who was acting as his sentry. All the others escaped.[28]

Another time we were in the Labis area. I was Bren 1 and my Limbu friend, 5495, a fire eater, carried a rifle. We two went on patrol and met a *daku* carrying a rifle who we shot at and hit in the foot. He threw away his rifle, groaning in pain, and started to tend to his wound but 5495 shot him dead. We took his corpse and rifle back to our platoon base in the jungle.

But the *daku* were in great strength, 360[29] to our 17. By 0900 hours they had surrounded us and we were pinned down until 1700 hours

---

[28] The chief personality was awarded a George Medal.
[29] A gross exaggeration!

when they withdrew. We fought back and had no casualties. We managed to kill three of them. We had to carry the corpses out for four map squares. The stink of blood, shit and guts was overpowering. We got rid of the corpses and waited in the LP area for three days until the OC, Tedford sahib, came. With him was a QGO who had come from 2/7 GR on a bad report. The OC ordered us to go back to the scene of the contact. He himself stayed behind. Captain (QGO) Khayalman Rai led us in. We met heavy fire and the QGO from 2/7 GR ran away. So heavy was the *daku* fire that the bullets knocked down the tree behind which Khayalman sahib had taken cover. He was unhurt. If he had not been with us that day we would have suffered heavy losses.

We went on for another 22 days. Aircraft came and dropped bombs and fired machine guns at the *daku* who were not all that far in front of us. We had an airdrop of food and ammunition but the *daku* collected some of the supplies, namely two tins of cooking oil and ten thousand rounds of ammunition. D Company was sent in to help us and eventually we found their main camp. We went to put an attack in the next day but it had been evacuated the night before. It was heavily defended with bunkers. The *daku* had eaten animals, including elephant. We found piles of elephant dung but no entrails, skin or flesh. We lost the tracks and were evacuated by helicopter. I was lucky not to have lost my life then.

In 1958 I transferred to the GMP and was posted to the 17 Gurkha Division Provost Company. My batch studied law for six months and, after being posted to 63 Brigade, learnt all about traffic control. We were then changed from being GMP to 5 Dog Company. Six months later I went on pension. I found that the British officers always looked after us with care and their administration was good. We were one.

Maitaraj Limbu, 2/10 GR, GMP, *had more than one battle to fight.*

2/10 GR were in Hong Kong and in 1949 we moved to Malaya. Some who had joined the army after me were promoted so I lost heart and volunteered for GMP. I had a lot of work with BORs, trying to keep them apart on a Saturday night from their drunken fights and away from the brothels in Kuala Lumpur. I couldn't understand why they were so worthless. Some white African soldiers[30] were very rude to a group of

[30] Rhodesian Squadron, Special Air Service Regiment.

us when we tried to stop them fighting in one bar and tried to attack us so that our group knocked one of them out by bashing a chair over his head. The others ran away. We then took the unconscious man out onto the road which was being made up and had lumps of concrete lying around. One man took a large lump of concrete and dropped it on the drunk man's face, breaking his nose and teeth. There was never any trouble for us Gurkhas after that.

Sometimes the Rhodesian drivers killed civilians. Then the driver would move his vehicle backwards and forwards over the dead person's face so that the body would not be recognized. The white Africans only stayed for one tour in Malaya.

One of my duties was escorting the passenger train from Kuala Lumpur north or south. On one trip north with some BORs we were stopped because the *daku* had lifted some of the track. We were then shot up. There was a one hour battle and we Gurkhas found ourselves on our own as the BORs had gone elsewhere. The *daku* left off firing and, after the track was relaid at about 1500 hours, we continued our journey north.

Once when patrolling a rubber estate when it was raining, the *daku*'s fire hit the wheel of the vehicle which turned over. My arms and ribs were injured. I was taken to hospital for a month. In the cold weather both still hurt me and I could never do a full day's work after I left the army. I "cut my name" for compassionate reasons in September 1953.

Indrabahadur Limbu, 1/7 GR, *remembered his service vividly.*

I joined the army on 30 September 1952 and went on a lot of operations. While I was still a young soldier I was escort to the CO.[31] He was inspecting rifle companies in their new locations after the periodic re-training. He had a scout car in front and one behind his open and unarmed Land Rover. I was gunner in the rear scout car. On the way back to Seremban the road was steep and winding, with thick jungle both sides. On the far side of the Jelebu pass the leading scout car was too far ahead and we in the rear scout car were too far behind. The *daku* ambushed him, killing him, the driver and the escort that sat with him. They descended, stole the weapons and the CO's watch. By the time the lead scout car realised it was not being followed by the

---

[31] Lt Col A.I. Forestier-Walker, MBE.

Land Rover it was too late and the road was too narrow and winding for it to turn round. As we came round the corner the *daku* were running away and the LMG jammed.

The CO was shot through his nose. I stayed there all night and only next morning did an ambulance come to take his body away.[32] I think both he and his driver, a Rai who had been allowed to re-enlist after wartime service, were wrong in not looking into their mirrors to see if we could go as fast as the Land Rover uphill.

I was involved in many more contacts and was awarded an m-i-d. Once in 1956 I was in the hilly country near Fort Chabai. I was a lance corporal and took the OP forward up a slope. I suddenly saw a Chinese man wearing a steel helmet and then I became unconscious. I heard the OC, Major Kelly, asking if I was dead. I had been hit a glancing blow up over my forehead.

The Malay soldiers were useless. If the British and Gurkhas had not been in Malaya the Chinese *daku* would have won. We Gurkhas are like brothers with the British.

---

[32] The RMO had put some plaster over the wound. The CO's wife was saddened to see the plaster and asked the RMO why it was there. He told her he had nicked the nose when shaving the corpse's face. She upbraided him but never learnt that her husband's face had been disfigured. His watch was recovered from a dead terrorist and OC A Company captured a rifle, 60 map squares away, which turned out to be the driver's.

CHAPTER 9

Brunei and Borneo

In the early 1960s the demise of colonial rule reached the island of Borneo, painfully. Borneo comprised four separate countries: the British territories of Brunei; North Borneo – soon to be known by its old name, Sabah, after it was absorbed into Malaysia; Sarawak; and Indonesian Borneo, also known as Kalimantan. The British trio covered the northern quarter of the island and had never been a separate political entity, nor had their inhabitants ever seen themselves as having a national identity.

Geographically most of Borneo is a vast expanse of jungle and mountain, even more so in the 1960s than now. One noted characteristic of Borneo, which is sparsely populated, is villages built under one roof, like one long house, hence references to 'longhouses'. Almost the entire border with Kalimantan is a natural watershed.

Britain wanted to be rid of Borneo; Malaya wanted it to redress a population imbalance and the whole to become Malaysia. Only Brunei demurred. The political wing of a dissident secret army, the North Kalimantan National Army, backed by Indonesia, won a critical election. Its commander was Yassin Affendi, a one-time client of the Japanese. The overall leader was Sheik Azahari and a rebellion broke out on 8 December 1962 in Brunei Town, since renamed Bandar Seri Begawan.

Indonesia's aim was to prevent the formation of Malaysia or, failing this, to attack it militarily, economically and politically while the new nation was too weak to react. In 1961 President Sukarno of Indonesia started to call his undeclared war a 'Confrontation' between Indonesia and Malaya, as it still was and Malaysia as it might become, and when Sheik Azahari rebelled against the Brunei Government in December 1962, Sukarno saw his chance. Military conflict was inevitable and Britain was sucked into it.

Two unusual military aspects soon evolved on the British side. One was the raising of auxiliary policemen to be the army's 'eyes and ears with a sting' on the border. These were the Border Scouts. Initially sections were commanded by Gurkhas. The second development was

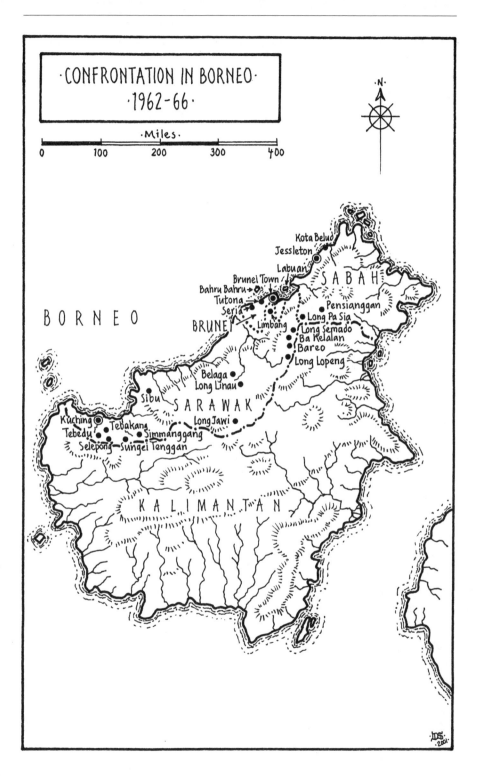

·CONFRONTATION IN BORNEO·
·1962–66·

·Miles·

0   100   200   300   400

·N·

the initiation of secret cross-border operations to keep the Indonesian Army at arm's length.

In the military sphere Malaysia could in no way have held its own without British and other Commonwealth support. Gradually agreement was established between Indonesia and Malaysia in 1965–66 and Confrontation ended, 'not with a bang but a whimper', but not before an Indonesian Army officer, Sumbi, had tried to lead a force of a hundred men through Sarawak to Brunei to sabotage oil installations. He had trained in England as a parachutist and in JWS. His saga is told in the soldiers' stories.

The ratio of Gurkhas to British troops was about 2:1. The standards achieved by every unit in the Brigade could hardly have been higher and would have been reflected in a greater total of awards had there not been a fixed quota.

Brunei Rebellion, 1962–63

Sukdeo Pun, 1/2 GR, *continued his story.*

In 1962 we had to go to Brunei. I was a platoon sergeant in C Company. We reached Brunei at 2300 hours. We reached police HQ at midnight and were told that the rebels were due to attack it. We took up defensive positions. The OC[1] then said that that would not do. The rebels did not know we had come so it would be far better to go and ambush them as they came forward. So he ordered some police vehicles. "If the rebels fire at you, do not fire back," were his orders. "Only fire a few rounds back if their fire is very heavy." I felt troubled at that order. How were we to manage if we could not fire back when fired on? We embussed and went towards Tutong. The OC's jeep stopped and my platoon went ahead. Our platoon commander, Lieutenant (QGO) Durgasing Gurung, told me to drive on in front and he dropped behind.

So I went ahead. As we reached Tutong the police driver, who lived there, stopped because he knew the rebels were there. He said "Stand by" and the rebels opened fire at us from an upper storey of a nearby

---

[1] Capt (later Lt Col) F.A. Lea, MC.

house. Bullets flew everywhere. I tried to return fire but found I couldn't lift my right arm as I had been hit near the shoulder and the bone was broken. I shouted out to the section commander to debus and take up defensive positions, that I was wounded and to send me the medical orderly. The orderly came, cut off my shirt with a razor blade and bound three or four first field dressings on the wound. I bled badly. I had no contact with the OC or the platoon commander as they were still in the rear.

There were another two or three wounded men and I told the section commander to put them near the vehicle and, if the rebels were to come, to hide themselves. By this time I was in the back of the vehicle and the driver had run away. The vehicle was on the main road. I saw the rebels advancing towards us in two sections, one on the right of the road, the other on the left, by bounds. I had the bayonet on my rifle. They came to the vehicle and inspected it. One of the rebels wore a peaked hat and made a noise "eh" as I pretended to be dead. Had the rebel wanted to use my bayonet on me that would have been that but he passed on doing nothing to me.

Another enemy group came up behind and looked inside the vehicle. I again feigned death. I still wonder how I stayed alive. By then there was so much blood in and on my boots that they had stuck to the vehicle floor and I could not move my feet. It was like wearing gum boots. I thought of my wife whom I had recently brought to the lines.

I stayed there till noon the next day.[2] At last the OC came. We had many wounded and many rebels had been captured. I had not lost consciousness but felt dizzy. We wounded were sent back to the battalion MI Room in Brunei. From there I was sent to a hospital in Brunei, where I do not know. I was prepared to go to Singapore. It was only then that I noticed a pain in my left side and I found I had been wounded there also. That was dressed. At the airport I felt utterly exhausted. I did not know any English but, when I saw a British soldier, I said "Orange, orange" to him and he brought me a cold bottle of orange. After drinking it I could see clearly once more, it revived me so much.

A special flight had been arranged for us wounded and the dead. The dead were wrapped in red cloth and, once in the plane, I was put in the middle of the dead. I thought I'd go that way also. We were taken

---

[2] The MT Cpl, Angatbahadur Rana, confirms that rescue was certainly not before 1100 hours at the earliest.

to the BMH and asked if we had fed. As we had not had any food we were operated on straight away. I am so glad you have let me talk about this. No British officer has ever asked me anything like this before. I regard you as heaven-sent, yes, heaven-sent.

After the operation my wife was brought to see me and wept. I told her not to weep as I was not dead and I could look after her even with a medical pension. I was in hospital for a long time, doing exercises and getting better. I was afraid I'd be sent on pension as I felt the battalion would not want me. The battalion was by then in Hong Kong. As soon as I rejoined I was taken out on the range to see if I could fire my weapon. Yes, I could and did. So I was passed fit and kept on.

I was sent on a CQMS course. I passed and on my return my OC[3] sent for me and said I had to go on a platoon commander's course. I knew him well, and as a friend. I looked after him when he visited Nepal. I kept my stores clean, neat and up-to-date. I worked on them every day. Even when the OC looked in late in the afternoon and asked me why I was not going to play games I told him I still had work to do getting the stores perfect.

I was promoted to Lieutenant (QGO) which surprised me as I thought I'd be going on a CQMS's pension. I was fit enough even though I found lifting heavy loads with my right arm difficult.

Nainabahadur Rai, MM and Bar, 2/7 GR, *turned out to be a hero.*

I was nearly 16 years of age when I enlisted, not as a boy soldier but as a man. After nine months' training I was sent to Kluang and posted to B Company. Soon after that we moved to Blakang Mati in Singapore. In due course we moved from Singapore to Hong Kong in April 1963.

We moved by air to Brunei as reinforcements to 1/2 GR, so it was said. Companies were scattered. B Company was on a small island off the coast called Bahru Bahru. Battalion HQ was at Limbang. We were sent into the jungle but did not find any traces of the enemy although we did hear about a Special Branch contact in Tutong. I, as a rifleman, did not know much about it. The target was Yassin Affendi, the rebel leader, as the other, Azahari, had gone to Indonesia.[4] A Special Branch officer captured a member of Yassin Affendi's ration supply group. B

---

[3] Maj J.J. Mole.
[4] No, he had been killed by 1/2 GR in Brunei town.

Company was sent to investigate about so many enemy in such-and-such a place.

At about 0100 hours on 18 May 1963 we were woken up by shouting to get ready to go on operations. The platoon commanders had an O Group with the company commander, Major D.J. Cutfield, while platoon sergeants fell the rest of us in with full scales of ammunition. I carried an SLR and I hadn't even put my jungle boots on properly when I paraded. We were then shown a model of where we were to go.

At dawn we embarked in boats all driven by officers of the Royal Engineers, lieutenants, captains and a major. It was full daylight by the time we landed. We moved off half an hour later into the hinterland and were put into ambush positions by the platoon commander, in a circle. We were in overgrown rubber which was marshy and it was no place to take up the prone position.

By 1100 hours I was feeling hungry and needed to stretch my legs. I had left camp without cleaning my teeth and had a bad taste in my mouth. I was cleaning them with my finger when I heard firing. The enemy's position was an island in a swamp in which was another island. I learnt that the firing was Special Branch at the enemy camp with a squad of B Company.

I stayed watching my front for a long time. I heard "Catch them" shouted three times but saw nothing. It was quiet after the firing. There was a small track where I was and I walked down it as my legs were restless to a tree to my front. I saw the undergrowth move and thought it was my men coming my way. I was afraid I'd shoot them if I had not applied my safety catch but also afraid that I would miss any enemy if I did not release my safety catch. I moved it on and off several times. The undergrowth moved again but I saw nobody.

I took cover behind the tree and saw four men. Were they rubber tappers or enemy? Then I saw one, dressed in black, who had a pistol on him and a bag of ammunition. Three others also wore black. I now knew I could kill them and at least one would fall to a couple of shots. But the four men disappeared. Then the undergrowth again moved so I had to kill them or I would die. But would I kill my own men on the other side of the enemy as our ambush was circular? I saw the four men talking but could not hear them. There was so much young rubber that I felt I'd only kill one with the first round and the others would hide. I hid my elbow behind the tree trunk so it could not be seen. I kept on changing my stance to get a better shot as they came towards me.

I saw a hat which I used as an aiming point. The four men came up the track towards me and I waited for them. Again they disappeared but soon came into view. I waited for them to come nearer still. They were in single file. From about 15 yards I fired one round and all fell. I went up to inspect the bodies and saw that my one bullet had killed three of them, the first man was hit in the stomach, the second in the chest and the third in the head. I looked at the fourth man who had no eye but also no hole at the back of his head. It was my lucky day.

I saw that the fourth man had spiked his eye out as he fell but I did not know if he was dead or not because he had no hole at the back of his head. I put my rifle to his chest and said "Hands up!" He opened his good eye and I was so startled I flinched and fired my weapon, hitting him in the left thigh.

I shouted out saying I had killed three men and had shot a fourth. The OC, in the distance, shouted "Where? where?" and I answered "Here, here." We shouted like that for some time and eventually the OC and others came on the scene. I had blood on my trousers and my boots. The OC asked the wounded man who he was. He did not answer for three times and then said he was Yassin Affendi. The OC shouted out in joy and slapped me on the back. He got into contact with battalion HQ and was told to keep Yassin Affendi alive at all costs. A helicopter arrived with the CO and the adjutant. Were they pleased! Two of the dead men were the general manager and the training officer.[5] The four, three dead and one wounded, were flown out.

Once back in Brunei I met a senior police officer who said I had taken much trouble and would get something, but what I'd get he didn't say. My CO, Lieutenant Colonel B.F.L. Rooney, told me I'd get an MM, which I did. From the next day R.L. Willis sahib made out a programme for me. I went by helicopter to meet General Walker,[6] the brigadier commanding 51 Brigade, and many others in many places to whom I had to tell my story. I thought the ADC to the general was Chinese and was surprised when he spoke to me in Nepali. I found out that he was Captain Lalbahadur Pun.

We finished that tour by going to Long Semado on the border, then

---

[5] They were the Assistant Secretary General, Party Ra'ayat, the Deputy Military Commander, TNKU, and a captain of TNKU. TNKU was the Tentara Nasional Kalimantan Utara, the North Kalimantan (the Indonesian name for British Borneo) National Army.

[6] DOBOPS.

it was back to Hong Kong. The queen gave me my medal in Buckingham Palace. She was pleased with me. I visited many places in Britain and was given much hospitality.

Back in the battalion I was promoted to lance corporal and sent on an anti-tank course at the JWS. I also learnt the 81mm mortar and how to be an MFC in Hong Kong.

Tejbahadur Gurung MM, 1/2 GR, *continued with his story.*

After my first leave there were fewer and fewer *daku* and as the [Malayan] Emergency came to a close we were sent to Hong Kong. After two years there we went back to Singapore and were called out suddenly to go to Brunei. By then I was in Support Company and attached to A Company. I found myself in Tutong. After that we went to Miri where there was a lot of swamp. We did not meet any enemy. We went back to Brunei town. There was some trouble when a young British officer was found trying to seduce Azahari's wife. He left the battalion very soon after that. My company was put to guard the sultan's bungalow. The sultan did not want any police there. We dug trenches and took up all round defence. The sultan left his bungalow only to pray at his mosque otherwise, except for an occasional visit to see us, he stayed underground. We spent three months there. We were told we were to shoot at any noise at night and on one occasion we did fire – only to find a dead cat.

But there was more to come.

Confrontation in Borneo, 1963–66

Manbahadur Thapa, MM, 1/2 GR, *had this to say.*

I enlisted on 20 November 1959, both as it is a tradition and for the money. After recruit training I was posted to A Company, 1/2 GR, in Burma Lines, Kota Tinggi, Malaya, and after six months I was posted to Support Company and served in the 3-inch Mortar Platoon for five years.

When the Brunei Rebellion occurred in late 1962 I was on leave. I heard that I had been sent a letter telling me to come back but it never came. I thought about the fighting but decided that, as ever, it was a case of living or dying so I was not scared. In 1964 I was promoted as a merit lance corporal.

From Burma Lines we went back to our peacetime location in Singapore, Slim Lines, and later went to Hong Kong. It was then a period of Confrontation between Indonesia and Malaysia and, with A Company, I was sent to the collection of longhouses at Long Jawi, in the Third Division of Sarawak. That was after an attack on the Border Scouts in that area. We were in defence around the longhouses for a week then were flown by helicopter to cut off the enemy who had attacked Long Jawi. We were flown about 40 miles, almost to the Indonesia–Sarawak border. The jungle was alive with prickly rattan and leeches. We didn't meet up with them so returned to Long Jawi. It was back to Kapit, the company base, after that.

I didn't like the longhouses as they were too crowded; as for the bare breasts, after a few days I did not notice them. It was time to go back to Singapore which we did by a boat that rolled a lot, then we flew on to Hong Kong for another six months, when it was back to Borneo again, this time in Sabah at Pensianggan.

In September 1964 we went by helicopter up to near the Indonesian border. I carried the GPMG which had just been issued. Only three men in the company had been trained on it. Once we had crossed the border our target was an Indonesian camp, a platoon position. We had practised the attack on a model. We surrounded the camp and my platoon was at the rear, in a cut-off position. By 1000 hours we were right behind the camp. An Indonesian recce scout first saw us but he was killed but not before shooting the hat off one of our men.

Heavy fire was then opened, including rocket launchers and machine guns. We remained alert. I left my GPMG with the No 2 and went on a local patrol to find out what was happening. I found out nothing and returned to the gun. I fired off a belt of 200 rounds at where I thought the enemy were. I loaded another belt. As I was loading a bomb exploded above us, either an Indonesian 60mm mortar bomb or my own platoon's 3.5-inch rocket launcher. I and four others were wounded. I was wounded in the right rear shoulder but as I was leaning over the GPMG some of the bits of metal were deflected.

I was unconscious for a moment. My friend put on a first field dressing. One soldier had his left upper leg muscle removed. I gave my GPMG to the No 2 and took his rifle, an AR15. My platoon sergeant wept and told me not to say it was our own round that had caused the damage by a tree burst. All the other soldiers had disappeared by this time. We were only four men by then. I was covered in blood, all down one side and in my boot. Six of the enemy had been killed and the rest of them had run away.

We moved off, I in front, and met the OC, Major Willoughby. As I reached a small river the rest of my platoon caught me up. The OC asked me if my wound was caused by the enemy or by our own troops and, as told to, I said it was enemy fire. The OC said that was the story we should stick to.

An SAS sergeant and an RAMC sergeant major put on a shell dressing. The OC ordered a helicopter, against the better judgement of battalion HQ. A bearded RN helicopter pilot flew in from over the border and flew us wounded to Brunei, Labuan. I signed a certificate with my left hand for an operation, which took place, then was flown to Singapore for another operation.

Thirty-five days later I was back in Brunei and had another week in Pensianggan. I was given the task of marshalling the helicopters. So it was back to Hong Kong for another six months before it was our turn again to go back to Pensianggan. I was given the job of mess corporal in the warrant officers' and sergeants' mess.

I trained on the 2-inch mortar for another cross-border operation and was flown into the same LP, in an area known as The Gap. The enemy were in two places, over the border on the other side of a hill. The OC, Major Duffell, took the left-hand position and the Company 2IC, Gurkha Captain Bhojbahadur, the right-hand position. I was on his right flank. At 0730 hours we heard the enemy making a noise – mess tins – on the other side of the river. We fed on biscuits and did not brew up. There were no enemy on the left flank, only on our right flank. As the 2-inch mortarman I did not go on a recce on the other side of the river but on this side. But before it was complete we opened fire on the enemy on the signal of the OC. We killed five of them. They were unprepared. I saw their rifles all stacked. Later the enemy fired back on both fronts. I gave my 2-inch mortar to my No 2 and took his rifle and went to encourage the troops and to direct their fire. By then the heavy firing had stopped and it was only light stuff. I opened fire as a precaution and probably hit where the enemy had stacked the ammunition. We searched their camp. I also directed the 3.5-inch rocket launcher fire. I found a Tommy gun that had been firing at me had one of my projectiles stuck in the centre of its barrel. That was really surprising.

I was awarded an MM for a combination of what I managed when wounded and for controlling the battle when the OC was not there, doing more than was expected of me, arranging fire positions for instance by using my kukri to cut the buttress roots of trees to get better fire positions.

One time the OC approached and the rest of the platoon said it was the enemy coming back but I said no, it was not. In fact we did fire on each other but caused no damage. Our men flapped. As the other side was firing, four of us tried to hide behind the same tree, arses wobbling as we burrowed for safety.

Hitbahadur Bhujel, 1/10 GR, *started at the beginning.*

As I was on my way back from visiting my aunt one *Dashera* I met someone who led me to the *Galla Wala* and I was enlisted on 27 November 1959. I did not know any English but I could write Nepali. There were about 1,600 recruits and our training lasted for 11 months. After passing out I was posted to the 3-inch Mortar Platoon of Support Company, at Majedee Barracks in Johore Bahru. My only jungle operational experience in Malaya was in the Grik area in the north but we did not make contact with any enemy. In 1963 we went to Sungei Udang camp near Malacca and relieved 2/7 GR. The drinking water was coloured red and not pleasant to drink but we managed to get it made normal.

In 1965 we were at Sungei Tenggan, in the Second Division of Sarawak. It was during *Dashera* and I was in the Support Platoon attached to D Company, commanded by Major Philips. By now our mortars were of 81mm calibre. I had broken my finger and a few other sick men were also in base and had not gone on operations with the others.

At a place called Selepong, not all that far away, Indonesians appeared and we were the only troops available to go and deal with them. We were led by Sergeant Birdhoj. I was armed with an SLR and had one man in front of me, 21148683. On our way to the Border Scout camp at Selepong we went through a rubber estate and I saw an Indonesian mortar bomb lying on the ground. 8683 picked it up but I told him to be careful. At the Border Scout camp was a 56-year-old in civilian clothing armed with a No 5 [Lee-Enfield] rifle and a grenade. He said that the enemy had made a reconnaissance of the Border Scout camp and he had fired at one of them but, although he had hit him, he did not think he was dead. It was the noise of that shooting that had alerted the commander in the Border Scout camp to alert us. It was thought that there were 35 enemy in the area.

We followed up blood trails and we found the wounded enemy. He was weak and tired but he had waited with a primed grenade in each hand, with the pins removed. One of our men grabbed both his hands, wrested the grenades out of his grip and threw them away. They exploded harmlessly. He looked like a commander and was taken back to the camp.

About a mile away we found a lot of '44 pattern packs full of pistols and ammunition. 8683 saw them and pointed them out. I said that there were enemy in the area and he asked me how I knew. I saw three enemy come into view to collect the packs and the corporal with us said he thought they were our men. I told him to be quiet but the corporal asked them who they were and they ran away. Two of us chased them and the rest were left behind. The enemy fired at us and we stayed still. One man, going forward, got caught up in some thorns. As he pushed his way forward he fell. I, following him, also fell near the roots of a big tree just as machine-gun fire was opened up on us and hit the tree trunk just above my head, tearing the bark off.

I returned fire at the one man I saw. He was firing an LMG and I hit him. He rolled over. By then I had regained all my confidence, having been a bit scared when the firing started. I saw an officer in a tree who was firing at me and I saw him fall as I shot him.

The platoon commander then caught up with us and I quickly briefed him. With him we were five and the enemy were many. "Whatever happens, if we die we die," he said. He told us we'd all open fire together and, as the Indonesians probably understood English, he would shout out fire orders, which he did. "3 Platoon left. 1 Platoon right. 2 Platoon, charge!" Our weapons were SMGs and SLRs. We fired all at once and they ran away. I said that there were dead men in front of us. We found one corpse and followed up another by tracking his blood. We caught him up and saw he was badly wounded. In his own language he asked us to kill him quickly. At that moment our signaller arrived but without his head set. The corporal caught us up and said we should kill the wounded man. I said no, that would be a sin to kill a wounded man but the corporal shot and killed him. We found a lot of '35 pattern packs, also full of US-type pistols and ammunition.

By then the Border Scouts from Selepong had come to find out what was happening and to tell us that the commander had ordered a helicopter. We said that we had killed three enemy and we were told to collect the bodies, the weapons and the ammunition. This we did, except for the ammunition which was too much and too heavy for us. We only evacuated two bodies that day as we had not found the third one which was recovered the next day. The OC and the police came and I told them all that had happened. We were sent back to camp and told that we could drink as much rum as we wished for free. We all slept well that night.

Next day the OC wrote a citation for a decoration but was told the name of a man who had not left camp. The man who was next to me said that I was the man who had done the killing, no one else. My name did not go forward and no one got a medal. The man who had claimed he was the killer of the enemy, a sergeant, had already reported he wanted to leave the army but he left as a Gurkha Lieutenant.

The battalion moved to Kalabakan in Sabah in 1963 and B Company's 5 Platoon attacked and killed 13 enemy with the loss of two of our men dead. I did not use my mortars in that engagement. I was in that area for six months. We heard that a Malay Regiment unit had neglected to post sentries and had lost 19 or so men in an Indonesian attack. We knew they were careless soldiers.

Nainabahadur Rai, MM and Bar, 2/7 GR, *continued his tale.*

In 1966 I was again in Limbang. We operated as a mortar section in support of rifle companies. It was easy – we moved by vehicle mostly and didn't have to go into the jungle. There were reports of six enemy and the mortar platoon had to go with C Company. Although I should have carried an AR15 I preferred to carry an SLR. One section went with each platoon. I met up with the OC, Captain Maniparsad Rai. We left at dusk and walked all night, reaching the enemy area at dawn. We had an O Group while the men brewed tea. The OC made a model of our target on the ground. I found myself on the very left edge of the company as we moved off in line, 7 Platoon on the right, 8 in the centre and 9 on the left. I carried a radio with me.

As we moved forward I saw some very recent tracks left by three people in the swampy ground. I stopped my section and reported it to my platoon commander. Was I to go on the original bearing given to me or to follow the tracks? I was told to move on the original bearing and not to follow them as they led out of my area. I advanced and the enemy tracks came back into my area and I reported that. The platoon commander did not tell the company commander and I was still not allowed to follow up. I felt it was dangerous to move forward as we were in almost open terrain with lots of fern. I had an attack of gooseflesh as I knew we'd meet the enemy, but how and where was uncertain. I wouldn't advance as I knew it was too big a risk and I had to follow the tracks. On the radio I was told I could but not to kill anyone.

I took my section off but beforehand I scraped a model on the ground for my section. We moved off by bounds and I was happier and lost my gooseflesh. We moved into a hollow and lost the tracks as the enemy had hidden them but we met them again as we moved up the higher ground on the other side. There was a small tree that had been uprooted as it was pulled on to help the enemy up the slope so I knew that the enemy were in front. There was more fern and one of the soldiers, Ganesh, saw what he thought was a tree stump and went to investigate and shouted out that it was one of the enemy. I told him not to fire.

I saw something flash on the enemy's back and thought it was the top of his water bottle but no, it was the handle of his knife. I went over and told him to put his hands up. He was a short man and, as he stood up, he took out his pistol so Ganesh shot him from about 25 yards away. I shouted to Ganesh to stop firing. The man looked up at me and said something about "fucking Gurkha" so I told Ganesh to fire one round and kill him. This he did.

I reported on the radio that Ganesh had killed one enemy and we were advancing to look for more. I told two of my men to stay near the corpse and I took the rest to look around the place, in a ravine and on some high ground. We found nothing and returned to the other two men. Now it so happened that another three enemy were lurking in the undergrowth and my two men nearly trod on them. Opening fire they shot the heads of the enemy, firing 20 rounds each. Again I shouted to cease firing. None of the enemy could be recognized, having no heads left.

I shouted out that we had killed three more enemy and were returning to our original bearing. When we all joined up I learnt that 7 and 8 Platoon had captured one enemy each so all of the six were accounted for.

The OC's radio operator reported to battalion HQ that I had killed four enemy. The CO came in a helicopter and congratulated me. We used branches and rifle slings to carry out the corpses to near a rubber estate and the helicopter took them away. The company 2IC mentioned something about an MM for me and I told him I had one already. That contact occurred on 3 June 1966 and in the *London Gazette* of July 1967 I was awarded another one.

The queen sent for me again. She was very happy. I told her that I had been one of her escort when she went shooting on an elephant after King Mahendra had died and that I had been her guide when she went to the house of the late king's mother. Queen Elizabeth was surprised to learn that.

You ask me about being Man of the Year.[7] That was after my first MM. Henderson sahib took me around many places. We had a meal in the Savoy Hotel. Sir Winston Churchill was there and he embraced me. He talked with me, using Henderson sahib as an interpreter. I saw Churchill sahib rubbing his right thumb in the palm of his left hand as though he were kneading chewing tobacco. I asked why that was and was told that that is where he got his thoughts from.

Nainabahadur Rai retired as an Honorary Lieutenant (QGO).

Kesar Pun, 2/6 GR, GIPC, *did not see action during the Malayan Emergency but had some interesting slants on his service before Borneo.*

I was enlisted on 21 October 1948 at Lehra. I was uneducated, the eighth child, and had spent most of my time up with the cattle in the

---

[7] Man of the Year: the British Council for Rehabilitation of the Disabled honoured those who had distinguished themselves in the preceding year. The services nominated a man each.

hill byres and knew nothing about any farming or house tasks. I went to join the army partly through peer pressure and partly because the *Galla Wala* had given me 2 rupees as a bond. My family did not let me go but I ran away. That first night an elder sister came and tried to persuade me to change my mind but I declined to go back home. I was illiterate and had envied the returning leave men, wearing smart clothes, so I wanted to be like them. I had no long-term thoughts. Once in the army I made new friends and only thought of my village and family when talk turned to Nepal.

We were a week in Lehra where we did some physical training but our real training only started in 6 GRTW in Sungei Patani. Then there was no war. On weekends we'd have singsongs and "village dancing". We all had to perform but, as I could not dance, I was let off and remained part of the chorus, clapping my hands in time with the rhythm and singing. Four months later we were sent to Hong Kong and finished the rest of our training, another four months, at San Wai camp. We had our Passing Out Parade there.

In those days there were no trees in Hong Kong and the houses in the New Territories near our camp were small. Even in that short time I noticed differences in the Hong Kong Chinese and the Malayan Chinese. For instance, the New Territories Chinese never got off the road for any vehicle, however much horns were blown. They only ran to the sides when the tanks moved along the road with a great clatter.

After recruit training I joined the Pipes and Drums. In 1953 I went to England for the queen's coronation. We were completely exhausted at the end of that day having marched smartly for 13 miles, playing our pipes for much of the time. Our feet! The next day we went to the palace to receive our Coronation Medals. The Contingent Commander, Lieutenant Colonel Murray of 7 GR, was given his medal by the queen and came to give us ours after that. After that we marched past the queen who took our salute. All COs and GMs also got the Coronation Medal.

The Pipes and Drums stayed on for an extra three months to take part in the Edinburgh tattoo. Everybody was so kind to us. Later on, in 1956, when I went back to do a six-months' Pipe Majors' course and again in 1958 for a six-months' Pipe Instructors' course in Lanark, based with the Cameronians of the Lowland Brigade, people did not make such a fuss of us as they were more used to Gurkhas by then. In 1958 I also took part in the Earls Court tattoo. A member of the royal family came every night and we had to welcome that person outside the tattoo hall.

Back in Ipoh, still a corporal, I fell and broke two teeth which put me off piping. I was all right playing with the others but, as a potential pipe major, I was afraid I would not be a good soloist. I was only allowed to leave the Pipes and Drums when promoted to sergeant and then I became the Intelligence sergeant.

In 1964 the battalion went to Borneo and I was sent to Bareo and put in charge of the aircraft tasking. This went on for six months. By then I had done a platoon commander's course and went to a rifle company as platoon sergeant. I only ever had one contact and that happened when the OC, Major Robinson, and the 2IC, Captain (QGO) Mitrabahadur, went to take rations to an OP. On the way back we made camp and at 1800 hours I and another sergeant, now dead, were sent on patrol to a place where a British soldier had been killed. Indonesian smoke was smelt so we did not go any farther forward but went back to the evening base.

Next morning, at 0500 hours, that sergeant and another man went to lay an ambush. I stayed behind in charge of the cooking. At 0630 hours heavy firing broke out and lasted for 30 minutes. The ambush had killed one Indonesian and slightly wounded another. The ambush party returned. We opened fire with our mortars and one bomb burst in the trees above us and wounded one man in the head. He was later evacuated by helicopter. Our mortars did a lot of damage to the Indonesians and they broke contact. There was a lot of blood not far from the camp when I went out later, sent on a recce to the ridge line; one GOR then another declined to go, so I went alone. I told them to give me covering fire. In our old OP at the top of the hill were more Indonesians. We both opened fire and the contact was inconclusive.

By early 1965 I had been passed over for Gurkha Lieutenant by one junior to me. I was still a sergeant. The OC called me over and said that there was a vacancy for a WO2 in GIPC so I should go and be a parachutist. So I did my basic parachute course with Major J.P. Cross in Singapore. Our GIPC base was in Kluang. We learnt many new and interesting aspects of war. Para company work and infantry work were different and I found para company work of more value for battle and commando-type work. After our training we took it for granted that we were at a higher level than other soldiers.

As far as para descents were concerned, I was more frightened by the "fan" during ground training than my first jump. Only after our first jump did we know what it was all about. Later, after about 20 jumps, including two at night, jumps became as normal as having our meals. However, I did find the night jumps harder than the daytime ones as we were never sure where exactly we were as we guided ourselves towards the lights on the DZ. We never jumped operationally but did drop on exercises, once, "against" 2/2 GR, at Kota Belud, Sabah, after a six-hour flight from Singapore.

In 1971, when GIPC was disbanded, I was made redundant by my parent unit, 6 GR. I was happy to go, with my 23 years' service counting as 28 – so getting a full Gurkha Captain's pension – as well as a £1,500 gratuity, that was fine by me.

Singabahadur Gurung, 1/6 GR, GIPC, 2/2 GR, *continued with his story.*

Indonesian Confrontation started and, stopping off in Singapore, we went to Lundu, in the First Division of Sarawak, Borneo. The CO, Lieutenant Colonel Hickey, told me I had to go to the GIPC. I was a lance corporal. Major Philips was the OC. He sent us out on five-man patrols, one commander, one radio operator, one medical assistant and two assault pioneers. We were sent out for between 45 and 60 days at a time. We would be infiltrated by helicopter, sometimes flying for 45 minutes, to near the border. It was dangerous. Our job was to observe enemy movement on or near the border but not to become involved in a fire-fight if we could avoid it.

We communicated with base by the use of one-time letter pads, opening our sets only once a day, generally in the late afternoon. We had a format to follow, I forget the various headings, but we had to report where we'd been, what we'd done and if we had anything to report of the enemy.

Once my patrol dumped our rations and, only taking three days' food with us, went to investigate some area. On our return we found that wild pigs had eaten or spoiled most of our dump. There was no ghee or pulse at all. We reported it and were told we could not be re-supplied until the due date, 14 days hence. We survived; having made sure that there were no enemy around, we went fishing with our mosquito nets and found edible jungle produce. One man, Kalbahadur

Gurung, became very ill with a temperature of 104 degrees [Fahrenheit]. We were unable to evacuate him by helicopter and had to make do with what was in our medical pack. He was in a bad way: "I've had no leave for four years and here I am, dying in the jungle," he said. I tried to explain the situation to him. Army life has its hard times and its easy times. He recovered. After 14 days we had our airdrop. As it was so heavy we only carried that which we knew we would need. For instance, we found we did not need all the solid fuel we were issued with. There was always some issue rum and we would pay for an extra bottle of rum, known as LS from the initials on the label.

At that time we heard a rumour that 1/2 GR and 2/2 GR were going to be disbanded but the GIPC was to be retained. We returned to Kluang and the company commanders changed. Major J.P. Cross took over and I was promoted to corporal. After retraining with a lot of new reinforcements we went back to Borneo, this time being based in Brunei, at the "Haunted House" not far from the sultan's palace. That was our base for all our four-month tours. Twice we handed over to the Guards Independent Parachute Company and once to a company of the Parachute Regiment. When Major Philips had been OC we had been in the Third Division, based on Sibu. Tactics were different now as we were sent across the border. However, we were never out for such long periods so there was less tension than before. Also we had more confidence and company morale was higher.

On one operation I had to go across the border from Ba Kelalan in Sarawak to see if the enemy were in a certain village. It took two days to get there. There was an enemy helicopter pad there and we moved south to the village to be looked at. A dog barked. We crossed a track, observed the village but saw no enemy. After we had got back into Borneo, my task was to lead B Company, 1/6 GR, over to attack that village if there were any enemy there, as it was thought that there would be. The men were surprised that we had gone all that way with only five men. In the event, there was no enemy in the village.

On another occasion an enemy force of around 30 to 40 came over the border, in Sabah near Long Pa Sia, and attacked a wooden police post. On a follow-up operation my patrol only missed them by half an hour. They had gone along a river and we came from uphill. We went back uphill, climbed a tree for better radio contact and reported back to HQ.

Even later, I had to take four patrols from Ba Kelalan over the border, in front of 1/6 GR's position. Once we were over we were to split into two parties of two patrols and, a little farther on, those two parties were to split into single patrols, each with its own mission. The OC, the CO, Lieutenant Colonel Hickey, and the brigadier came to see us off. In front of me the brigadier turned to the CO and asked him if he was happy in sending such a large group over the border commanded by a corporal. I heard him say that, had it been a British unit, he would have insisted that the commander had to be a lieutenant. The CO said that he was happy if the OC was happy and the OC said he was. The brigadier then turned to me and said, "Corporal, are you happy?" and I told him I was.

And then there was another occasion when I took my patrol over the border, again in front of that company of 1/6 GR. I made a recce, came back and led the company across. Once over the border the man behind me, a captain of the artillery, was talking into his radio set, for "silent registration" as he called it. We were all greatly surprised when two 105mm shells from our own gun at Ba Kelalan landed 25 yards in front of us. The OC told me later that the Indonesians had somehow broken the radio code and had issued orders to fire the gun from their position their side of the border.

The OC took four patrols over the border to see if the Indonesians were using a track that ran parallel with the border and mounting attacks from anywhere along it. Two of the patrols had one task, after which they were to lay a Claymore mine[8] ambush in front of their position and the nearest known enemy position at a place called Waylaya, maybe three miles away to the west. It was thought to have around 300 men of the Para-Commando unit, RPKAD, there. Our patrol's task was to recce a track off to the east to see if it had been recently used. Unfortunately the OC fell off quite a high rock and bent his rifle. I could see it was no better than a stick. Just before the patrols split, we ran into a local who could easily give notice to the Indonesians of our presence. The OC could talk that man's language, Iban, and told us that he had told the man that we were going some place where we were not, as a deception plan.

We split and our patrol searched for telltale signs of movement. On our way back we found that there were, in fact, two tracks, not one as marked on the map. We passed a longhouse but, because it was getting late and we had not come across the other group, we did not investigate

---

[8] A particularly lethal contraption that was mounted on a tree or similar object and fired a blast of pellets shotgun-fashion, but much more powerfully.

it. By then it was obvious that we had gone beyond the ambush and were between it and Waylaya. If we turned back to look for it we could walk into our own ambush. We were following the track that led us through a thick band of bracken to a wooded area at the top of a ridge. I saw the OC suddenly turn round at the first tree and look at its base. He beckoned me over. "Singé," he said. "Look at what has been scratched at the base of the tree by a soldier in ambush and who would have covered all our movement through that bracken." I looked and saw the initials RPKAD with the previous day's date.

We had to make base soon. It was dark by the time we found some water, cooked a meal and settled for the night. We guessed our position on the map and the OC said he had sent a message for the other group to come there early next morning. When it was light we saw we were in the only patch of trees in an expanse of long grass, covered with masses of buffaloes. Two hours after the others should have arrived they had not appeared and I suggested to the OC that he make a monkey or a cuckoo noise with his hands. This he did and a few minutes later the others came. We were all most relieved. The map was so inaccurate that we would not have found each other without that noise, which, in fact, was what they were waiting for.

As we moved back to the border we went to investigate that house and found some old people in it but no enemy. An old crone went up to the OC and stroked his cheeks; we were amused but he was embarrassed. They gave us a banana and some warm peanuts to eat. Outside one of the sentries reported he had seen an enemy soldier slip away after we had entered the longhouse. We left them, saw a place where 1/2 GR had had a battle, the OC climbed a tree and sketched the place and then we quickly moved away to the border. We climbed up a hill and below us an Indonesian helicopter, escorted by a fighter aeroplane, came looking for us. The OC said he did not know if it had been our radio call that had been intercepted or the man we had met who had given our presence away. We were all happy to get back over the border next day.

The OC kept up all happy with his smiles and jokes. We never felt tired at the end of a hard day when he talked to us like one of our own, working just as hard as we did. We never had to go 14 days without rations or not be able to evacuate a sick man as had been the case before he came to the company.

Our last job was to act as demonstration troops and exercise enemy for courses held in the JWS. J.P. Cross sahib now commanded JWS and Major Niven was OC of GIPC. By then I was a Gurkha Lieutenant. Major Niven called me over and said that GIPC was to disband and what did I want to do. I said that if I could not rejoin 6 GR I'd go on pension. Neither happened and I was posted to 2/2 GR as a platoon commander. I was promoted to Gurkha Captain and put in charge of the families. As the battalion was to go to England without the families, it was a very big job. I handed over the family lines to 10 GR after I had arranged for all the families to be returned to Nepal.

I went on pension in 1977. British Army life is good, especially the management.

Hombahadur Thapa, 2/2 GR, *found the worst parts of work in Malaya …*

were the difficult terrain, mud and the thorns that kept one back. The operations finished in 1958 when we went to Hong Kong.

In 1964 we went to Borneo. I was in Support Company, renamed E Company, and we were in Sungei Tenggan in the Second Division of Sarawak. It was not far from the border with Indonesia. One morning at 0500 hours we left to set an ambush near the border.[9] We were 22 and we carried five LMGs. We reached where the artillery, 105mm, was and the gunner officer told us we were too late to go up to the border that day. Better to stay there, have a meal and move out early the next morning. "I'll take you the first two map squares," he said. Early next morning we had a drink of tea and moved off. I was doubtful so I asked the officer what would happen if help were needed. He told me not to worry as that was why he was there. "Hurry up and come back. If you want support, be quick in asking for it," he said.

---

[9] 'The area was Batu Lintang in the 2nd Division of Borneo and an ambush was set up on the Borneo side of the border, not in Indonesia. Information had been received that some Indonesian guerillas were to cross the border that night to attend a cock fight in a Sarawak longhouse adjacent to the border. In the event a company of Indonesian troops came in and were duly ambushed. The ambush stood its ground and inflicted significant casualties. My platoon and the rest of the company were helicoptered in at first light the next morning and we picked up nine Indonesian dead with signs of many more wounded and dragged away.'
Brig C.J. Bullock, OBE, MC, in a letter of 14 September 1999.

We moved all day and only reached our objective at about 1800 hours. I saw a man and a woman carrying vegetables. I asked the woman if there were any enemy around but she did not answer. The man did, saying there were many, and immediately fell to the ground. Through binoculars we saw about 300 Indonesians in and around a school, some eating biscuits, and on the far side three mortar base-plate positions. There were LMGs on fixed lines. Their sentry was slow to see us but when he did we found that the enemy were already in ambush positions in a rubber estate.

The commander said there were too many enemy to be taken on and we had to leave as quickly as possible. By that time the enemy had seen us and started to chase us. We ran uphill, clutching on to the rubber trees for support. The enemy cried out, "Hullo Jakarta, hullo Jakarta, the enemy are in front of us," which I heard and understood. They came towards us.

My LMG 1 was so slow that Rifleman Reshambahadur, who had won an MM by then and later an m-i-d, took the gun off him and fired at the enemy. I and another joined in. The enemy shouted out in pain as the bullets hit them and nine were killed but the others came on.

The platoon commander first ordered us to go 200 yards forward and then to go 200 yards back but it was too dark to move, although there was a little light left. We stayed where we were. On the radio we heard the gunner officer tell us not to be afraid and he would fire two or three rounds all around us every five minutes or so. We also kept up fire to keep the enemy away. Remember, we were only 22 and I was only a rifleman. Even so, I stood up and for about five or six minutes shouted out fire orders for five companies as I fired. "1 Company, left side, 2 Company, right side, 3 Company, front side," like that. That kept the enemy from closing in on us.

Then the aerial of our set was shot off. I told the 2-inch mortarman to fire but he said how could he in those trees. I took the weapon myself and held the mortar straight and fired some bombs that way. They all burst but still the enemy came on. It was almost dark by then. I took out a grenade, still holding my rifle, and pulled out the pin with my teeth, then threw it at the enemy.

It was just light enough to see that the enemy had put their hats on sticks for us to fire at while they crawled around towards us to a flank. I saw them and killed three of them. By then it was about 1900 hours.

That night a helicopter tried to land but was unsuccessful. Next morning the gunner officer and the OC, Major Laws, came in and congratulated the platoon commander, Lieutenant (QGO) Nandaraj Gurung, who won an MC.

We got back. I was made a lance corporal for that but did not get a *bahaduri* and even my pension is a rifleman's.

Bhimraj Gurung, 2/6 GR, GIPC, *continued with his narrative.*

When Confrontation started 2/6 GR was sent to Seria in Brunei but we operated near the border with Indonesia. I had no idea why there was a war there. All I knew was that it was my job to kill the enemy. Our platoon had one bad incident. The platoon sergeant had been in the Signal Platoon for a long time and had little experience and a potential Sandhurst cadet, Lance Corporal Lachhimbahadur Gurung, son of Major (QGO) Dambar, was careless and inexperienced. We were attacked by the enemy and Lachhimbahadur had his head cut off while the platoon sergeant had his arm severed. The enemy escaped with both and we never got the bits back. We could not find the LP that had been reported and had to make a new one, which took some time.[10]

I only met the Indonesians twice and the other time was a chance encounter with no casualties either side.

Then we were told that there were some vacancies in the GIPC. I was tired with rifle company work and those junior to me had been promoted over my head. I volunteered and was accepted. On the first jump I hurt my foot. I reported sick and the doctor said I was all right. An RAF parachute instructor told me not to be afraid and even the women in England were parachutists. I took him to mean I was less than a woman and determined to pass the course. So I tried very hard, passed and, after eight jumps, got my wings.

The training in GIPC was more interesting than work in the battalion had been and the OC, Major J.P. Cross, made conditions, in and out of the camp, happy, convenient and much more personal with us. All the arrangements were efficient and all the soldiers were happy. One day

---

[10] A party of Royal Engineers was detailed to make a number of LPs in the border area but only cut them quite a way in the rear. They gave the grid references as being on the border, some two or three map squares from where they had, in fact, been made. This was told me by a Gurkha Engineers sapper who accompanied the Royal Engineer team.

he called me over and said that I was the oldest rifleman in the company and he was the oldest anyway, so why not us two old men be together, I as his batman. This I agreed to. One Sunday morning, there was some pilfering in the lines and the OC had two shirts stolen when he was playing basketball and I thought I'd be blamed. There had been other thefts and the culprit could not be found. The OC arranged that a Tamil boy medium be put in a trance and asked to find out where the stolen kit was. And it was found. Which other OC anywhere would have thought of that?

One time in Sarawak the OC and I went to liaise with a Police Field Force company. We spent two nights in a place infested with small sand flies. I took the OC's mosquito net but not my own and had hardly a wink of sleep that night. Next morning the OC asked me where my mosquito net was and I told him I'd not brought it. He said that I would not have had a good night's sleep and I agreed. He told me to find some chillis, cut them lengthwise and hang them around my head that night. This I did and the sand flies, mosquitoes and all other bugs kept away from me because of the pungent smell of the chillis. I had a wonderful sleep!

I left the army at the end of 1966, with 15 years' service, the last two in the GIPC. I'd have served there much longer if I had had the chance.

Rambahadur Limbu, VC, MVO, 2/10 GR, *told his story.*

My father, a wartime soldier with four years' service who had been wounded, died when I was eight years old. He had taught me how to read and write Nepali on a slate and I would practise when I was overseeing the cattle in the byre. The *Galla Wala* contacted me and told me that service in the British Army was good and I should contact him at a certain place at a certain time. It was better not to tell one's parents about being recruited as it meant many houses would go short-handed in the fields. After I had married my mother told me I was on no account to be a soldier.

On 21 November 1957 I enlisted, at the age of 22. There were 22 others, including two going for boys' service and my younger brother. Only 21 reached Dharan as one was the son of the *Galla Wala*'s brother and, were he taken from home, the *Galla Wala* would not be welcome there again. We had been told to say our ages were 17 so both I and my brother said we were 17. A clerk checking up asked if we were from the same father and we said we were. I therefore put my age up to 18. My brother, who became ill on the journey, failed his medical examination and returned with the *Galla Wala*.

After two days in Dharan we went over to the western depot, Paklihawa, where the British doctor spoke in Rai to the Rais and in Limbu to the Limbus. After being accepted and taught how to put on our uniform, we moved down into India and went to Gorakhpur for our X-Rays. We staged in Calcutta, embarked on SS *Santhia* and went over to Malaya, staying in Rangoon for a day where we were allowed to go on to the quay for some exercise.

Training in Sungei Patani started after we had been there for a week. That first week we were shown around the place. The weaker lads were given extra milk. We were only allowed one mess tin full of rice and when we found we were still hungry we would go back for a second helping, having washed our mess tins first as though we had not been there before. Once the cooks started to recognize us we took our first lot of rice bareheaded and put our hats on for the second time round. The cooks soon rumbled to that ruse also.

After our evening meal at 1800 hours we would have company roll call, then a platoon lecture, then a section lecture that sometimes lasted till 2200 hours. I joined 2/10 GR in September 1958 and was posted to C Company. By 1965 I was a lance corporal commanding 2 Section of 7 Platoon. [By 1966] I had nine years' service and had my wife in the family lines with an infant son. We went over to Sarawak and took over from 1/10 GR in Serian camp. Soon afterwards, with seven days' rations, we crossed the border from the Bau district into Indonesia and made for the area of Gunong Kepai, which we called Hilltop. Others had been there before. First of all we made a recce of the enemy camp for three days. The countryside was steep and there was a strong enemy platoon on the top. The camp was well fortified with walls of felled trees, trenches and sentries.

On the fourth day we went back to the company base and the company commander told battalion HQ that the recce was over and that he was about to put in the attack as already planned. The 105mm artillery was ready. A sand model was made and we were all briefed in detail. That night I had a bad dream and woke up worried. I heard the noise of a bird, three times, a different sort of noise from usual, a sad noise. I felt that was a bad omen and I had to be especially alert during the operation. Next morning we rose at 0300 hours, washed our faces, prepared some tea in an out-of-the-way place and drank it before the water had boiled. We put some biscuits into our pouches and checked we had our full scale of ammunition. The LMG 1, a strong and experienced man, did not want any tea. He looked pale and spoke in a small voice as though his spirit had already left him. I tried to cheer him up as we moved off at 0400 hours.

I was in front, parting the undergrowth as I went and, using scissors [*sic*], cut the vines that got in the way. We were some 150 men strong. We got near the enemy camp. It was still dark. As we climbed up to the first lot of felled trees the LMG 1, in a small voice, asked me why we were always in front. "Why?" He sighed as though he was already defeated. As he was the strongest man there I was amazed. I told him that we were in front because we were the most trusted and were the best in the company. "Don't worry. On!"

On we went until we were about 30 yards from the enemy and we saw their mosquito nets. They were still asleep.[11] The OC stopped us and I heard the platoon commander talking on the radio. Why had we stopped? Was it because the enemy were too strong for us? I only heard the platoon commander, Lieutenant (QGO) Purnasing Limbu, say: "No sahib, we have reached as far as this, now it's on and kill them." 9 Platoon was to give covering fire with all the company GPMGs. These had only recently arrived in the battalion. The other two platoons had Bren guns. 8 Platoon was on the right and 7 Platoon on the left. An observation post for the 105mm artillery was up a high tree 500 metres behind us. They were ready to fire.

One of the enemy woke up and, with his rifle slung, walked towards us as we were crawling towards the camp. He came near but did not see us. He had a piss and took his rifle off his shoulder as though he had seen us. We opened fire and killed him. Then 9 Platoon started with the covering fire and we moved forwards. I needed to keep in touch with the sections to left and right of me, one of 8 Platoon and of my own 7 Platoon. But we did not see anyone to right or left and we were near the enemy trenches.

The man on my right was wounded, one of two new riflemen. The LMG 1 and 2 were on my left. Enemy fire then hit the LMG 1 in the stomach and his guts fell out. His arm was also shot off above the elbow. He was still alive and gave his gun to the Gun 2. I put on a first

---

[11] Other narratives give the time of the attack as in the afternoon.

field dressing but it took quite some time to get it out of its case as it was new and I had neglected to tear it open in readiness. Then the LMG had a stoppage. Gun 2 took the magazine off and changed it. As he was doing this I told him not to raise his head but he did and was shot in the forehead. He managed to say, *"Aiya, ustad,*[12] a bullet ..." and died. He fell on top of me.

I did not know where the next enemy trench was and the enemy were firing at us. I took out a grenade and pulled the pin out with my teeth and threw it. It hit a tree and rolled back quickly on the slippery earth, towards us. I told the others to keep their heads down but I had to watch it. It slipped out of sight down the hill and exploded in a group of Indonesians who were moving round to infiltrate us. I threw more onto them and firing eased. I paid attention to the wounded man. He said, and I can never forget it, *"Ustad,* I won't live, please kill me." I told him I was about to rescue him and detailed the other two to stay there and give me covering fire while I went back to get help. I saw my platoon commander down below and shouted to him: "Gun 2 dead, Gun 1 wounded. Come and help," but no one came so I went back to my section, crawled up to Gun 1 and brought him back. He was heavy and it was difficult. I went back a hundred yards to the first of the felled trees. He wanted water. I told him I'd come back and give him some then I went back and brought the Gun 2 back. He was lighter and so it was easier. My hand was cut by the jutting bone of the broken arm of the wounded man but I only found that out later.

I did all that on my own. I saw a lot of dead enemy where we had fired before. The third time I went back and cleared the whole area then withdrew the rest of my men and the LMG. I called for help but no one came. I went to where I had left the wounded man by the felled trees and tried to get him over them but I couldn't. I had put my rifle to one side while I tried to get him over and it was then that the OC came forward. He asked me about the weapons, including my rifle, and I said all weapons were accounted for. While the medical orderly was coming forward the wounded man died.

It was time to get out of it. I later learnt that the artillery was five minutes slow in opening fire because of a radio fault. Three others were wounded from other sections.

---

[12] *Ustad,* a title of respect used to NCOs in units recruited in eastern Nepal. In western units the equivalent is *Guruji.*

When we got back on the flatter ground the artillery was still firing. That night I dug a trench and we waited where we were. The OC told us to eat but there were only biscuits which I ate. A helicopter could not come at night for the other wounded but a party came from the rear and carried them out all night using torches. They saved their lives.

My *jori* kept away from me that night and next morning when it was light I looked at the LMG and saw it was covered in blood but I had no idea about myself. I made my own tea with what was left of my water bottle water but no one came to sit near me. I wondered why not. They did not say anything. It was only an hour later, at 0700 hours, that I realized I was covered in blood, intestines and human skin and my pouches were full of the same stuff. My hand was hurting by then and I saw I had been cut by the shattered arm bone of the LMG 1. I wanted to undress and clean up but there was no water. I had a change of clothing but the platoon commander did not let me throw the old stuff away because we were still in Indonesia. He told me to carry it out in a plastic bag.

I later learnt that, in all, 24 enemy were killed. The next day we reached Serikin. The brigadier and the CO came to congratulate C Company and gave us two days' rest. After that it was back to another ambush.

We were back in Blakang Mati, Singapore, on 28 January 1966. On 2 February my wife fell ill and was admitted to hospital. Four days later she died. My son was six months old. I asked to go on leave. I had to show my son to my in-laws. I was told I could go but not quite yet. My son was looked after by a Chinese woman, arranged for by the Gurkha Major's wife.

We were then told that there was going to be a Champion Company competition but there would be no training for it nor was a fixed programme announced of what it would be. We thought it would probably be drill as we were ordered to fall in on the square on 22 February at 1000 hours. At 0700 hours that day the CO, the adjutant and the Gurkha Major gave me a *shabash* telling me I'd done well. By then it was almost a habit as it was the tenth time someone had said that. Fine, but by then it didn't mean all that much to me.

The adjutant gave me a briefing and showed me a table on the parade ground. The companies were to parade on various parts of the parade ground but C Company was to be in front of the table. I was told to stand in the middle of the front rank and shown where the CO and others would be near the table. I was to be called and then I was to give my rifle to the man on my right. I was also shown a white spot on the ground where I would have to stand. No reason was given and, as it was an order, I did not ask what it was about.

The adjutant handed the parade over to the CO and, at 1000 hours when General Sir Alan Jolly[13] arrived on parade, in full dress, the CO reported to him. The adjutant then called out my number, rank and name and I was told to come forward. I gave my rifle to the man on my right and went forward. I stood on the white spot in front of the C-in-C and he announced in English that I had been awarded the Victoria Cross. The Gurkha adjutant then read out a Nepali version of what the C-in-C had said. I was surprised.[14] The C-in-C pinned a new set of ribbons on my shirt.

That night nobody slept at all and parties were held everywhere, British officers' mess, QGOs' mess, warrant officers' and sergeants' mess and all the company lines. I was in two minds. I was very proud of having won a VC but when I thought of my dead friends in my section and was sad.[15]

Later I was given the medal by Her Majesty Queen Elizabeth.

Rambahadur Limbu retired as an Honorary Captain (GCO).

✗

Hindupal Rai, DCM, 1/10 GR, *joined the army on 30 October 1953.*

I was taken by the *Galla Wala* to the western recruiting depot in Paklihawa and then we were taken to Lehra. After nine months' training I was posted to D Company, 1/10 GR, and was deployed on operations against the *daku*, chiefly ambush and patrolling. I was only involved in two contacts which were both unsuccessful.

The battalion moved to Malacca and to Hong Kong where we had IS training. My OC was Major C.J. Pike. I was sent on a drill course at Sungei Patani and only had one night in my family quarter on my return as the battalion had been detailed to go to Sarawak the next day. By then I was a local lance corporal. In Sarawak we moved to Bokah camp

---

[13] C-in-C FARELF (Far East Land Forces).

[14] Rambahadur Limbu showed no emotion when he got to this part of his narrative but words failed him.

[15] He later added, 'Of course I was sad about my wife. That was so natural I don't have to mention it.'

in the Second Division and were flown to the border with Indonesia with ten days' rations. We were later given another five days' worth.

We were on the border, the other side of the River Separang which we crossed by a rope spread from one side to the other. We were in a cut-off position. The CO told the OC, on the radio, not to cross the border.

Indonesians came by boat. Pirthibahadur sahib shot two boats into the water. Indrajit Limbu said he'd give Pirthibahadur sahib a sign to retire. Pirthibahadur started to retire and did not give the signal. He was killed by Indonesian fire.

Next day D Company went to Sempadang and moved off at 1000 hours. We moved all night. My section checked an enemy camp on a small track. On that patrol we saw trenches in the camp with some men doing PT and others cooking. We went back to our overnight camp and 30 Indonesians came up to us. There were two sentries, one an old soldier and the other a new one. The older took the news to company HQ and I went up to be sentry. I had been told not to open fire on the enemy.

That night the OC held an O Group and at 0300 hours we withdrew. We had not eaten but had a packet of biscuits between two men. We disposed of the wrapper in a pit we came across on our move. My section then had to go back to where we'd been. My orders were to see what I could do and to choose my own position. I went back by compass bearing and at dawn put my section to the right of the track by a big fallen tree. There were stones and mud and no big trees. The OC and my platoon commander, WO2 Jamanbahadur Rai, were to have come up later but I did not see them. I deployed my section with the LMG 1 and 2 on the left, then the rifle group's two men and I took a position at the other end. I was armed with an SMG.

When it was light some civilians came carrying some pumpkins. There were children and a couple of dogs. We drank some of our water and nibbled biscuits All felt sleepy and I told my men to take turns in closing their eyes. But I soon saw everybody had their eyes shut so I took pellets of mud and threw them at my men, telling them not to go to sleep. The 30 Indonesians came again and my men watched them. The OC had said that we were to let the enemy come and not to open fire. The rest of the company would open fire and then we would kill any who ran our way. So we stayed quiet.

However, they came up from behind us.[16] I saw them carrying their rifles at the ready. I saw three and decided to fire at them. I was afraid that if I aimed at the leading man's forehead the gun would shoot high so I aimed at his stomach and he fell, dead. A 2-inch mortar bomb landed near us. I heard one of my men laugh so I asked him why but he was trying to keep quiet in his pain as he had been wounded. In two more breaths he died. The enemy came on again and the gun group killed 12 of them and I killed five. One of the gun group was also wounded.

Eventually fire stopped and we tried to make our position into one of all-round defence. I did not know where the rest of my platoon and company HQ were and I wondered what to do. One of my men said we had been left by ourselves and I told him that was not so but, in any case we were self-contained with rations and ammunition, and I had a map and compass. I told the men not to show themselves and to keep their heads down. Then our 105mm artillery opened fire so we couldn't move. We all kept our heads down and got covered with mud.

I took my men back along the Indonesian tracks as we made our retreat but we had three bursts fired at us. We fell flat. None was hit. Up and on again and we met a civilian whom we thought was a spy. We blindfolded him and took him back. I met the platoon commander, reported my casualties and realized that I had been fired on by my own men. I said I wanted to report that to the OC but the platoon commander said I was not to as there had been no casualties.

I went back to my wounded man who asked for help. I clamped my feet in the mud to retain my balance on the sloping ground and comforted him, telling him I'd bind him up, give him an injection and have him taken back. He had his hands over his crotch and I asked him if he had been shot there but, no, in his arm.

At that time there were three more bursts of mortar fire and the section 2IC was hit as he made his way towards me. A fragment of mortar shell made a groove up his face to his ear and it took his hat off. He fell down on top of me. I thought he was dead. I injected morphia and told him not to lose heart. One of the others suggested we leave the place another way but we were fired on again so we dived down the slope. That was hard on the wounded but we saved ourselves.

Five minutes after the 105mm artillery stopped firing the enemy also

---

[16] It was only later realised that this group was another party and had nothing to do with the deployment of the 30.

stopped firing.[17] We got back to the platoon and I told the commander that I was going to report being fired on by my own people to the CO. The expression on the platoon commander's face changed and my own voice dried up. I couldn't talk. Someone brought me some water and only then could I talk. The platoon commander did not want to go and report to the CO as he himself had fired at us as he was scared. I told him that if he had killed us he would have told the OC that it was the enemy who had done so. I had no time for that platoon commander who was sent out of the battalion on pension.

I did go to the OC to report but I only met the company 2IC who sent me back with some other men to get the dead in. I told him I would go but I was so tired I had no strength left. None of the others wanted to go back so I went back with a Limbu who had joined the army in 1960. We saw an Indonesian leaning over a tree stump with his hat on the back of his neck. On looking at him we saw he had no head.

We collected our wounded, dead and weapons. In all we lost three dead and two wounded. The OC said he'd call in a helicopter with a fighter escort to help carry the dead and wounded out but this was refused as the place was not suitable for landing. That day we dug trenches and, except for sentries, had a day's rest. We had a meal and cut open all our unexpended rations to bury them prior to our going back over the border. We only got back two nights and a day later.

We moved to two other places before returning to Hong Kong and peacetime activities. The OC, C.J. Pike sahib, was awarded a DSO, one Jagatbahadur an MM and I a DCM. We went to England for the queen to give us our awards. I learnt that the British officers did all the work and the QGOs did nothing in comparison. The British are always impartial and work on merit. Our Brigade of Gurkhas would be nowhere without British officers.

I went on pension of my own accord in 1968 as my father was paralyzed and my mother dead.

---

[17] News came through from London about then that Confrontation was over and no more contact was to be made.

Ranbahadur Limbu, 2/10 GR, *'had' to talk.*[18]

It still gives me nightmares. It was like this: two platoons, 4 and 5, were sent over the border to recce an Indonesian camp. We walked for two days and made camp on a small hill. My platoon commander was Gurkha Lieutenant Jaiparsad Rai, a man from Darjeeling, and the 5 Platoon commander was a sergeant. Both men elected to stay back and send their platoons forward under the next senior. I was, therefore, commanding 4 Platoon. Our orders were not to open fire.

We moved forward over a river, much bigger than was shown on the map. We came up to the camp and were surprised to find ourselves surrounded by about 50 Indonesians who fired on us from the direction of the river we had crossed. Our orders were not to fire but here we were being fired on. I had to make a plan, which I did. I opened fire and killed five of them.

I got back to the hill camp but five of our men never appeared. Where had they gone? Were they dead or alive? We stayed on that hill for five days and on the fifth night we moved back to a higher hill. The CO, Lieutenant Colonel Myers, told us on the radio to move back in the direction of Sarawak and fire shots in the air to give the lost ones a bearing. We moved in the small hours and the jungle was alight with phosphorescent plants.

After five days all five did come out. One found his way into a 1/7 GR camp, two went to C Company in Bokah camp and two went to Rasau where D Company had been but was then empty. All the men had their weapons with them.

The Gurkha Lieutenant and I quarrelled. He said he had given orders that I was not to fire and I had disobeyed him. For my part I told him I had had to fire to stay alive. He said he would have me stripped of my rank. Next day the CO and three officers came in a helicopter and landed below us. It took us an hour and a quarter to get down to them. There was a lot of talk. The Gurkha Lieutenant told him that there had been no enemy but the corporal who had taken 5 Platoon across said that that was a lie. The Gurkha Lieutenant lost his case. The sergeant kept quiet.

Our punishment was to have to walk back to camp. Once back I was called to the office and thrashed it out with the OC, Captain Johnson.

---

[18] This story was told me when we stopped for a night at the narrator's house. I had forgotten we had known each other from JWS days 32 years earlier and that, over eleven years before, he had walked a day to give me some cardamom seeds.

Once more I told him that our task was a recce and we had been told not to open fire but the Indonesians had opened fire first, we were outnumbered and we had suffered no casualties. The Gurkha Lieutenant had to pack his bags and leave.

That incident still gives me nightmares all of 34 years later.

Surdhoj Gurung, 1/10 GR.   Many of the lads of my village went to join the army. I heard them talk about playing games, going to the cinema, learning how to talk properly, how the British officers ran good programmes. I heard about wars so I thought I'd go. When I joined the army in October 1957 I was 17 years old and knew a little Nepali [writing]. On the boat over to Malaya, a clerk from Darjeeling taught me my Roman alphabet.

After I was promoted to lance corporal, we were deployed in Tebakang in the border region, where I went on patrol but had no contact with the Indonesians. Later, with 105mm artillery on our side of the border we crossed over on a series of day patrols. We carried grenades and had our meals ready to eat in our mess tins. We would go up to a big river three hours away. I became sick with septic mosquito bites and was evacuated to Kuching hospital, then back to Singapore for a week and spent two weeks in the cool of the Cameron Highlands getting better. By then that tour was over and the battalion was back in Malacca.

I was sent to Calcutta as a ration storeman and because the [British] quartermaster knew no Nepali nor Hindi, it was my job to go to the Indian supply depot for our rations. I spoke in English as much as I could and switched to Hindi when unable to continue in English. At the end of that duty I went home for five and a half months and brought my family back with me. I was posted to C Company.

After training for Borneo for 15 days, we left for Kalabakan in Tawau Residency. The enemy had killed a lot of Malay troops and I saw dried blood all over the walls when I got there. We followed up by helicopter to the River Serudong but did not make any contact as the enemy, who had looted the nearest village of all stores and livestock, had just left. We followed up, found their cooking places which were still warm but still did not make contact.

We were sent to Kuching and on to Bokah camp before being sent over the border. Our task was to recce a camp. There was double barbed wire around it and it was in a swamp. We went back and the whole company went in. My weapon was an AR15. An FOO came with us and climbed a tree to give direct fire orders. The Indonesians were on a PT parade when the artillery started ranging. We fired our weapons at them but the wire was too thick for us to get through and the swamp made it too difficult. We returned.

Our next task was in the Tebakang/Tebedu area, both our side of the border. Indonesians were in Tebakang and 17 of us had to make a recce for their base camp. We left our camp at 0400 hours and by 0900 hours were in the suspected Indonesian infiltration area.[19] We left our *joris* cooking the food and set off on our recce. We met a group of Indonesians and asked them in English and Malay who they were and, if they did not say who they were we would open fire on them. They opened fire on us and killed one and wounded six of us. I carried the first aid pack and patched up the wounded and asked HQ for reinforcements. Until we were sent help I tried to hide in a hollow tree but found my weapon had jammed so I changed my position to one behind a fallen tree.

I cleared my weapon, looked around and saw the other men. I was fired at and my hat was shot off my head as I put my head down below cover. I was No 2 of the LMG group. We were on the point of attacking the enemy and had crept forward. I decided to go some 20 yards to the left and fired several bursts. The Indonesians cried out and their fire stopped. We again asked for help from those who had stayed behind cooking the meal. They arrived with the rest of the company and the wounded were taken back on stretchers for evacuation to hospital.

We found a dead Indonesian. His weapon had been taken. His hat was there with a red star in it as a badge. I brought the hat back and gave it to company HQ. The enemy had left tracks which we followed. Our packs were still where we had left them when we started the recce. The rest of the company arrived. We were hungry. Each platoon was in the lead for a quarter of an hour. By 1600 hours, Hughes sahib, the OC, saw we were tired so he gave us a ten minutes' rest. I carried two water bottles, one had water, the other rum. I drank a lid full of rum and revived my spirits.

By 1700 hours we were up a hill and 50 yards away was secondary

---

[19] About 30 Indonesian regulars (RPKAD shock troops) and Chinese infiltrators took part in the incursion on 16 February 1966.

jungle. Our section was at the rear. They opened fire on us and we all shouted "Charge!" as we went in. My LMG 1 was hit in the chest and died. One of my men stepped on an anti-personnel mine and was hurt in his foot. In all three of us were wounded and one was killed. It started to rain heavily and night fell. Then it stopped raining and a full moon shone. We were all very hungry. There was a cultivated area there and the locals had sown cucumber, guava, peach and papaya. We scrounged as much as we could and ate it, although most of it was still unripe. We stayed there all night and I drank my rum.

Next morning a helicopter came with four big flasks of tea, biscuits and bread. We felt revived and moved off again. Where we had had ten minutes' rest on the previous day we laid an ambush. We went with anti-personnel mine-detecting "prods" and found some old uniforms that had been thrown away. We radioed HQ about the dangerous situation. Ten yards away was a dry ravine and we saw a pile of cut saplings. We wondered why they were there. We put out sentries while we discussed with the OC what to do about it. How could we pull away the saplings without exposing ourselves to danger. I suggested we cut saplings with curved ends and use them like hooks. "Good idea, Surdhoj," said the OC. We uncovered five dead enemy, aged between 18 and 40. There were no arms, no documents, no maps, no compasses. They had a red star in their hats. We reported back to battalion HQ.

We moved off to a big open space, covered with long grass. There were tracks all over the place. So many men! They had done that to trick us. We tried to follow up but it took too much time. We then met a timber track.[20] By then we said we were so tired we could move no farther forward. We said we'd go forward if we had a meal first but we had not had a decent meal for three days and we'd run out of strength. We were too tired to talk. We put out sentries and rested where we were. We were told to wait there for two hours and a relief would be sent. Two hours later a company of 2 GR relieved us.

We went back to our base, had a meal and a wash. We were all given some rum from a cask. We relaxed. We went back to battalion HQ where we still had to go on recce patrols. We also had to play basketball with the local Chinese.

My senior NCO gave my name in for a decoration as I had killed all five of the enemy whose corpses we found under the saplings. Nothing came of it.

---

[20] A track cut to haul out timber by vehicle.

I had no real fear when I went on such operations. I knew that the British officers would do as much as they could to have a good organization. I also worked with Border Scout sections whose only use was one of local knowledge. They only had basic training and two of us Gurkhas had to be with each section of them.

I went on pension in January 1970.

Jasbahadur Rai, 1/10 GR.   I joined the army on 7 September 1949 and was in the 3-inch Mortar Platoon for some time. By the time the battalion went to Sarawak on operations I was a corporal. We went there to keep it for the Malaysians against the Indonesians. I thought the Indonesians were better soldiers than the Malays. I was in D Company then and attached to a Border Scout position at Selepong. The Indonesians attacked the post and D Company went to reinforce it. One of the Iban scouts killed an Indonesian, cut off his head and brought it back. The government was offering a reward of S$500 for each head and that was a lot of money for anybody.

The Ibans take the heads, then they dry them and hang them in their houses.

The longest battle I had as a corporal was for 32 minutes after 25 Indonesians tried to attack a Border Scout position at night. They failed and, in the dawn, a scout on OP duty saw one of them and fired at him. We all moved out, taking grenades with us. We followed the blood trail and captured him. He told us where the others were, up a hill in the jungle. By then the OC, Major Philips, and the 2IC, Captain (QGO) Dhojbir Limbu were on the scene. They said we would attack them and I was to go in front. This I did but found myself on my own as both officers stayed behind.

I came across the Indonesian ambush position with an LMG post and attacked it, killing two enemies. The others took fire positions as did I, crawling forward. One Indonesian was crawling forward towards me and came very near. He aimed at me but I killed him also. The others did not withdraw so I shouted fire orders in English to make them think there were more people there than one man.

I went forward and saw two more Indonesians by another gun post in dark jungle. I saw bullets flash and I fired at them, killing one. By then the rest of the platoon had caught up with me. The Indonesians had left an LMG and ammunition behind so we took it all back. In all there were four dead and three wounded. The CO flew over in an aeroplane and gave orders over the radio to continue chasing the others but Major Philips told me not to go. The battle was over.

A week later the Director of Operations and one other came and I took them to the scene of the battle. "What a difficult place on that hill to attack. How was it you did not get shot? Amazing!" I did not answer as I could not tell them that the others had let me go on ahead. The OC and the 2IC also said nothing nor did they put me in for a *bahaduri*.

A year later, after Major Philips had gone to GIPC and Major Robertson had taken over, Captain (QGO) Dhojbir Limbu told me that he had tried to get my name forwarded for a *bahaduri* but without success. "I'll have a whiskey in your name," he said. "No, have one in your own," was my answer. So I got no *bahaduri*. Getting one is not only earning it but also being recognized by the officers. "The government's order: the alarm of the tiger" is our Nepali proverb.

When I was the company QM, as a sergeant, I went with the OC, Major Pike, ten map squares into Indonesia. Major Pike was a strong character and a leader. I asked what would happen if we suffered casualties? Nothing on the way in but we will be able to get a helicopter after a contact. We moved very slowly for a week, over hills and across rivers. I was near the OC and the FOO. I am a small man and in the river we crossed for a close recce of the Indonesian camp the water washed my hat off my head. I was told off for making a noise! We did the close recce and rejoined the rest of the company on the near bank. We waited.

We were due to attack the Indonesians at 1100 hours but they already knew of our presence and they attacked us at 0900 hours. They shouted "Pig Gurkhas" in their own language which we understood as they attacked our gun post. The artillery was not ready to give supporting fire and we had a big battle. Two of our men were killed and two wounded. Bombs fell about us but I do not know if they were ours or theirs.

I left the two dead men behind and took one of the wounded with me. The firing I went through was both theirs and ours. Later we had four dead. We managed to take the corpses out of that area and fired on the Indonesians as we did so to stop them from taking them. They did capture a 2-inch mortar. The OC asked for a helicopter for the corpses, as well as for any wounded but one was not sent so the corpses had to be carried out to the border.

We wrapped the corpses in poncho capes and, hanging them from poles we had cut, we moved off at night and slowly carried them for two days until we reached the border. The stink was overpowering. 2nd Lieutenant Dawson had arrived on the border and had an LP cut so the corpses could be taken away by helicopter.

I did not get a *bahaduri* but I did get a *shabash* and direct promotion to lieutenant (QGO). Before leaving the army on pension I served in UK, Cyprus and Dharan.

Tejbahadur Gurung, MM, 1/2 GR, *had been 'blooded' in Malaya. He continued his story.*

The battalion deployed in Sarawak. By then I was a lance corporal. I was put to command a group of Border Scouts at Long Jawi. I found out that the head man was on the side of the Indonesians. This group of longhouses was some three days by boat from company HQ at Belaga. On the way up, we stayed the first night at a house where the Ukit people were. The girls were very fresh and rubbed our faces with lampblack – all in good fun.

The third day three British officers arrived and had a look at the defence of Long Jawi, which was threatened from Indonesia. There were no trenches when I arrived and I had started to have some dug. There was no wire. The British officers had a meeting in the longhouse with all the inhabitants and told them of the way my group of Border Scouts would defend the place. None of us knew then that an enemy recce group was sitting at the back and so found out the plan.

There should have been 23 Border Scouts at Long Jawi but I only saw four or five for the first two days. I called them all in on the fifth day and 11 arrived. I used one man as an interpreter and made him my deputy. I made all those scouts who had turned up fire five rounds with their rifles. It was a dangerous place.

Apart from a Police Field Force radio operator we were eight Gurkhas, including Kharkabahadur Gurung, Chandrabahadur Gurung who was our radio operator, Dhanbahadur Gurung, Belbahadur Gurung and Amarbahadur Thapa, LMG 1. After the three British officers left a local came to me in our post. I was suspicious as I thought he was not of the village. He offered us sugar cane. I asked about him and was told he was a local but I did not believe that and I felt he was an agent who had come to spy on us.

That evening the Border Scout who acted as interpreter told me he had to go and spend the night in his own house as his wife was expecting. I told him I would prefer him to stay with us but he said he had to go. I had sent a message to HQ warning of an enemy attack and next morning early I learnt that we were to be attacked soon. I could just make out an enemy group sorting itself out on a helicopter pad on the opposite side of the small valley and went to alert the signallers, mine and the Police Field Force operator, and ran back up the hill with a box of grenades. The enemy opened fire with a 60mm mortar and I was knocked down. I lost the box of grenades in the gloom and only managed to pick up a couple of them which I put in my pouch. I regained the post.

The enemy[21] then attacked the longhouse and killed the two radio operators. At first light fire became heavier around us and all the Border Scouts bar one slipped away. Our main post was not at the top of the hill but some way down. We had started to dig trenches around it. We slept and cooked there. The Indonesian machine gun kept on jamming. We returned fire, both automatic and single shots from rifles and this caused enemy casualties. Dhanbahadur was killed, so was the Bren gunner and Kharkabahadur's thigh was shattered. Enemy fire became more intense and I decided that we had to leave and go to the top of the hill with our weapons. We made a quick escape but without our packs and no food. Belbahadur was also wounded but not so seriously.

After quite a time, when it was full daylight, I decided that we had to leave and we escaped up to the top of the hill with our weapons but without our packs and no food. We had to leave the dead men. The wounded said they could not move and were ready to die there but I told them we would get them to safety and they would be rescued. From the top of the hill we moved as silently and as quickly as we could down a small incline, over a stream and up into some thick jungle. We stayed there all day while the enemy still fired on our evacuated post. Eventually they charged and, finding everything empty, burnt the place down.

It rained all night and we had no cover. It was a very, very long time before the dawn. I decided to leave the two wounded men there and

---

[21] It was later discovered that there were about 150 Indonesian raiders.

move away with the other two Gurkhas and the one Border Scout. I bandaged the men up again as best I could. Kharkabahadur begged me to kill him but I managed to quieten him by saying I would return with others and rescue him. He would get better and be all right.[22]

My small group set off and we moved all day, picking up a few edible berries as we walked through the jungle. The second night we slept in the open and on the next day, when we were by the large river, we saw some locals coming downstream in a small boat. There was a woman in it and I signalled them to come to the bank. I told them I would keep the woman as hostage while the others, who were very afraid, went off to find a boat to take us farther downstream. They did come back with a boat after some while and the woman rejoined her husband.

The boat had a boatman and we reached Long Linau that evening. We did not go to the longhouse but stayed in a travellers' hut where we found some chillis and salt, which we ate. There was, of course, water from the river for drinking. On the third day we reached company HQ.

The company commander, Burlison sahib, was very anxious. I found out that no helicopter had been sent and I wondered why. The radio operator, who seemed to do most of the work there, said that he had received my message about the threat and had passed it on. He would not know what had happened to it after that. I was distressed that no action had been taken.

The CO came to see us and he seemed angry that we were not still in our post. I told him what I could and then reported to the IO, Mole sahib, in the operations room. He gave me a drink of rum and then debriefed me. I understood that if my message had reached him some action would have been taken. Only after I reached Belaga did a reaction force go out.

I ate, washed and was re-kitted before going back to be a guide. One worry was that the way I had got the boat might be adverse. It was not. We reached Long Jawi and rescued the wounded and the corpses. The next 19 or 20 days were spent farther south after the enemy.

Lieutenant (QGO) Pasbahadur Gurung and his platoon were flown in to where a fast-flowing river could take the raiding party by boat back into Indonesia to see if he could intercept them. I went with the platoon. The ambush was laid just before the two boats containing the

---

[22] The two would still meet up collecting their pensions when the story was recorded in late 1999.

raiders[23] came into view. All were killed.[24] We went up to the border but did not cross it. After we returned to Belaga I had a rest. Soon afterwards the battalion returned to Hong Kong and I went on home leave.

On my return I found I had been promoted to sergeant and had been awarded an MM. I went to UK so that the queen could give it to me. She gave me a *shabash* and shook my hand. After that I was promoted to Gurkha Lieutenant and posted to C Company. I finished my service as 2IC in Support Company as a Gurkha Captain.

Ojahang Limbu, 1/10 GR, *saw more active service in Borneo than he had in Malaya. Quite why he made the next remark was uncertain as there was no context.*

Over in Hong Kong my platoon commander said that bad soldiers had a red ink entry against their name and should be ready to die. After two or three years in Hong Kong we moved to Sarawak. Ambassadors in Malaya said that there were many illiterates in Sarawak and the Gurkhas had to have an IS parade in Kuching. We marched by, rifles at the high port with our Gurkha hats on, in threes, with IS banners in front. A Company were in the lead and were fired on, with the two front GORs being killed. The platoon commander gave orders to open fire but the enemy fled.[25]

We then started operations on the Indonesian side of the border. One time I told Gibson sahib that there were enemy ahead and should we not open fire. He said "No, let's capture them." I said not that as they would kill us. As we were talking the enemy shot at him and knocked his hat off. We GORs couldn't make reports but he left the company a few days after that and Haddow sahib came instead.

B Company under Major Niven went to Stass[26], took 12 days' rations and went I don't know how many map squares into Indonesia. We took

---

[23] There were 26 armed Indonesians. All were killed but only one body was recovered. A Border Scout who had been tied hand and foot and taken with the raiders managed to jump overboard and make his escape.

[24] Lt (QGO) Pasbahadur Gurung was awarded an MC.

[25] His company commander, Maj (later Col) B.M. Niven, MBE, in a letter dated 26 October 2000, wrote 'news to me ... I doubt the authority somewhat!'

[26] In fact B Company was in the Simanggang sector. *Vide* Niven letter.

cutting pliers. Supply for the Indonesians we went to ambush was by boat up a river. But the Indonesians were clever and their boats were separated by 25 to 30 yards so could not be covered at the same time. We sank some of them, packed up all the traces of our camp and went back over the border.

On another tour, Major Niven took us back, with another 12 days' rations, to near where Rambahadur Limbu had won his VC. It was in grassy country with only a few trees. 5 Platoon was on higher ground, 6 Platoon was lower down on a narrow path and 4 Platoon, where I was, was in reserve. 5 Platoon opened fire and the enemy tried to outflank it.

We were called forward and an enemy mortar bomb landed in the middle of us. We took positions of safety and counted. When we had got to 150 we shouted out that it was a misfire and continued. The enemy were beaten off and we captured two prisoners, both of whom had claws instead of thumbs. We brought them back blindfolded, hands tied behind their backs, to Stass and then a helicopter took them away.[27]

Another time Major Niven with four others went on a recce near Babang in Indonesia. With him was an FOO, his BOR radio operator, Lieutenant (QGO) Gajurmani and me. Two 105mm pieces were ready at Stass and three 5.5-inch pieces were ready at Simanggang. We watched our front all day, picking a target.

We went back to Stass and were given four days' leave. On the last day we were told to write a letter and leave it under our pillow. What sort of letter? If we die, we die. We took another 12 days' rations and got to Babang. The 105s fired across the area which surrounded the enemy at Kengdom. The FOO gave the fire orders to the 5.5s. Many rounds were fired but we found nothing when we followed up. We got back to Stass five days later. That was the end of Confrontation.

---

[27] The two prisoners were hunters (or civilian Indonesian scouts?). It was not claws they had but six toes on each foot. They were released while still in the area but farther off. Niven letter.

Balman Gurung, MM, 2/6 GR, *was involved in three contacts during the Malayan Emergency, once when six* daku *were killed and the other two accounting for one each. His service continued during Confrontation.*

In 1963 the battalion relieved 1/7 GR in Brunei but we had no contact with the enemy.

On 18 August 1963, in the Long Lopeng area of Sarawak, we were told that there were six Indonesians without rations or arms. My platoon was in Long Semado, not far off, and at 1600 hours that same day we moved out, reaching Long Lopeng at 0400 hours. We spoke to the headman and by 0600 hours had captured the six men. They were sent out to Kuching. We learnt that there were still three enemy in the jungle. We went back to Long Semado.

On 19 August a helicopter brought two of the captured six back and they were to guide us to the remaining three. 1 Platoon returned to Long Lopeng and set off for the enemy camp but could not reach it. We spent the night at a river junction and I had a bad dream which worried me as it boded ill. We moved off at 0830, and were in the target area by noon. The two Indonesians would take us no farther. The platoon advanced to the enemy position. One section was to be in ambush and the other to attack the camp. There was no one in the camp.

The Indonesians were 25 yards away and they opened fire. I was with four men, two GORs, both young soldiers with no experience, and two Border Scouts. I put them in fire positions by two big trees and one Border Scout was shot in the chest. He died at 0400 hours that night.

I shouted "*Ayo Gorkhali*, charge!" and ran forward about 15 yards. I was alone. My two GORs were still by their tree. I shouted out for them to cover me with single shots. One of them shouted back that an enemy was very close, he could see him but I couldn't. I learnt later that he was referring to an Indonesian who had taken a fire position on the other side of the same tree as I had. The enemy kept up their fire for some ten minutes but from where?

After five minutes I realised I was bleeding and saw I had been wounded in both thighs, four fingers of my right hand and my left arm. I thought that, as I was wounded and covered in blood, I would die and so I'd better take some enemy with me. I got up and charged them for about ten yards and saw 15 to 20 men with back baskets disappearing. I finished my magazine and, trying to change it for a new one, found that I could not take the old one off. A bullet had shot the safety catch and the old magazine off. My pouches had been shot off me; I carried a grenade but had put it in my pack, as taught. Had it been in my pouch I would have been killed when it exploded.

I returned to my two men by myself and fell down. I told my men to follow up about 50 yards and this they did. Although I had fired 19 rounds and killed several men no bodies were found yet 5,000 rounds of ammunition, a Japanese rifle and pistol and eight bundles of documents were. I was wounded at 1350 hours.

I could not be rescued that day although the platoon tried to cut an LP that night. Next morning at 0930 hours a helicopter came overhead but could not land, only hover. Two doctors were lowered. They patched me up and I was winched on board and flown to Brunei.

It took a long time to get better. I was told I had been awarded an MM on 1 August 1964, a year later, and a year after that it was pinned on my chest by the UK High Commissioner in Singapore.

I left the army on 28 December 1967.

Balman's courage was evident in his village where three times, unaided, he killed predatory leopards.

The Sumbi Incident

Jitbahadur Rai, 1/7 GR, GIPC, *was instrumental in alerting the security forces to an expected threat.*

On our last tour in Borneo my patrol was in support of 1/7 GR, based at Bareo in the Fourth Division. We were briefed about a threat from an Indonesian commander called Sumbi who was thought to be about to infiltrate from Indonesian Borneo, through Sarawak and into Brunei to sabotage the oil pumping.

One day, not far from the border, I and another man went on a patrol and noticed a piece of tinfoil. My companion, Rifleman Dharmalal Rai from 1/10 GR, sniffed it and said it smelled of coffee. We did not have coffee in our rations, although maybe the British soldiers did in theirs, but there were no British troops in the area. I thought it might be Sumbi's group so we rejoined the other three men and looked around. We found tracks for two men but they were jungle boots, just like ours. Even so we tracked them from midday 29 July until the evening of the 31st. Eventually we discovered a pile of sacking and two discarded pairs of old British Army jungle boots. It was Sumbi's gang who had bandaged their Indonesian type footwear to hide their movements.

We did not follow them up but reported it. We had a proper meal and rest that night because I had forbidden hot meals or making a camp for the past two nights in case we disturbed the enemy in front. It is cold up in those mountains. Next morning we got a radio message saying that 1/7 GR did not believe the report and we were ordered to go back to the border, backtracking to make sure that the group had crossed over from Indonesia. We did this and confirmed that that was the case.[28]

I thought it was a small enough matter but the OC thought otherwise. Before we left for Kluang the OC, Cross sahib, told the company that Major General Lea[29] was coming by helicopter from Labuan to visit the company in the Haunted House. The OC told me and Dharmalal to fall in separately and led the major general to us. The general sahib shook our hands and told us how well we'd done and that without our work Sumbi might have been successful. Much later the OC told me that he had tried to get me a medal for what I'd done, had been told that was not possible and had asked the general to come over and congratulate us instead.

I was not at the capture of the last four of Sumbi's men but Sergeant Chandrabahadur Rai, who had been with me in C Company before we both went to GIPC, told me about it. "One of my patrol, Rifleman Jamansing Rai, had to be evacuated by helicopter and, in his place, the OC joined the patrol. On patrol next day, after a night's rain that caused any traces of movement to look older than they were, the OC, moving as No. 4 in the patrol, saw a leaf, lying on the jungle floor, that had been folded. He called me back and said that nature never did like straight lines so it had to have been made by man. We cast around and saw what could just possibly be men's tracks. We followed them to the border between us and the Royal Brunei Malay Regiment. The news

---

[28] *The Times*, of 7 December 1966, published an account of the Sumbi incursion. It was headlined 'Courage of the Gurkhas Foiled Saboteurs' and continued, 'Details of one of the most brilliant actions in the history of Gurkhas have just been released' and went on to describe the Gurkha Para Company patrol's meticulous attention to detail in sniffing the tinfoil that smelt of coffee.

[29] Maj Gen H.G. (later Sir George) Lea, CB, DSO, DOBOPS.

was passed to them. The end result was the capture of the last of Sumbi's men."[30]

Dharmalal Rai, 1/10 GR, GIPC, *told of the part he played.*

I joined the army in October 1958 and the Malayan Emergency was over by the time I finished my recruit training and joined 1/10 GR. I trained to be a parachutist and joined GIPC from the very start in that I was already trained when it was raised on 1 January 1963.

Some time in 1966 my patrol was operating between 1/7 GR in Ba Kelalan and the border. We had been warned about a Lieutenant Sumbi of the Indonesian Army who was reported to be planning an incursion with 50 men as far north as the Brunei oilfields to sabotage them. One morning my patrol commander, WO2 Jitbahadur Rai, took me with him on a patrol to see what we could find while the radio operator contacted company HQ and the other two cooked the morning meal. We were in high country which was chilly in the morning. It had rained the night before and as we two set out lots of little drops of water sparkled as the sun rose.

By the time of our return all the sparkling drops had dried up but my eye was attracted by something that glinted. I went over to it and found it was a piece of tinfoil. I sniffed it and it smelt of coffee. Now that was not in our rations. It may have been in BORs' rations but no British troops were within miles of us. I talked to Jitbahadur about this and we presumed it was Sumbi's group. Once we were back with the rest of the patrol we ate our meal and cast around and picked up tracks for two wearing British type jungle boots. It was slow work tracking them which we did for the rest of that day, all next day and part of the day after that.

Jitbahadur was convinced there were more men than just those two, although we found no definite signs. That first night we did not make camp nor did we cook a meal but we did brew ourselves tea and eat some hard tack. That was what we did on the second night also.

On the third day we met with success. We found those two pairs of old jungle boots and 48 pieces of wrapping that had hidden the tracks of the rest of the group which had to be Sumbi's. We sent the message

---

[30] In his debriefing, one of the four men admitted he was a 'compulsive twig-snapper and leaf-folder'.

to company HQ who relayed it to tactical HQ 1/7 GR. We were all amazed to be told that 1/7 GR's CO did not believe our story! A group of their soldiers was sent to where we were and we were directed to backtrack the prints all the way to the Indonesian border to prove that people had crossed from Indonesia into Sarawak.

The OC was angry that we were disbelieved. I believe he wrote us up for an award but none was forthcoming. When he learnt that no GIPC names were on the list he arranged for General Lea sahib to fly over to our camp, the Haunted House in Brunei opposite the sultan's palace, to congratulate WO2 Jitbahadur Rai and me personally.

I stayed in GIPC until it disbanded in October 1971.

Bhaktabahadur Rai, 1/7 GR, *was an eye witness to the 'Sumbi Saga'.*

I joined the army in 1962 when I was 16 and so found training hard work. I was sent to Ipoh and posted to 4 Platoon. We soon moved to Sarawak and went on many jungle operations. Carrying two weeks' rations in a rucksack hurt me so I had to walk around with a stick for a week. B Company was based in Stass. I was LMG 2 and had a rifle as my personal weapon. I had no fear in the jungle except of insects, snakes and scorpions.

River crossing was hard. We strung rattan over the river and hauled ourselves over by clutching hold of it. Once the rattan snapped and two of us slipped into the river but we held on and managed to get out.

I went on operations over the border, into Indonesia, with a British captain. We moved forward for seven days, very quietly. I was with Gorbadhan, Pembu Sherpa and Bombahadur Limbu. They were not with the rest of the platoon when we were fired at by the Indonesians while we were cooking. We moved elsewhere, unfed. Pembu and Gorbadhan caught up with us later but Bombahadur stayed firing at the Indonesians, shouting out orders for imaginary troops to confuse the them. After a while he jumped over a stream and caught us up. The enemy also left off firing. The Gurkha Captain, company 2IC, got in a flap, telling us we were not to open fire but he himself was firing bursts into the ground as he spoke. An enemy helicopter came looking for us. We got back to the border in one day, it having taken us a week on the way in. Bombahadur was awarded the MM.

We moved northeast to Ba Kelalan. One day when I was on sentry duty in an observation post, I heard the alarm signal, a tin being beaten, so we knew the enemy were on us. I waited, being eaten by mosquitoes but only our own troops met up with us.

The OC was Major Jenkins. News of Sumbi's incursion had already been given by the patrol of GIPC which was working in 1/7 GR area. Major Jenkins said he had had a letter from Sumbi who was his classmate. "I'm coming into your country." So we had to go on an 18-day operation. On the twelfth day we came across a steep outcrop covered in vines and rattan. The enemy had bent saplings so were easy to follow up. We moved over a difficult hill, across a ravine into easier country, all in jungle. We knew the enemy were in the area. We followed up the signs and met an Indonesian in a poncho cape. We closed in on him and ordered, "Hands up", but then we saw he was dead. He had died of starvation. Sumbi's group had not brought enough rations and were living off the land. We examined him for documents and looked at his weapon. We continued, on and on, and met two more dead men who had died of hunger.

We met Sumbi and two others in close country and all said "Hands up". The OC also said "Hands up." Sumbi's group aimed at us but then the other two put down their arms. In English Sumbi said "I will kill you first then I will die." He had something like an AR15. We had taken up fire positions and the position was surrounded. Nobody opened fire. We moved forward but then Bombahadur, carrying his LMG, rushed ahead. We said not to go, but seeing him advance like that, Sumbi laid down his weapon and Bombahadur caught him.

Major Jenkins and Sumbi talked. The two captives took the biscuits we offered them but Sumbi declined. We made arrangements for a helicopter as the two who had surrendered first were too weak to walk. We bound Sumbi's hands behind his back with toggle rope. There was a big flat stone in a nearby river and we made a helicopter landing site on it. The helicopter came and Major Jenkins and Sumbi went off in the first flight, the rest of us following later.

At no time that I saw did our men nor the military who came in the helicopter lay hands on any of the Indonesians. There had been no shooting at all since we left the camp. The only person who showed any bravery was Bombahadur but he did not get a *bahaduri*.

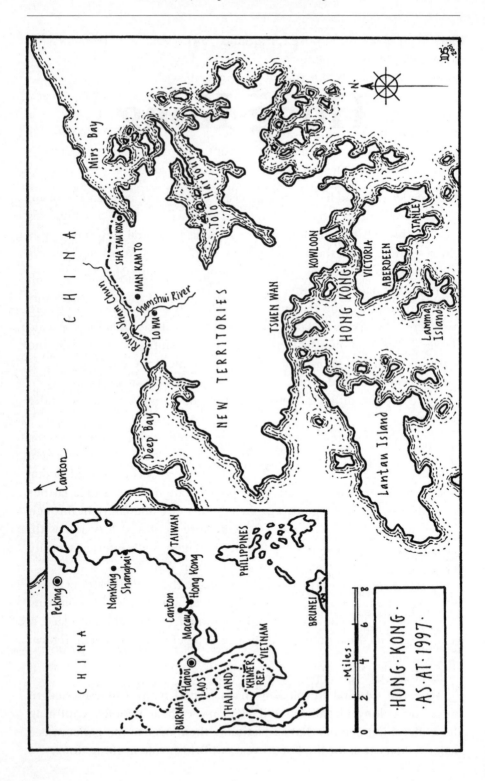

·HONG·KONG·
·AS·AT·1997·

CHAPTER **10**

Hong Kong

The treaties that had led to the establishment of European settlements in China were long seen by the Chinese as 'unequal'. In 1967, as China was passing through the turmoil of Mao Zedong's Cultural Revolution, this old resentment and the violent tactics of Chairman Mao's Red Guards combined and spilled over into Hong Kong when, on 1 May, Labour Day, a typhoon of hate and rioting hit the colony.

The pretext for the flare-up was a relatively small industrial dispute between the workers and management of two factories that made plastic flowers. The communists seized this opportunity to exacerbate the situation until, in a short time, major disturbances were taking place at several points around Hong Kong island itself and in Kowloon. Then followed a most difficult four-month period, a long time to be under pressure.

On 8 July 1967, really serious trouble started at the extreme eastern end of the frontier on Mirs Bay at the normally sleepy and picturesque little fishing village of Sha Tau Kok, where there was a forward police post near the frontier and the main police station about a mile farther back. By a stroke of misguided genius, the frontier line ran right through the village itself. 1/7 GR and 1/10 GR were deployed forward, with, farther back, 1/6 GR as reserve frontier battalion, with internal security responsibility for the resettlement area of Tsun Wan.

In Man Kam To both the CO of 1/10 GR and the British District Officer were snatched and held as hostages over the border. A company commander of 1/6 GR also suffered the same fate in a different place. A very dangerous situation was only just settled before a 'point of no return' was reached.

Later 2/7 GR was deployed from Malaysia.

After the Cultural Revolution chaos abated many Chinese tried to enter the colony illegally, as did Vietnamese 'boat people'. Capturing these illegal immigrants (IIs) and handing them over to the police was a major military task for the last 25 years of British rule in Hong Kong.

Much of the action was low key and only isolated incidents of bravery were worthy of being recognised for awards. It is fair to say that the renowned discipline of the Brigade of Gurkhas was responsible for a delicate situation never spilling over to become wholly unmanageable.

Jaiparsad Rai, 1/10 GR, *remembered the tension.*

I joined the army in October 1949 and I want to tell you about Hong Kong. The accommodation was not good but, to start with, relations with the civilians were. Then Red China started to cause trouble at Sha Tau Kok. That is a difficult place because the international boundary runs down the middle of the road in the village. The Chinese had killed some Pakistani police. I was sent to an upper storey of the bank building. 1/6 GR had previously prepared sandbag bunkers and we reinforced them. After a night there we moved to the railway bridge at Lo Wu over Shamshui river. The bridge was short but the drop to the river was deep. The Chinese threw grenades at us from the far side.

At Man Kam To bridge grenades were also thrown and the CO, Lieutenant Colonel McAlister,[1] who had gone to see his sentries, was snatched by a party of Chinese and taken over the bridge. The 2IC, Major Philips, and Major Niven, wanted to fire artillery if the Chinese did not release the CO by 0555 hours on the morrow. Madankumar sahib was allowed to go to see the CO who sent a message that one dead CO was no worry but World War III was no good. I think the officers who suggested artillery flapped and would have started a war for that is what the Chinese were banking on. Our morale was low with the CO in their hands. The brigade commander, Brigadier Martin, flew overhead in a helicopter. Eventually the CO was released. All Hong Kong was in danger if he had been killed by the Chinese.

Bishnukumar Rai, 1/7 GR, *also remembered what happened.*

Confrontation finished and the battalion returned to Kluang and, in 1968, went to Hong Kong. In November the Chinese communists fired on the police at the border village of Sha Tau Kok. We were rushed up as reinforcements. That was a period of much turbulence. We dug

---

[1] Later Maj Gen R.W.L. McAlister, CB, OBE.

defences by night and tried to rest by day, keeping quiet. First we dug section weapon pits, then gun posts and finally the command post. We had to fix wire and overhead cover. Food in hot containers was brought up by mules as we were not allowed to cook. For 21 days life was hard but the Chinese did not fire on us. They were about 600 yards in front and we could hear them. I was afraid to start with but I lost that when I realised that my death would be reported back home by one of my friends who was with me and I would do the same for him.

There was always more activity shown by the Chinese in front of British battalions in the forward area than when we Gurkhas were there. The Chinese seemed to be friendly to us.

Later on we were engaged in work against IIs. We adopted new tactics to counter them. We operated in bricks, each brick being three or four men. At night one man would keep alert and the others sleep. We would have eight bricks in one ambush area. We caught many IIs each night, my brick as many as 11 and my platoon catching between 40 and 45 nightly. When the man with the night vision glass saw them coming he would either alert the platoon or, if there were too many for the platoon to deal with, HQ in the rear. Some surrendered more easily than others; some ran away wherever they could. Some of those we captured said they had been on the move for two weeks. The ones we captured were often tired, hungry, unarmed and weak. They travelled lightly, using ground meal for food and Tiger Balm for medication.

We were armed with batons. After some time the IIs became more aggressive, using knives and chains against us. In one hand-to-hand struggle when IIs came to surround me and one man attacked me I broke an II's skull. One day I saw some branches moving over the border river when it was not flowing quickly. I looked hard and saw that men were holding cut branches in front of them as camouflage. Six IIs crossed over and hid in the jungle. HQ sent a helicopter to take us to look for them but trees hid them. Eventually we picked up three, two males and a female. They were cleverly hidden, lying down covered with undergrowth. I never heard of children trying to be smuggled over.

From our OP we could observe the Hong Kong police in action against the IIs. They would use dogs to bite them and beat them with batons. We could hear their cries.

Aimansing Limbu, QGM, 1/7 GR, *was a young soldier when he first experienced difficult situations.*

Once I reached the battalion in Hong Kong I was posted to A Company. Our main duty was to capture IIs. The first time I was on duty against them I kept on wondering how they would come, when they would come and whether I could capture them or not. Their weapons were knives and meat choppers. We were not afraid of their weapons as ours were stronger. There were more males than females. They were running from their own communist country, not that I understood much about that because that's politics. I caught them because that was what I was ordered to do. Nepalis in Nepal are, compared with them, only "show" communists.

One particular night in 1979 there were six or seven groups of four men in each. We went to Tolo Harbour, by the sea, opposite Sha Tau Kok. At around 2300 hours eight IIs were seen approaching by boat. I gave my mates a warning and I waded out to the boat which was near the shore by then and tried to get on to it. It was raining and there were medium waves. The water came up to my waist as I reached them and they tried to escape. The IIs only saw me, not the others, so they attacked me, trying to drown me by putting my head under water and stamping on my fingers.

I managed to climb onto the boat. I did not use my kukri on them but I hit some of them with my baton, fist and feet. They seemed to lose their senses but I didn't so I subdued them and made them get to the shore. In all the action lasted about twenty minutes, that is from first seeing them to getting them ashore. I learnt how to cope with such a situation by a combination of experience and new skills, such as taekwon-do. That was more use than rifle bullets.

I captured many IIs, so many I lost count. We used a piece of kit we knew as IWS to see better at night. It was about one foot long and heavy. It gave us vision up to about a hundred metres and, once our target had been seen, we put it down.

When I was awarded the Queen's Gallantry Medal[2] I was surprised. I got many congratulations from my friends and from England. I went to England to collect my award from the queen. That was my second time in the UK. I was there on a course in 1971. Going to the palace

---

[2] Aimansing Limbu is the first, and at time of writing, the only Gurkha to be awarded the QGM. The citation makes a more compelling narrative than this story. Reticence and modesty in the telling were obvious.

made me think how proud I was to have shaken the hand of the British queen when I had never met the royal family of my own country.

Dalbahadur Rai, 1/7 GR. In 1967 we were in Hong Kong, up on the Chinese border. I was due to go on leave but that was cancelled. IIs had started coming over in numbers. I was an acting sergeant, Support Company, but attached to D Company. We operated at night and went back to barracks by day. We worked in three-man groups, armed with large truncheons and kukris. There was one rifle for each three-man group and one radio. One night my group was in ambush in a patch of trees about 200 yards behind the border. It was raining. We caught 30 people, male and female aged between 20 and 25, and sent them back to HQ. Some tried to fight and some tried to run away. Around midnight I saw, through my night-vision glasses, about half a dozen people coming our way. I alerted the other two. Two IIs went into a small outside latrine and two moved over to the other side of the track. I caught the two in the latrine and two others near a small fishpond nearby. Two ran away and one went into some swampy ground. I told my radio operator to be near me and I went to apprehend the lone man. He was big and strong and had two knives. I closed in on him and he attacked me. We wrestled. He then slashed at me, cutting my jacket. I took my kukri out to deal with him. I raised it but, as I brought it down, it snagged on a branch so hitting him in the back and breaking his spine. If I had not hit the tree, he would have been killed.

He fell and couldn't get up. I disarmed him. There was blood everywhere. I bound him up as best I could with my first field dressing. I called one of the others and took him to the road. I called up the company commander and sent him off to HQ. From there he was sent to hospital and later became a citizen of Hong Kong. He was a lucky man and, as he might have killed me, I also was lucky.

I was the centre of an enquiry. I took my interlocutors to show them what had happened. I was exonerated and was given a Queen's Commendation. That is shown by my wearing an oak leaf. I was the only Gurkha to have one. No other Gurkha had won one when I left the army.

CHAPTER 11

Cyprus

In colonial times the British regarded Cyprus as 'the key to western Asia'. 1/2 GR formed part of the original garrison at Larnaca in 1878 and Gurkhas were stationed on the island in both World Wars.

As a result of the Greek Cypriots wanting *Enosis,* or union, with Greece there was much anti-British activity in the 1950s and in 1958 the Turks intervened. Independence, within the Commonwealth, came in 1959. By the terms of the treaty which established the Republic of Cyprus in 1960 two British Sovereign Base Areas (BSBA) were set up, at Akrotiri in the west, and Dhekelia in the east, amounting to 99 square miles of territory.

In 1974 renewed calls for *Enosis* were followed by a coup by the Greek National Guard against the president, Archbishop Makarios, and attacks by the Greek National Guard on all the Turkish communities in Cyprus. In response the Turkish regular army invaded the island from mainland Turkey to assist the Turkish Cypriots.

10 GR, in the UK, were put on 72 hours' notice to move to Cyprus and went there at the end of July 1974. The Turkish government complained that 'mercenaries' should not be used and the 'mercenary' aspect was correctly rebutted. The Turks then accused the British of wrongly using Turk against Turk because the British were deploying Gurkhas who, as everybody knew, were really Turkas.

For the first week a ceasefire held, then broke down as the Turks advanced on the coastal town of Famagusta and the Dhekelia Base Area was imperiled. Thousands of refugees poured into the base. 10 GR manned road blocks, searched vehicles, put out mobile patrols to let the two ethnic communities see who, in fact, 10 GR were and how they operated.

In the face of the Turkish advance on Famagusta, the Greek National Guard was expected to withdraw into the apex of land south of Famagusta and east of Dhekelia, known as 'The Triangle'. A and C

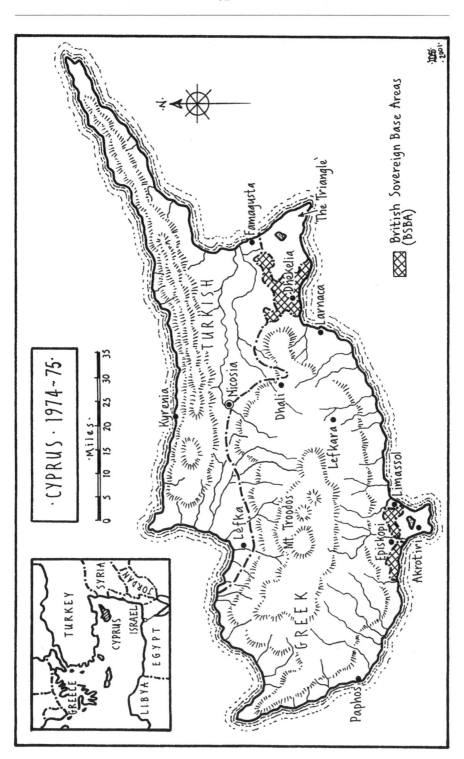

Companies were deployed to meet them, disarm them, escort them through the BSBA and then return their weapons to them on the far side.

By 27 February 1975 10 GR were back in UK.

Hitbahadur Bhujel, 10 GR, *continued his story after Borneo.*

It was peace time soldiering in Hong Kong after that. I was promoted to lance corporal, went on courses in Sungei Patani in Malaya and later, as a corporal, went on three courses in England. At the end of July 1974, when the amalgamated battalion was in England, we were given three hours' notice to move to Cyprus.[1] We flew from Swindon to Dhekelia. Our task was to protect the British Sovereign Base Area. Some of the roads were good but others were very narrow. I also did duty guarding the radar installations which were in a restricted area.

For the past six to seven months the Turks had bullied the Greeks and driven them away from their homes. The ruler, Makarios, was a Christian Greek and his deputy, Rauf Denktash, a Turkish Muslim. The Turks were in a minority. The Greek ruler said that Cypriots were all one but, even so, the Greeks had turned out Turks from villages in the Greek sector and had tried to kill the villagers. They had used bulldozers to make trenches and then tried to bury the Turks in them, dead or alive. Makarios couldn't control them and the Turks bombed his residence, the Peninsula Hotel and government buildings.

The Greeks said that they did not like the British troops and that, I suppose, is why the Gurkhas were sent. The refugees liked us Gurkhas and there were many refugees. It was not a very happy time in Cyprus.

We set up road blocks and the Turks were told not to come south from Nicosia. Famagusta and Larnaca were untouched. Makarios' house had a cellar to hide in but he escaped to Britain by British Airways. Denktash went to Turkey. His enemy was called Nikos Sampson. The Greeks had weapons in their houses. We set up road blocks and established a curfew. Greek police were armed with [Lee-Enfield] Mark V rifles. The Greeks were wicked. The code word for us putting up a road block in a hurry was "Pink Panther" with the grid reference of where it was to be.

I was on stand-by. Our weapons were AR15s and SLRs. I was a sergeant and I had a corporal and 15 riflemen under me. I was ordered

---

[1] Maybe this refers to the actual move to the airhead.

to set up a road block and away we went in a three-ton lorry. A Greek police lieutenant colonel had come through another road block where Lieutenant (QGO) Manbahadur was. I didn't know how he had managed to get through but I had to stop him. He drove up to me in a police vehicle. He was in uniform. The corporal checked the vehicle but the police officer would not let him open the boot. I was called down.

I said that he should open his boot and, as he was an officer, saluted him. I told him it was an order that he had to open it. "I won't open it," he answered. "I'm a lieutenant colonel. You are only a sergeant. Are you a lieutenant colonel?" I saw he was trying to pick a quarrel with me so I took out the ignition key. "You are a lieutenant colonel, Mr Makarios' man. I am Queen Elizabeth's man. I am also looking after Makarios."

I sent a message to the OC, Major Watt. He was a great sleeper when he had nothing else to do. Major Watt was also on a road block and he told me to bring the Greek police officer to him. I knew that his boot was full of weapons for the villagers. "You won't open your boot? Follow me to HQ." He agreed and away we drove, he following my vehicle. We passed a turning to a village, Ormadia, where the largest Greek police station was. It was completely out of bounds to all of us. No one was allowed to enter it. The police colonel followed me a short while but accelerated and drove off to the police station in Ormadia.

I made a radio call to Major Watt and reported it, telling him the vehicle number. "Follow him," he told me in English. I told him that it was out of bounds. "No worry. Follow him." So, no matter what, that is what I did. There were 300 policemen there and I told my driver to go to the police station as fast as he could. Once there I pulled out my SMG and loaded it. I was surrounded by policemen and, as I had no idea what else to do, I brought my weapon up to the fire position and the policemen ran away. The police colonel had gone inside. I sat in his vehicle with my cocked weapon. Police majors and captains came out to me and later on so did the lieutenant colonel.

I asked him why he had run away and he said that he had just wanted to visit his people. I told him to get into his vehicle and that he had to drive to my camp. "If you don't get into your vehicle and go to my HQ I will shoot you," I told him. Away we went. He tried to escape again but drove into the road block where Major Watt was. "Here he is, please don't shoot him, please don't shoot him," Major Watt said to me. I was so angry with the police officer that is what I wanted to do.

I went to see the CO, Lieutenant Colonel Pike, who asked me if I wanted to go and see the brigadier? Then I was told that the Greek police officer would not come back to the British base but was going to Larnaca. I was to take his photograph, thoroughly recognise him and note details of his vehicle. By then it was evening and the Greek had to be escorted to another road block, called Whiskey Three. No one wanted to take him so I said I would. Major Watt said "Please, please don't hit him." I took the Greek police officer away and let him go at the last road block.

Next day the CO called me in and asked me if I had gone into the Greek police station. "Yes, I did. If I follow an enemy I go with a Commonwealth order." He accepted that but the brigadier took action. "On whose orders did you go to the police station?" he asked me. "The OC's," I told him. "Didn't you know the order NOT to go into the police station?" "Yes." "Why, then, did you go?" "I was following the OC's orders. I have to follow orders. In that case why were we allowed to cross the Borneo border and go into Indonesia? After the enemy, surely."

I turned to the CO and said "If we had not crossed the border you would not have the DSO." In a quiet voice he said "Keep quiet." I don't know what he said to Major Watt. I was also CQMS and the Naafi manager and that evening we all met up in the Naafi, the OC, CSM, platoon commander and the company 2IC. I was told not to worry. Sure, the CO was angry. Back in England I received the Queen's Commendation, the only one of 10 GR.

After we got back to Hong Kong I was guard commander of the magazine guard and one of my soldiers, discharged five rounds from his rifle when he was sleepy. I was determined to save him; why ruin a soldier's career for such a thing? I had the weapon cleaned, threw away the empty rounds and managed to get five more for him before I was approached by the duty officer to find out why the shots had happened. I stuck to my story that it was fireworks from a Chinese village. I was not believed by anybody and was leant on heavily by everybody, right to the top. But no one had proof so, in the end, the case was dropped. If I had been discovered, I would have been court martialled. It is very hard to cover up for anybody. That man was eventually promoted to Gurkha lieutenant. He refers to me as his saviour. He is now in charge of the Sultan of Brunei's brother's bodyguard.

CHAPTER 12

The Falklands

Everyone who heard about it was surprised when the quarrel over the Falkland Islands erupted, so it is worth recalling how those islands were invaded.

After the British had dismissed protests and ignored previous incidents, five frigates with 1,600 soldiers aboard left Buenos Aires undetected, arrived off the islands and delivered an ultimatum. This was rejected and the invading troops landed under cover of a bombardment by the frigates. The British marines ashore – two officers and 21 other ranks – fired a few shots for honour's sake then, seeing the impossibility of defence against such a force, capitulated.

In London there was intense indignation, not only at the invasion, but at the Government's failure to foresee and prevent it. The Foreign Secretary had to resign and, without waiting for a reply to diplomatic protests, a powerful task force was quickly fitted out in Portsmouth.

The Foreign Secretary's name is of no concern for that invasion took place in 1770.

Those who will not learn from history are doomed to repeat it, as happened during the 1970s and culminated in armed conflict in 1982.

A neat encapsulation of the problem put it that 'The Falkland Islands' misfortune has always been to be wanted more than they are loved. One can draw a neat balance between years of diplomatic negotiation with an unstable Argentine polity, on the one hand, and the irresponsibility of a British House of Commons on the other.'[1]

The Falkland Islands' dispute was not about 'colonial Britain': there were no Mayan, Aztec or sub-continental Indian masses being subjugated there, no African tribes, no imported slave races, no debauched Polynesians or Aborigines, not even any Chinese refugees escaping over a wire – merely a small population of settlers of British blood.

That having been pointed out, it is also true to say that seldom has a

---

[1] Review article (of Hastings, Max, & Jenkins, Simon, *The Battle of the Falklands*) in *The Economist*, 19 February 1983.

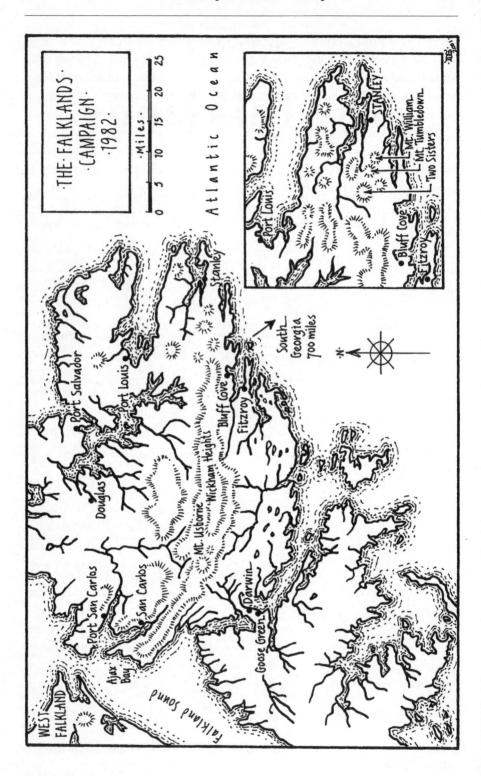

shorter war produced such opposing views about the rights and wrongs of it all. Experts on Latin America tended to find it more difficult than most to judge it in an unbiased fashion, if only because a number of Latin American countries quietly applauded the British action – very quietly, but applaud it they did. It is also not known how many of Argentina's neighbours knew about that country's nuclear plans and potential.

Much as these experts might deplore the conduct of the Argentine military junta, they tended to sympathise with the populist anti-colonialism which brought Argentina the amount of moral support that it did, overtly, despite the considerable criticism in private, on the Latin American sub-continent. Argentine claims to the islands can be traced back to the papal partition of sovereignty in the New World in 1494, but these are unfounded. However, it cannot be gainsaid that the Argentines were more patriotic about the Islas Malvinas, as they know the islands, in that 149th year of their being British (once more), than the British were about the Falklands.

1/7 GR, stationed in the United Kingdom since 1981, had been made part of 5 British Airborne Brigade – one of the two brigades that were deployed in the Task Force to recapture the territory – and, in fact, the battalion played only a small part in the fighting during the 45 days it was deployed on land. It only got a mention, as being part of the Order of Battle of 5 Brigade, three times in the first two books to be produced after the fighting was over. The reason is that the Gurkhas never did anything worthy of being written about in the eyes of those two, British, authors. There was a certain amount of embarrassed murmuring behind hands raised to mouths in high military circles that the battalion was badly misemployed but only those intimately connected with events have the right so to say. In any case, victory covers a multitude of wrong decisions as well as emphasizing many correct ones.

Argentine troops in front of 1/7 GR melted away and refused contact. The following extract contains a clue to Argentina's fraudulent and uncomplimentary propaganda about the Gurkhas: 'The [Gurkhas'] fighting record is virtually second to none, although in the eyes of the uninformed they are perhaps credited with magical powers, as witnessed by the Argentine reaction to them in the Falklands.'[2] The Gurkhas are probably the only soldiers who can win their battles on their reputation alone.

---

[2] See the *Journal of the Royal United Services Institute for Defence Studies* March 1983.

The stories featured here reflect not only the paucity of action but also how the Gurkhas saw themselves, warts and all.

Interestingly, despite much shrill leftist propaganda in Kathmandu during this period, the Nepalese Government made no adverse comment, nor did the Indian Government. In London, Third World representations tried to prevent any Gurkha troops being used. However, it was more important to win the ensuing battle than to listen to nit-picking prattle, so no notice was taken and the decision was made.

Barajit Rai, 1/7 GR. I trained for nine months in Hong Kong and joined 7 GR. We went to Brunei and had some good and interesting training. As my father had been a driver I was interested in vehicles and got a transfer into the MT Platoon. That was from 1979 to 1982.

And then it was time to go to the Falklands. I had always wondered if I would go to war and see the enemy. I was called to the office and told that as A Company was short of NCOs I was to go there, it was my original company, to be a section commander. We were on the *Queen Elizabeth II* for 22 days and 22 nights. We transferred ships and landed on the north side of the Falklands. I liked the place. It was a good place and I was ready for war. We all had about 65 or 70 pounds to carry. We went to Goose Green by Chinook in one day. 2 Para[3] had taken it a week before and the Argentine dead were still lying around just as they had fallen. We took some POWs and they put the bodies in trenches that were dug by dozers.

Once we were at Goose Green I felt we had, at last, got to the war. 2 Para were ahead of us; we were in the rear, in a supporting role. We went ahead ten days later but our stores had been sunk in the ship by the Argentines before being unloaded so we returned to where we had been. We moved off to the north-west and at last came under 105mm artillery fire, rounds dropping at five-, ten- or 15-minute intervals.

It rained and we dug trenches. 1/7 GR had no face-to-face contact with the enemy but, at the end, for the final assault, we were sent to Mount William where the start line was. The soldiers were very tired and the LMG pair in my section did not want to dig their trench. I dug mine and the platoon commander was angry with those two. The 105mm shells came nearer and nearer and those who had not dug

---

[3] 2nd Battalion, Parachute Regiment.

trenches fell into ours! We had three trenches with nine men each and were so squashed we had the greatest difficulty in getting out. One shell landed in the middle of three of us and one man was thrown into the air and landed unconscious in a trench. One man was hit in the foot by a splinter.

A Company were to give supporting fire from the top of the feature. It was hard work getting some of the men forward. One man, a Sherpa, hid. A bomb splinter hit a stone and ricocheted off onto his water bottle. He thought he had been killed and shouted out "Aya, aya, I'm dead, I'm dead." I gave him a rocket. The top of the hill was still half an hour away. The battalion 2IC was there and sited the weapons. He told us to stay ready but not to open fire. Our company commander was Willis sahib, the man who had enlisted me. But I never did open fire.

Whether it was good luck or bad luck, the war ended then. Three weeks later, filling in trenches, a corporal's tool exploded a mine and he was killed and two men were wounded. We embarked on the *Uganda* and got to Southampton. Major General Chapple, the MGBG, welcomed us. We had not had much war experience but had a tremendous welcome from the public. It was glorious. We had a two-hour march through Fleet to the lines. Normally our men get tired carrying the rifles in the trail position after 15 to 20 minutes but none of us felt tired at all. The public took us into their homes, into the pubs and did not allow us to pay for anything. One club sent two or three barrels of beer to the battalion. All were very happy.

Forty men were given a free 3-star and 5-star hotel holiday. Especially the ex-members of the Brigade welcomed us into their homes. In fact, the British battalions had done the fighting and taken the casualties. I felt we had not been used correctly, nor had we deserved such a wonderful welcome from the public for we had not done as much as they thought we had.

I finished up as a WO2.

Aimansing Limbu, QGM, 1/7 GR, *continued his story.*

The next time I had contact with hostiles was in the Falklands. I was a section commander then. The battalion was in England and 2 Para went to start with. We, in 1/7 GR, thought it would be all over before we had a chance to get there. We went a month later with only 15 days' notice.

It was good that we went before any other Gurkha battalion[4] was sent. During those 15 days we trained hard in Wales on field firing ranges with live ammunition. It was so cold there we felt it was good training for the Falklands. One of our men was killed in a motor accident after the training. Everybody had their own thoughts before we left England; some went to the temple. I didn't but I did think of my god.

We went by the *QEII* having packed up our belongings and locked our barrack rooms in our camp in Church Crookham. On our way out the public gave us a great farewell. I felt moved when other ships "wept", "waaai waaai", at our departure. As we approached South Georgia we had been warned that the Argentines had sent a submarine to attack us. We had air support and other boat's AA guns.

Once at the Falklands we disembarked at night. We had been warned to disembark the following day but a moment later we were told to move immediately. No time even for a cup of tea! At San Carlos we took up positions and dug trenches, all in the dark. The earth was soft and we met water about two to three feet down. At dawn we saw high ground to left and right with the sea behind us. There were no trees, only grass.

We moved to Goose Green in Chinook helicopters. These are normally a 45-man capacity but we were a hundred in one lift. It was a great squeeze and lasted for 30 minutes. At Goose Green there were no trees, only grass. 2 Para had attacked there and we went to guard it. The Argentines had left their rations. I set up a defensive post. There were many dead Argentines there. Later Argentine prisoners of war came and buried the corpses in pits dug by dozers.

We moved off to Black Cock for a day then went forward about 10km on foot. We spent two days on higher ground where we were shelled. We had two wounded. The Argentines fired 120mm artillery only and there were no aircraft.

The last attack was to go in on Mount William. We left at night. A Company gave covering fire to Tumbledown. Argentine artillery kept our heads down as we advanced. We were covering D Company which was going to make the attack. Argentine snipers delayed us but a little while later the Argentines surrendered.

One of our signallers was killed by an Argentine grenade left as a booby trap, primed with the pin out and lodged so that it would explode when moved. This happened while we were filling in trenches.

---

[4] Some of the battalions in Hong Kong volunteered to be sent to the Falklands.

We had a great welcome in Southampton and in Fleet when we marched through the town. The people were most appreciative. Although normally our rifles would have made our arms ache by marching that way for so long, none of us felt tired.

Dalbahadur Rai, 1/7 GR, *continued.*

We had to prepare in a great hurry. I was Support Company CQMS but I had to go to D Company, never having a proper hand-over. We had a lot of preparation to do, including arctic clothing which was very heavy. This was the first time any of us had experience preparing for real war and it was not easy. Our soldiers all wanted GPMGs, even in place of rations, and the OC said he wanted to have one GPMG between two soldiers. However, that was not allowed and we had to take what was the authorised scale of the weapon.

The boat we went on was the *Queen Elizabeth II*, much bigger than the one I had gone from Calcutta on, and much better furnished. Cloth was put on the velvet cushion covers to keep them clean. We were always a bit scared of sinking as there was a war on and rescue would be difficult. The men said they probably would not die on land but there was a bigger chance of dying at sea. Look what happened to the *Belgrano* later!

On the *QEII* we were not very seasick. In fact the Welsh Guards were more seasick then we were. At my level we did not find the Welsh and Scots accents all that hard to understand but at soldier level there were some problems with the Scots.

However, our minds were prepared to go anywhere and eat anything as we had sworn an oath to obey all orders. As for our traditions and discipline, each regiment has its own, as the Guards battalions had theirs and kept to them. Even so, we Gurkhas made less noise and drank less than did the British soldiers.

We called in at Cape Town in South Africa and, two days before the end of our journey, transferred to the *Norland* near South Georgia. We did not land but went over by a kind of bridge. There was more movement on that boat but we managed. The great thing was that everything was duty free. Brandy was 3p for as much as we wanted. We all got drunk, as did the British troops with us.[5]

---

[5] This boast is not borne out by anyone else.

After three days we landed at San Carlos. D Company was the leading company. The CO had said that we would move to Goose Green by helicopter but our OC opted to go by foot. The loads were very heavy[6] and it took three days for them to get there. I stayed in B Echelon.[7] We all prepared trenches and shelters. There were no vehicles, only light aircraft and helicopters. The only guns were ships' guns and our own 81mm mortars.

There were great difficulties such as no ration supplies on the way forward to Mount William. Helicopters were in very short supply and the weather was not good. Gurkha re-supply was the lowest priority. Solid fuel was used and men would cook their meals in pairs, in mess tins. Sometimes they had to eat their rice uncooked. Self-heating food was mostly given to the British troops as such stuff was not in the Gurkha scales.

During the critical time of contact with the enemy we only had one re-supply. It was not an easy time for the forward companies. They found some Argentine rations in deserted trenches and in positions still full of dead men. Back in B Echelon I never saw any enemy and only heard bombardments from the air and the guns.

We were all happy with the cease-fire, the happiest being the battalion 2IC, Major Dawson. He came and shook us all by the hand. But we were also disappointed; no face-to-face action, no contacts and no medals for bravery. We felt incomplete. In fact one man was shot dead by an Argentine sniper. It was much easier after the cease-fire and we were all sent back to Goose Green. Then we were sent to clear West Fox Bay. Our welcome back to England was great, especially when we marched through Fleet.

In my 28 years' experience I felt we were trained properly for any kind of warfare, from tropical Sarawak to arctic Falklands. As for field commanders in Borneo, had they introduced swimming training earlier we would have had fewer deaths.

I left the army in 1992 as a Gurkha Captain and was promoted to

---

[6] The loads were so heavy because 1/7 GR carried weights of over 120lbs because the men had more weapons and more ammunition than anyone else in the theatre. They had 2 GPMGs per section, for example, and the battalion had learnt, on its last exercise in Wales, that it could not trust helicopters or the weather, to help move heave gear forward so the men had to carry it all themselves. Only in the attack were they stripped down to 'fighting order'. Letter from Lt Col (later Brig) D.P. de C. Morgan, OBE, CO 1/7 GR, 30 August 1985.

[7] Rear administrative area.

Honorary Lieutenant (GCO) on retirement. Since then I have been an AWO looking after ex-servicemen's and serving soldiers' home problems and an ARO, helping to recruit. Both jobs are harder than any I did in the army.

Jagandhoj Limbu, 2/7 GR, 1/7 GR, *had been to a number of places before he went on active service.*

I joined the army on 7 October 1964 and, after nine months' training, was posted to the Recce Platoon in Support Company of 2/7 GR in Malacca. One night, in the middle of a large exercise, we were called back to camp to go to Hong Kong immediately to quell trouble. In the event we landed in the Philippines which we all thought was Vietnam. After three and a half hours at the airport we took off again for Hong Kong. Typhoon conditions had prevented our landing earlier. We were stationed, along with battalion HQ, at Kai Tak airport.

After that we returned to Malacca and handed over to 2/10 GR, and I went on six months' home leave. We had several overseas exercises, one in Australia and one in Papua New Guinea, as well as in Singapore, Brunei and Malaysia. After another spell of home leave we moved to Brunei in December 1975 and as a corporal I was part of the demonstration platoon of the Training Team Brunei[8] for two years, until December 1977. In 1972 the battalion, by now the amalgamated 7 GR, went to England and my platoon was part of the Demonstration Platoon at Mons Officers' Training School. One time we spent two months in Cyprus as Exercise Enemy to cadets from Sandhurst.

In 1974 we handed over to 10 GR in Church Crookham and moved back to Hong Kong. I went on six months' home leave. In 1978 I went to England to help with the battalion shooting team at Bisley. By this time there were two battalions of 7 GR once more. When I was promoted to WO2, I was sent to D Company, 1/7 GR. On 2 April 1982 we heard that Argentina had invaded the Falkland Islands. We didn't believe it until we had heard officially but we saw it on TV in the Naafi.

We started various activities, preparing for war. These included administration such as checking nominal rolls and family details. D Company went to Sennybridge for dry training and live firing. There were eight ranges there and the range warden said, in English, to me

---

[8] This was what was left of the JWS (1948–71) from mainland Malaysia.

"Johnny, the Argentines have twisted the lion's tail. Careful. The lion is roaring now." I understood what he said but I did not answer him as I was busy. For our final training we were at Sennybridge for a week. We trained individually and collectively, dry and live, in sections, platoons and companies, day and night. One night we had a night attack exercise. C Company was on our right. We reached the FUP around midnight and heard a Land Rover driving our way very fast, engine roaring and tyres screeching. It braked and we heard it roll over three times. We knew that something serious had happened. It was the ammunition vehicle bringing stores for C Company. Sergeant Ranbahadur Limbu was killed.

We advanced by leap-frogging and reached our objective where British troops, acting as enemy, opened fire at us. I was carrying my rifle across my chest and my right foot stuck in a hole. The rifle hit my nose and I became unconscious. A little later the OC called me and I told him I had broken my nose. We were back in camp next morning then, at the end of training, went back to Church Crookham. B Company had to be recalled from Belize.

By the 12th we were ready to go to the Falklands as part of 5 Brigade. We went to Southampton and embarked on the *QEII*. This was a very big ship and I had never seen anything like it. Welsh and Scots Guards, along with some supporting elements, embarked first. We were given a tremendous send off and it did not seem as though we were going to war but we knew we were. I felt uncertain about being hit when at sea as there was nothing to tread on nor to catch hold of. As we are bad sailors and suffer from seasickness we were put in the lowest deck where the rolling was least felt. Our schedule was PT first thing. The ship was so big we were tired out after running once round the deck. We had weapon training lessons and live firing. After five or six days we stopped at Freetown for three or four hours for refuelling but we were not allowed off the boat. The BBC gave so much news that the Argentines had to know where we where. I got really angry as I listened to broadcasts and I wanted to smash the loud speakers to try and keep them quiet! When we reached the edge of South Georgia we changed ships and embarked on the MV *Norland*. It was very rough. We were all given something to drink but I saw no drunkenness, any sickness being due to the rough seas.

We disembarked at San Carlos and D Company moved nonstop to the high ground. This time there was no leap-frogging. On our right was swamp. It was useless country, the land was no good, no trees but swamp and stony hills. There were trees at Goose Green which we reached later. We took over trenches that had been dug by 2 Para. Our task was to guard the southern perimeter. Milan[9] ammunition boxes were strewn all over the place. It had not been easy to make a beachhead but there was no other place available with equally good facilities. Hospital ships stayed there till the end. The area was just big enough to accommodate brigade HQ.

We advanced for three days. We were the only company not to go by helicopter for part of the way. We went to Goose Green and I think that 2 Para had done very well there. The forward company was on a small rise making a good defensive position. They had made a night attack there and won two Victoria Crosses. We modified the trenches they had dug with *sangars*[10] but did not dig new ones as other parts of the ground were too wet. We stayed there a day and a night. There were still some dead Argentines and blood-stained clothing in the area. Battlefield debris made us move carefully and much ammunition was strewn around.

We advanced from Goose Green, always on foot. I suppose we managed to move four or five miles a day. It was light from around 1000 hours and dark soon after 1500 hours so there were only around five to six hours of daylight. We moved to Fitzroy by civilian trawler, SS *Monsuman*, with elements of 2 Para, as a temporary brigade patrol unit.

RFA *Sir Galahad* was sunk. The Scots Guards had secured the beachhead and went up to some higher ground on the right with the Commandos on the left. We went up the ridge and took a defensive position. An Argentine aircraft came over twice but we thought it was ours. The British command system was very good to warn us so quickly about such an attack. There was nowhere to hide except behind boulders. Harriers drove them away. We knew that the next attack would be by an Argentine aircraft and the third time an Argentine aircraft came over the company signaller and one other fired their SLRs at it. The company commander shouted out, "Signal cowboy, don't fire at it with your rifle." The sky was black with the smoke of shells trying to shoot it down and all were ineffective, including the anti-aircraft Blowpipe system. I saw it all happening through my binoculars. The Welsh Guards were in the *Sir Galahad* when it was sunk. Sea King

---

[9] Milan, wire-controlled anti-tank missile, used in the Falklands to destroy bunkers.
[10] Defensive breastworks.

helicopters did valuable work in rescuing people. Many of the crew were Chinese and there were many deaths.

Three days later we moved to Bluff Cove. B Company was on our right and the Scots Guards on our left. We were in the middle, on a ridge line. Each evening Argentine artillery was fired at us but luckily on our ridge line all shells went overhead. B Company was hit and had some casualties when a shell landed in a trench.

Orders came for the final attack. The start line was Goat Ridge. A helicopter brought rocket launcher anti-tank and other types of ammunition. I was clever; the company commander had told me to get the maximum ammunition and I got so much that B Company complained that we had taken their share. We moved at night and the axis of our advance was the high ground between Mount Tumbledown and our FUP at Goat Ridge. We walked on and on. It was very cold. Some of us stumbled on bodies, dead or sleeping, Argentine or Scots Guards? We did not stop to find out.

The brigade plan was for the Scots Guards to take Mount Tumbledown before dawn and then 1/7 GR would pass through them, being given covering fire onto Mount William. It would be a difficult task as maximum enemy trenches were on Mount William. It was easy for the enemy to hide among the boulders and so not be seen by us in time. .50 Browning MMGs had been given to the Pipes and Drums Platoon and they were part of a fire support group for the Scots Guards. In their attack the Scots Guards had 14, or was it 17, men killed. However, the Scots Guards were late onto their objective by when it was well after daylight.

We had to move off for the final attack still in the dark and were not to linger. As we crossed the edge of a minefield enemy artillery fired on us and this held up A Company, to our front, for an hour. One man had his equipment shot off his back. It was light before we reached our final objective and the enemy were so afraid of us they surrendered, put up a white flag and accepted unconditional surrender. They were mentally ill-equipped for us Gurkhas.

The CO came up with the FOO and the Anti-Tank Platoon commander. They stood up on a high stone and suddenly the CO said "hide, hide", but in Nepali, "*luk, luk*". That sounds just like the English "look, look" and the FOO, not understanding, stood there, looking around. A bullet from a Scots Guard hit a rock close by, ricocheted off and wounded him near his heart. He was evacuated by helicopter. A Guardsman asked me who were those on the left flank coming down from the ridge and I said I had no idea. He looked through his telescope and was ready to fire but I restrained him. The group was the CO's.

We were ordered to go to Stanley to disarm the Argentines and the Scots Guards were sent away then and there. We Gurkhas had to spend one more night on the mountain and it was the hardest night of all. Mount William was the most difficult place to attack and if the Argentines had been as courageous as the Gurkhas they'd have stayed there and we'd have had maximum casualties and possible defeat, such a difficult place to attack was it.

Argentine administration was weak and the Argentine soldiers were not happy to fight, so it was said. Looking at their rations, their trenches and their tactics, they were not up to much. The soldiers were raw. There was nothing wrong with their weapons and their boots were excellent, much better than ours. Our boots were the worst part of our clothing. They were DMS, not Combat High, and were no good for terrain such as the Falklands. Had we had a rubber cover for our boots, our feet would not have hurt so much, nor would there have been a danger of frostbite. Our feet hurt so much that, after we had rested, they still hurt when we had to be on the move again.

Our return to England was stupendous. As for the battle honour we were given despite no fatal casualties during the fighting, we deserved it as our reputation alone drove the Argentines away so victory was ours. I am sure that if 1/7 GR had not been sent to the Falklands victory would not have been so easy. On my next home leave my wife told me she had heard that all the Gurkhas who had gone to the Falklands had been killed.[11] I told her that I had come back!

What I understand from the Falklands war is that GORs in future must maintain regimental traditions and spirit.[12] Our bravery is well known already.

Bishnukumar Rai, 1/7 GR, *had been in a rifle company in Hong Kong.*

By the time of the Falklands crisis I was a trained anti-tank gunner. I

---

[11] The buzz in Kathmandu was that all bar one soldier in 1/7 GR had been killed. The rumour was eventually traced to the Soviet embassy.

[12] This spirit is known as *kaida*, the proper way of doing things in the tightly-knit, well-organised extended family that a good unit is.

was the first man of 1/7 GR to be taught the Milan anti-tank weapon. We heard that the Argentines had asked the Falkland Island authorities for training facilities and then some of them would not leave. One shipload of troops was sent to the Falklands and the month's anti-tank range firing that had been arranged for us in Cyprus was cancelled. We managed to have two weeks there before being recalled when 5 Brigade, of which we were part, was detailed to go to the Falklands.

We had a great farewell from Southampton and eventually reached the Falklands. My lot had to jump into the sea near Goose Green when Argentine fighters attacked us. Our fighters drove them away. We were ferried by Chinook helicopter up a hill where we dug defensive positions. We stayed there a few days, how many I can't remember. I was attached to A Company.

Later we were moved up on to the features Twin Sisters and Goat Ridge to give support to the British battalions. The Scots Guards were to take Tumbledown and we were meant to go to Mount William, but we were late in starting and only arrived when it was light. There was a heavy bombardment and the British battalion took casualties. In the battle I heard all sorts of weapons being fired. In real war tactics break down, people get lost and I heard shouts asking where sections had got to. We saw men lying down but we did not know if they were asleep or dead. As we passed we saw they were dead. We had one man hit and the medical orderly was called. I heard an English voice shout that the fire was too hard and he was not coming to fetch the wounded man. The 2IC of A Company gave first aid until a medical orderly arrived.

One Scots Guards sniper opened fire on us. One of our men had his water bottle shattered and the FOO was wounded by a ricochet. One of our LMGs fired at a friendly helicopter which was flying much too high to be hit. Then the white flag was flown over Stanley and the war was over. We were surprised by firing from a flank and thought that the British troops had not heard that the fighting was at an end but they were firing their weapons because they were happy. We had to stay around there for two more days.

We had a tremendous welcome from the British public when we arrived at Southampton and later when we went around.

I left the army as a sergeant on 31 October 1985.

CHAPTER 13

The Gulf War

On 2 August 1990 Iraq annexed Kuwait. To free it Operation Granby was mounted to move troops to the region as a prelude to Operation Desert Storm, which took place from 24-28 February 1991.

The British Army contingent amounted to some 45,000 all ranks and contained an element of the Brigade of Gurkhas. Unusually this was not composed of infantrymen but a logistical unit, 28 (Ambulance) Squadron GTR. Even that unit was a temporary one, made up from the two squadrons of the regiment, with elements of the Queen's Gurkha Signals and the Band of the Brigade of Gurkhas also being involved.

Of interest is a comment from an influential American reporter that the Ambulance Squadron was the smartest of all units he saw in the Gulf.

Krishnabahadur Gurung, MVO, MBE, GTR. I served in many places, from the Far East to Europe and took on my responsibilities in many places but I never gave myself even one per cent chance of being involved in a war. In April 1990 I went on a Royal Corps of Transport Troop Leader's Course in UK, the first QGO so to do and, much the wiser, was posted to the Gurkha Mechanical Transport School in Sek Kong. In the November I was sent for, at very short notice, by RHQ. After reporting to the CO I found he, the 2IC and I had to report to the Royal Hong Kong Police Training School for Press Interview Techniques instruction. I was very surprised. Why such instruction? I had never had such training before, especially for such minor matters, and it had to be connected with my instructing job.

On the third day talk of war came with such questions as what effect would involvement in war by Gurkha soldiers have on their families and what sort of feed back would there be and what would the families think about it? I could not see how any of that was relevant.

Back at RHQ the two British officers whispered to themselves that it was about time the news was broken to me and I was told that there was a possibility of one of the squadrons being involved in the Gulf operation. "However, that has yet to be confirmed. Wait, out!"

The CO stressed that the news was for us three alone. Over the next couple of days I became more confident and could see the relevance of that course. At that time there were some senior to me and that surprised me. I wondered how it was that I had been appointed for the task of being Squadron Senior QGO but I accepted it.

Then a signal came from MOD saying that a squadron was required. We three then told our families. When my 12- and 13-year-old children were out of the house I told my wife I was going to the war. She asked me where and I told her it was the Gulf and she said that that was an aerial war so how could I be involved? I was more confident after my wife gave me her support.

Next day the CO told me to choose four senior QGOs and troop commanders. I told him that my choosing commanders was invidious as all the QGOs were capable so he could detail them, but the rank and file needed to be combed for the best available.

We made up the ORBAT[1] for what was to be 28 Gurkha (Ambulance) Squadron from both 28 and 31 Squadrons. We started training the command element while the rank and file of the squadron was chosen. After two weeks' training the OC squadron was due for posting so a new one came, Major R. Gilroy. At the time the advance party was due to go to UK he became father of twins so I was sent instead. I had had no training for any type of Northern Ireland situation nor had I any knowledge about ambulance training – we had no such equipment anyway. Never mind. OC 29 [non-Gurkha] Squadron was given the task of collecting kit in UK.

I took 30 men to the UK in mid-November and Major Gilroy stayed in Hong Kong supervising the rest of the squadron in low-level training. The whole squadron had reached UK by 5 December 1990 by which time the advance party had collected all the ambulances and stores which filled a whole gymnasium in Church Crookham.

All was new to us but I found I was daily becoming more interested and more confident, and with higher morale. Most of the men seemed happy to be going to war. After training started and we realised the war would be different, the men started asking about mechanised warfare and the effect of aerial bombardment, even what chance would they

---

[1] Order of Battle.

have of survival if Saddam Hussein started in earnest. So far our duties had been normal transportation work going from A to B and back in jungle terrain.

Training continued and we sent our stores to Saudi by boat. After that we had a Christmas break and the British officers went away for three days. I had a bit of a problem with the men as now time would hang heavily on their hands. Our GTR Liaison Officer, Lieutenant Colonel Bridger, made a great effort such as getting the men tickets for soccer matches and tours around London. We were all able to take our minds off the future.

Then came training for the main threat: NBC warfare. We also had to experience it live, including anthrax and its long needle. My NBC instructor was a British staff sergeant from 31 Squadron and he had the anthrax injection first of all in front of the soldiers. He fainted but none of us had any bother.

We did not have our unit fitter section from Hong Kong with us so a new one joined us in UK, as did 12 radio operators from the Queen's Gurkha Signals and 40 stretcher bearers from the Band of the Brigade of Gurkhas, a total of 214 Gurkhas in all.

We arrived at Al-Jubail in Saudi Arabia in the first week of January 1991 and went to a holding area. After we had collected all our kit we started our training phase. We did not stay in Al-Jubail but went to Al-Qaysumah. After that the men realised just what mechanised warfare involved, only having seen films of it in UK. In Saudi we had "live practice". Our role was road casualty evacuation from the Field Dressing Station to the Field Hospital. For that we had two troops, one, X, was to support 4 Armoured Brigade, the other, Y, 7 Armoured Brigade. Z Troop was to support the Field Hospital. We deployed to our operational areas.

The first problem we found in the desert was navigation, even simply going from A to B, but satellite navigation gave us much help and we practised a lot with it. At first during our Friendly Force battle preparation the Americans had difficulty in distinguishing us Gurkhas from Egyptians as they saw similarities – short, stocky build and colour of skin. Sometimes, when our men got on the wrong road, say in the American base camp area, there were doubts, even when checking identity documents. It was only when we showed the kukri which all Gurkhas carried that the Americans were satisfied we were Gurkhas and not Egyptians. "What is the proof?" "I have kukri," then, "He is Johnny Gurkha."

However, we were all ready for the start of operations. One month passed but nothing happened. We all wondered when we would reach our objective. From 16 February 1991 the aerial attacks started, then a second and a third week passed. It struck me that what was needed most in war was mental discipline during the waiting period. This period was not easy for us. We asked ourselves when we'd be off and how we'd manage. To get to our objective was the intention we all had.

We had a lot to do even when waiting. I'd be asked when we'd be off, is the sky the only place for action, when do the land forces start? Our men were spread over a wide area. My OC, the squadron sergeant major and I visited the forward troops from time to time to find out how the men were and their problems. The troops were a day's journey away from us and each other.

The war started. The most unusual aspect, as I saw it, was in mechanised operations, the fuel for the tanks and other vehicles had to be pre-placed out in front. One of my corporals asked me how could this be? I didn't know much about these tactics either. That section was in support of an artillery battery. I asked the battery operation control officer about it but he wasn't sure either. In the end an artillery officer told me that, if there was no fuel ready out in front when the vehicles ran dry, we'd all be dead. However, when it is clear in front, that is what happens in the first phase. After that all our men understood.

When the war actually started we were all happy. Our squadron HQ was with 1 Armoured Division HQ and my troops were advancing in front, left was 4 Brigade, whose commander was later Deputy Commander Land Forces Hong Kong, and right was 7 Brigade. On we went. After our forces had entered Kuwait we were still some distance away. We wondered when we would get to Kuwait. We had to stay where we were in case there were casualties as mines had still to be cleared. One of the young British soldiers picked up a mine and it exploded in his hands, killing him. The Christian priest buried him in a simple, temporary ceremony. It was sad.

The OC and I were ordered to return to HQ immediately. However, we could not go forward because of those mines and movement back was slow as all the roads were completely cluttered with American vehicles and masses of Iraqi POWs. It was night when we got back.

Our next task was not driving ambulances but taking those due back to UK to the airport holding area. My OC and I went back to Kuwait. One of the orders was not to leave the places marked out for vehicular traffic. We met our men in X Troop who were very happy with the result of the fighting. It was time to go to Y Troop and it was dark by the time we started. I said it was inadvisable to go by night but the OC said it was alright. We were in a group of three Land Rovers. We started off but missed our turning when we failed to see the white marking tape. We soon realised we were unable to move as it was too dark to get out of the minefield. One hour, two hours – stuck.

We were in the middle of a minefield that had anti-personnel mines in it also. We were stuck. We heard people calling to us. But we were stuck. We'd have to stay there until daylight. We then heard a jerboa scuttling by. My squadron sergeant major said that the track was from where the desert rat had come from. "Possibly so, but don't let's go," I said, as the sergeant major was strong-willed. "No, it is this way," he insisted. "Let's see about it," I said to the OC.

The sergeant major was correct. We found the way out successfully. I said to the OC that not only was our formation sign a jerboa but a mouse was the bringer of advice from the god of wisdom, Ganesh, and the jerboa was sent to save us.

All ended quietly and we returned to the UK in the first week of April, handed the kit in and returned to Hong Kong. We had suffered no casualties and only been involved in three minor traffic accidents. There were, in fact, more casualties from these accidents than from enemy action. What was so very satisfying, apart from my own personal activities, was that many had doubted the Gurkhas' ability to perform in such a novel role in such a modern setting and we proved that Gurkhas are "all weather soldiers".

The Gurkhas will always be successful if their British and Gurkha officers are of sufficiently high calibre. I learnt three things from the Gulf War: 1. Gurkhas can operate under any conditions; 2. If the commander knows how to handle his men, they will operate under any condition; 3. Mental discipline and mental balance are essential in a commander to know fully how to handle his men, especially when there is so much waiting about, so many rumours and no firm orders. Finally, the Royal Logistic Corps has full faith in the QOGTR.

I was promoted Major (QGO) in 1997, made MVO and MBE, and finally retired on pension in 1998 as an Honorary Captain (GCO).

FORMER·YUGOSLAVIA·
·BOSNIA·KOSOVO·
AND·MACEDONIA·
·1997-99·

Chapter 14

Former Yugoslavia

The end of all empires brings problems to liberator and liberated. The collapse of the Soviet empire was no exception and there was a 'domino effect' in reverse when Yugoslavia disintegrated. So ancient was the hatred, so fractured the communities, so severe the massacres, so harsh the regime and so palpable the fear of the vast majority of the population that the outside world, first in Bosnia the UNO, and later in Kosovo NATO, had to step in to try and restore sanity where madness had reigned.

Hitman Gurung, 1 RGR.   In 1996 we were part of 5 Airborne Brigade for out of area operations. In August 1997 we were given a warning order to go to Bosnia for two months. We left for Bosnia on the 28th and our first tasks were vehicle preparation and area familiarisation. We were the first Gurkha infantry to be sent there. There had been a lot of fighting and, now it was over, we were to boost the international peacekeeping force during the run-up to municipal elections on 13 and 14 September 1997. They were the first elections after the war.

The CO briefed us and we had some training. Our mission was to take sensitive and non-sensitive material and ballot boxes to polling stations and then escort them back afterwards. It was decided that soft-skinned vehicles were unsuitable so we were given Saxon armoured vehicles and 15 men from the QOGTR as drivers. In all we were in groups of 120 men. Three platoons were under command of 2 RRF[1]

---

[1] Second Battalion, The Royal Regiment of Fusiliers. Capt (QGO) Hitman Gurung was singled out for special praise by the Fusiliers' CO, Lt Col G.P. Cass, in a letter, dated 9 October 1997, to CO 1 RGR, Lt Col Bijay Rawat: '... outstanding: he is experienced, highly motivated, intelligent and more importantly, well able to use his common sense to solve difficult problems. He has proved extremely popular throughout the Battle Group.'

who were under strength and could not cope with the large area for which they were responsible. We were at Donji Vakuf.

The other platoon, 5 Platoon, were with King's Royal Hussars at Banja Luka. Their mission was crowd control and controlling any large amount of traffic. The 5 Platoon commander was Lieutenant (QGO) Belbahadur Pun. They had stones thrown at them while doing this job.

After the election we were on stand-by for a few days to see what the reaction to the result would be. There was no trouble so we stood down. After that our task was to go to Jazce to help the Bosnian Muslims who had suffered a lot of *dukha* and been driven away from their homes. So much damage had been done to property. They were threatened on their return and we had to keep order in our area of responsibility by foot and vehicle patrols of up to two to three hours at a time. At first we wore full combat dress but after morale became better we merely carried our helmets and body armour, wearing regimental berets.

At Dibichani there had been a school for about 1,600 students. It had been destroyed. We based ourselves there and repaired it. The platoon from Banja Luka rejoined us. We were given 33,000 Deutschmarks from London to help us buy materials. There was an impressive opening ceremony when it was rebuilt.

It was a big success. We Gurkhas were liked and trusted, and we made a good impression. The languages were Croat and Muslim [sic] and we had interpreters with us. On 18 September 1997 our tour ended. We were given a good report.

Hitman Gurung was made 2IC of A Company, 1 RGR, on his return from home leave in 1998. His recollections continued with a description of the Kosovo operations.

1999 was a good year for Gurkhas. 1 RGR went to Kosovo on operations. We were put on stand-by in April during the NATO airstrike period. Battalion HQ and A Company left UK on 6 June with 5 Airborne Brigade. We were the leading battalion and mine was the leading company. We went to Macedonia, landing at Skopje, and were sent about four kilometres to a brigade assembly area.

We practised the battle procedure for crossing the border into Kosovo. High level talks were going on and, five days later on 11 June, we were all ready to fly to Priština airport in a TACO,[2] NATO wanting

---

[2] Tactical Air Land Operation.

to get there before the Russians. There were many helicopters in the wheat fields ready to take us. We carried extra ammunition. It was very exciting. Kate Adie[3] was there so it had to be a proper war. We were ready for take-off but it was cancelled. General Jackson had high level discussions and let the situation cool off by allowing the Russians to get to Priština first.

On 12 June, at 0530 hours first light, half the battalion moved off by road and half by Chinook and Apache helicopters. We had to seize, then search the Kačanik defile. It was the toughest operation there was and that is why we Gurkhas were sent on it. It was hilly country, full of trees and dangerous. B Company led the way, clearing the road and, having secured the bridge, let the tanks and other transport through. A and C Companies landed and C Company, the Assault Pioneer Company, cleared the bridge.

A Company stood by twice. Once when the Pathfinder Platoon had heard that Serb troops were in the area, which was a false report, and once to collect UCK[4] weapons. The locals in that area were afraid of us Gurkhas. That was the first time any UCK weapons had been collected.

And then the situation changed. We had gone to fight a war but there was no war to fight. We had a peace enforcement mission because, by then, the Serb military had all gone north of Priština. The locals were very happy to see us and welcomed us with flowers. People shouted out "NATO" and "the Gurkhas have come". We were sent to Lipljan and given individual company areas.

We came across the Russians several times. They were careless and had low morale. They got drunk with Serbians. They did not look the type to have won World War III. The Albanians, being poor, were hard-working like us. The Serbs were richer. After the Serb Army had gone north, it was Albanian versus Serb so the Serbs became pro us.

Our tasks were patrolling and to cordon and search houses for suspected war criminals and weapons. We had photographs of offenders. Only once did we nearly have a firefight. WO2 Thaman was the patrol commander that time and did well. Tactics used in Northern Ireland were of much use. We had not served there but there was enough residual knowledge of Hong Kong IS parades for us to manage well.

---

[3] A certain television news reporter.

[4] Kosovo Liberation Army.

At first the Serbs had been the enemy but those Serbs who lived in the area were happy to be protected by us. They would invite us into their houses for meals.

On 31 August 1999 we were welcomed back to UK.

In June 2000 I became GM of British Gurkhas Pokhara. *How wonderful!*

Looking back on it all I felt proud that we carried out the traditions of our forebears. The young lads were not afraid. Their fighting quality was still tops. Some people may have thought GOR were not up to that sort of war but we managed in Bosnia, Kosovo and East Timor.

CHAPTER 15

East Timor

Timor island is the largest and easternmost of the Lesser Sunda Archipelago. The eastern half of the island, East Timor, had had a Portuguese presence since 1512 but latterly it suffered from neglect, mostly benign, until the Indonesian invasion in 1975. Despite international pressure, a protracted military campaign was conducted by the Indonesian Army, known as TNI,[1] aided by guerillas, against the separatist forces who disliked the Indonesians intensely. The major independence movement, FRETELIN,[2] was initially matched against three other groups but eventually became the dominant opposition

The government of Indonesia, as represented in Dili, capital of East Timor, was corrupt as high as the head of state. Apart from the policy of transmigration that brought many non-Timorese into the province, the situation was further exacerbated by the religious aspect. The East Timorese are mainly Christian and the Indonesians Muslim. The Indonesian Army was also a political force so giving it a dimension of activity not normally associated with a military organisation. Many of the militia who supported the TNI were civilians who had been brought over from other states, mostly Java and Sumatra.

A referendum was held to decide whether East Timor should remain within the Indonesian ambit and about four-fifths of the population gave a negative answer. The ensuing backlash of fermentation of accumulated bigotry, bias and bombast produced such a bitter brew that fighting reached an intensity of sustained atrocities that could not be overlooked any more by the rest of the world. An Australian-led force, with a contingent from 2 RGR stationed in Brunei, went to the rescue and later handed over to the UNO.

---

[1] Tentara Nasional Indonesia.
[2] Frente Revolucionário de Timor Leste Independente.

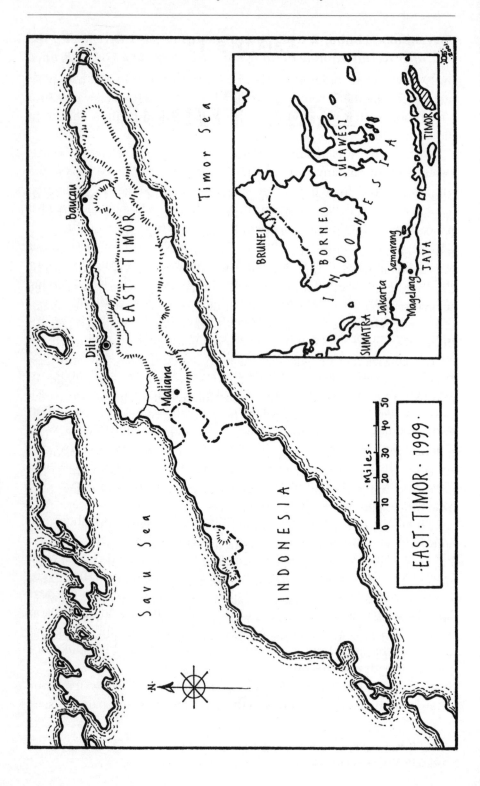

Suryakumar Limbu, 2 RGR, *joined the army on 3 December 1986 and, after recruit training in Hong Kong, was posted to 7 GR in Brunei.*

In 1999 we were ordered to stand by for East Timor. We had been training for another exercise at the time so when we were warned for East Timor we felt it was just more overseas training with a change in the destination.

A Company was detailed to go with a support element. I was attached to A Company as a corporal in command of two GPMGs in the support fire role. In all there were six guns under a sergeant. We trained for a week. We flew to Darwin in RAF Hercules aircraft and spent a week there in Robinson barracks. It was very hot. We were under 3 RAR.[3] We ate their rations. They had more juice than we had in our rations and we ate meat every day. We were lectured about East Timor and told that the country was like Nepal as regards hills. The language was like Malay which we already knew from our time in Brunei.

On 19 September we flew to Dili, an hour and 20 minutes away. We were fully equipped for war. We carried 600 rounds for each gun and our load weighed between 50 and 60 kilos. We arrived at 0500 hours. The airport had been in Australian hands for about 20 days. We marched away to a camp 10km away. It took us 3½ hours to get there.

As we marched along we saw ruins everywhere. Not a house and no walls standing, not a pane of glass unbroken. The inhabitants were sitting about. They waved to us. The smell of death was everywhere. We were amazed. We did not see any human corpses. The inhabitants were not like the Indonesians; Timorese were smaller and darker. We reached the area to be taken over.

Our GPMG position was not in the camp so we did not go there. We took positions around the camp up a steep hill that overlooked the whole of Dili. We were about 800 metres from the camp. There were some TNI in the position we had to take, in the open. They were friendly and shook hands. We had a night together and they left the next day. Meanwhile A Company had to go to the United Nations Mission East Timor camp which the TNI had taken over but the lieutenant colonel in charge did not let us in. OC A Company[4] and he spoke but it took three days to resolve.

We were on our hill position for about 26 days. We had to fetch our water from the camp, an hour's journey for the downhill part. To start

---

[3] Third Battalion, Royal Australian Regiment.
[4] Maj C.F. Warren, later made MBE.

with rations were insufficient, nothing fresh, all tinned. Later we got some rice from the camp the Indonesians had been in.

One time we heard a radio report about an A Company patrol that had mistakenly moved into an area that was full of Indonesian Army men. They were challenged, two GORs were jumped on, thrown to the ground and their weapons snatched. Luckily there was an interpreter with them and the whole business was settled quickly and amicably.

By then we had moved to Maliana, to the west of the country, not far from West Timor. It is like southern Nepal, the Terai. It is a good, fertile place. A lot of fruit is grown there. It is flat but there are hills to the north and we Gurkhas were sent to the high ground. Many refugees were hiding in the hills because their houses had been destroyed. They started to come back and we distributed rations to them. We dug trenches and took up all-round defensive positions. Our mission was to check the refugees to see if they had weapons on them as some of the militia could have been posing as refugees. Some had pistols and some had parangs. Those without weapons were afraid of us. The Australians gave us mineral water which we gave to the refugees.

Fifteen days later we were sent to the north of the country, over in the east, to Baucau which is near the sea. We went to find out if there were any Indonesian Army, militia or FRETELIN but we did not find anyone. TNI was careless, more so than the Australian Army. Its soldiers were untidy and took no care of their equipment. They put two magazines on their rifle, one loaded and the other strapped on by plaster. The Australians did not seem to be able to operate for any length of time without either looking for shade or taking their equipment and hats off. There was nothing smart about them. They did not strike me as being able to win a war though they treated us well.

We were stood down and based at Government House which was not far from the United Nations mission building. We wanted to go and have a look at it but were denied entrance. We had a farewell parade on 13 and 14 November and on the 16th we flew back to Brunei.

The public were happy with us and were sorry to see us go. "We'll remember you," they said. It was a most interesting time for us, a new place and everything different.

CHAPTER 16

Final Thoughts of an Old Soldier

Gurkhas are a product of the past. If they did not exist no one would now invent them. They have survived by persuading people that they achieve standards higher than those the modern world normally sets itself.

From the mid-1990s a movement has grown up in Nepal that has been antagonistic both to the difference in the terms and conditions of service between British soldiers and their Gurkha counterparts, and, more politically motivated, the anachronism of the whole concept. The former grievances have, I am delighted to say, been rectified – and accepted by all less a fringe minority – while the latter complaint is more motivated by those who learnt their politics between the early 1950s and 1990 when Nepal was in a time warp. Retention of the Brigade of Gurkhas or its demise will be a political decision but, were it to go, those in the mountains – like those whose stories you have read – will be ineradicably sorry.

Only one-third of all stories gathered have been reproduced here and, for reasons of space, some in truncated form. I have once again been very forcibly struck that never has a nation had such loyal and good soldiers for so long at so cheap a price.

J. P. Cross
Nepal 2002

Further Reading

Malaya, 1941-45
Barber, N., *Sinister Twilight*, Eyre & Spottiswoode, 1969
Chapman, S., *The Jungle is Neutral*, Chatto & Windus, 1949

Burma
Allen, L., *Burma. The Longest War, 1941-45*, Dent, 1984
Bickersteth, Maj A.C., *One Damned Thing After Another*, published privately
Brett-James, A., *The Ball of Fire*, Gale & Polden, 1951
Calvert, M., *Prisoner of Hope*, Hamish Hamilton, 1969
Fergusson, B., *Beyond the Chindwin*, Collins, 1945
Fergusson, B., *Wild Green Earth*, Collins, 1946
Kirby, S.W., *The War Against Japan*, vol. III, HMSO
Masters, J., *The Road Past Mandalay*, Michael Joseph, 1961
Mead, P., *Orde Wingate and the Historians*, Merlin Books Ltd, 1987
Slim, Sir W., *Defeat into Victory*, Cassell, 1956
Tuchman, B., *Sand against the Wind*, Macmillan, 1970

Malayan Emergency
Barber, N., *The War of the Running Dogs*, Collins, 1971
Cross, Lt Col J.P., *In Gurkha Company*, Arms & Armour Press, 1986
Henniker, Brig, M.C.A., *Red Shadow Over Malaya*, Blackwood, 1953
James, H., and Sheil-Small, D., *A Pride of Gurkhas*, Leo Cooper, 1975
Smith, E.D., *Counter-Insurgency Operations. 1: Malaya and Borneo*, Ian Allan, 1985

Borneo
Dickens, P., *SAS: The Jungle Frontier*, Arms & Armour Press, 1983
Geraghty, T., *Who Dares Wins*, Arms & Armour Press, 1980
James, H., and Sheil-Small, D., *The Undeclared War*, Leo Cooper, 1971
Smith, E.D., *Counter-Insurgency Operations. 1: Malaya and Borneo*, Ian Allan, 1985

Communist Revolutionary Warfare
Bateman, M-E., *Defeat in the East*, OUP, 1967
Kramer, M., (ed), *The Black Book of Communism: Crimes, Terror, Repression*,
    trans. Jonathan Murphy and Mark Kramer, Harvard University Press, Cambridge,
    MA, 1999
Thompson, Sir Robert, *Defeating Communist Insurgency*, Chatto & Windus, 1967

General/World War II
Bloodworth, D., *An Eye for the Dragon*, Secker & Warburg, 1970
Bloodworth, D., *Chinese Looking Glass*, Secker & Warburg, 1967
Bryant, A., *Turn of the Tide*, Collins, 1957
Dear, I.C.B., and Foot, M.R.D., (eds), *The Oxford Companion to the Second World
    War*, Oxford University Press, 1995
Keegan, J., *The Second World War*, Arrow Books, 1990
Miller, D., *Great Battles of World War II*, Greenhill Books, 1998
Pocock, T., *Fighting General*, Collins, 1967
Weinberg, G.L., *A World at Arms: A Global History of World War II*, Cambridge
    University Press, 1994

Index